*the cinema of* JOHN CARPENTER

**DIRECTORS' CUTS**

*the cinema of*
# JOHN CARPENTER

*the technique of terror*

edited by ian conrich & david woods

**WALLFLOWER PRESS** LONDON & NEW YORK

A Wallflower Book
Published by
Columbia University Press
Publishers Since 1893
New York • Chichester, West Sussex
cup.columbia.edu

A complete CIP record is available from the Library of Congress

ISBN 978-1-904764-15-1 (cloth : alk. paper)
ISBN 978-1-904764-14-4 (pbk. : alk. paper)
ISBN 978-0-231-85035-3 (e-book)

Columbia University Press books are printed on permanent
and durable acid-free paper.
Printed in the United States of America

Book and cover design by Rob Bowden Design
Cover photo by Neil Jacobs

CONTENTS

ACKNOWLEDGEMENTS

The editors would like to thank the contributors, the staff at the British Film Institute library, Wallflower Press and John Carpenter's office in their support throughout the completion of this book.

**Ronald V. Borst** is a film archivist and advisor living in Hollywood, USA. He has contributed to *Famous Monsters of Filmland* and *Castle of Frankenstein*, and was co-editor of *Photon*. He is the author of *Graven Images* (1992), and Associate Producer for the A&E Network documentaries on Boris Karloff and Bela Lugosi.

**David Burnand** is Principal Lecturer in Screen Music at the Royal College of Music, London. He is a film composer, sound designer and researcher, with publications on a range of subjects, including British film composers, attitudes within the musical establishment towards film composition and sound design in Andrei Tarkovsky's *Sacrifice*. He has written for *Sight and Sound*, *Electro-Acoustic Music* and *Performance*. With Miguel Mera, he is currently co-editing a volume entitled *European Film Music*.

**Ian Conrich** is Senior Lecturer in Film Studies at the University of Surrey Roehampton, an Editor of the *Journal of British Cinema and Television*, Guest Editor of a forthcoming special issue of *Post Script* on Australian and New Zealand cinema and the co-editor of six books, including the forthcoming *Horror Zone: The Cultural Experience of Contemporary Horror Cinema*. He has written extensively on the horror genre, with his work appearing in *The Modern Fantastic: The Films of David Cronenberg* (2000), *The Horror Film Reader* (2001), *British Horror Cinema* (2001), *Cauchemars Américains: Fantastique et Horreur dans le Cinéma Moderne* (2003), *The Horror Film* (2004), *American Independent Cinema: Critical Perspectives* (2004), and the forthcoming *Japanese Horror Cinema* and *Horror International: World Horror Cinema*.

**Omayra Zaragoza Cruz** is Lecturer in American Studies at the University of Nottingham. Her research centres on nineteenth- and twentieth-century African American culture. Publications include 'Orchestra Seats: Cinema/Cast/Culture', in *Women and Performance* (2004), and the forthcoming *Popular Culture: A Reader* and *Popular Across Culture*. Her work also appears in *The Visual Culture Reader* (2nd edn., 2003).

**Barry Keith Grant** is Professor of Film Studies and Popular Culture at Brock University in Ontario. He is the author, co-author or editor of numerous books, including *Film Genre: Theory and Criticism* (1977), *Planks of Reason: Essays on the Horror*

*Film* (1984), *Film Genre Reader* (1986), *Voyages of Discovery: The Cinema of Frederick Wiseman* (1992), *The Dread of Difference: Gender and the Horror Film* (1996), *Documenting the Documentary: Close Readings of Documentary Film and Video* (1998), *The Film Studies Dictionary* (2001) and *John Ford's Stagecoach* (2003). He is currently editor of the 'Contemporary Approaches to Film and Television' series for Wayne State University Press.

**Raiford Guins** is Senior Lecturer in Contemporary Screen Media at the University of the West of England and Principal Editor of the Americas for the *Journal of Visual Culture*. His work has appeared in *West Coast Line*, *Television and New Media*, *New Formations* and *The Visual Culture Reader* (2nd edn., 2003). Publications include the forthcoming books *Popular Culture: A Reader* and *Popular Across Culture*, and he has begun work on a third, entitled *Edited Clean Version: Censorial Procedures in the Age of Digital Effects*.

**Sheldon Hall** is Lecturer in Film Studies at Sheffield Hallam University. He has recently completed a book on the making of the film *Zulu*, and is co-author (with Steve Neale) of the forthcoming *Epics, Spectaculars and Blockbusters*, and co-editor (with Steve Neale and John Belton) of a forthcoming collection of essays arising out of the 2003 conference 'Widescreen Cinema', held at the National Museum of Photography, Film and Television, Bradford, of which he was co-organiser. Other publications include contributions to *The Movie Book of the Western* (1995), *British Historical Cinema* (2002) and *Unexplored Hitchcock* (forthcoming).

**Miguel Mera** is Senior Lecturer in Screen Music at the Royal College of Music, London. His publications include papers on humour in film music, the use of silence and space in Toru Takemitsu's film scores and the representation of historical period in film music. Miguel is currently working on a book examining Mychael Danna's score for *The Ice Storm*, and co-editing (with David Burnand) a volume entitled *European Film Music*. As a composer he has written music for a variety of film and television productions.

**Marie Mulvey-Roberts** is Reader in Literary Studies at the School of English and Drama at the University of the West of England, where she teaches Gothic Literature. She is the author of *British Poets and Secret Societies* (1986) and *Gothic Immortals: The Fiction of the Brotherhood of the Rosy Cross* (1990), and has edited over thirty books including (with Roy Porter), *Pleasure in the Eighteenth Century* (1996) and *The Handbook to Gothic Literature* (1998). She is co-editor of the forthcoming *Gothic Fiction*, selected from the Sadleir-Black Collection of Gothic Literature, and *The Guide to the Gothic*.

**Anna Powell** is Senior Lecturer in Film Studies in the Department of English at Manchester Metropolitan University. Her interests include Gothic culture, horror film and literature, subcultures and experimental film. She has published articles and book chapters on *The Blair Witch Project*, narcophile vampires and Kenneth Anger and the occult. She has contributed to *Screen* and *The Body's Perilous Pleasures: Dangerous Desires and Contemporary Culture* (1999) and is the author of *The Vampire Libertine as Sovereign Subject* (2002) and *Deleuze and the Horror Film* (forthcoming).

**Robert Shail** is Lecturer in Film and Media Studies at University of Wales, Lampeter. His work has appeared in the *International Journal of Sexuality and Gender Studies* and *Film and Film Culture*, and is a contributor to *The Trouble with Men: Masculinities in European and Hollywood Cinema* (2004).

**Steve Smith** is a lecturer in the Department of French at the University of Nottingham. He has edited and contributed to *Nottingham French Studies* and contributed to *The Year's Work in Cultural and Critical Theory* (vol. 2) (1996) and *Crime Scenes: Detective Narratives in European Cultures* (2000).

**Tony Williams** is Professor/Area Head of Film Studies in the Department of English at Southern Illinois University at Carbondale. He has written for *Cinema Journal, Wide Angle, Jump Cut, Movie, CineAction, Journal of Popular Film and Television, Sight and Sound* and *Films and Filming*. His books include *Hearths of Darkness: The Family in the American Horror Film* (1997), *Larry Cohen: Radical Allegories of an American Filmmaker* (1998), *Structures of Desire: British Cinema 1939–1955* (1998), *The Cinema of George A. Romero: Knight of the Living Dead* (2003) and *Body and Soul: The Cinematic Vision of Robert Aldrich* (2004).

**David Woods** is Senior Lecturer in Media and Cultural Studies at Nottingham Trent University. He is the co-editor of *New Zealand – A Pastoral Paradise?* (2000) and has contributed to *Translation, Theory and Latin America: Dimensions of the Third Term* (1995) and *The Background to Critical Theory: From Kant to Lévi-Strauss* (2002).

**Suzie Young** is Associate Professor at York University in Toronto. She has interests in critical theories and practices of 'place' (digital diaspora; the 'international film'), 'body' (cinematernity; Nature-TV), and the 'grotesque'. Her work has appeared in *Asian Cinema* and *Science Fiction Studies*.

INTRODUCTION

# Ian Conrich and David Woods

An anthology on the cinema of John Carpenter may appear inappropriate to some, when considering the critical reaction to his more recent films. Productions have become infrequent and there is continual reference to the 'better days' of the films earlier in Carpenter's career. A review for the 2001 production *Ghosts of Mars* said 'it's a shame that the film should be yet another clunky reminder of past greatness from a filmmaker whose decline continues apace' (Newman 2001: 52). In interviews, Carpenter appears at times frustrated by the lack of recognition for his screen achievements and at the ways in which his films have not always reached their intended audience. There is, though, a distinct regard for many of his productions, and Carpenter is a director recognised, more than most, as possessing an ability for crafting genre films and a screen technique of terror. His career has spanned much of new American cinema, but to understand Carpenter there is a need to see him as more than just one type of filmmaker and to consider him within a manifold conceptual framework.

Horror is the genre with which Carpenter has been most associated, though *Ghosts of Mars* is a horror/science fiction hybrid, as is *The Thing* (1982). *Ghosts of Mars* is also a western, as is the Gothic horror *Vampires* (1998). *Starman* (1984) mixes science fiction with romance, and *Memoirs of an Invisible Man* (1992) is more a science fiction thriller. *Assault on Precinct 13* (1976), *Elvis* (1979) and *Big Trouble in Little China* (1986), are variously examples of the crime movie, the music bio-pic and the martial arts action film. Carpenter's employment of genre, and his generic referencing of a director such as Howard Hawks, are such that Carpenter has become regarded as a filmmaker with closer associations to classical, as opposed to post-classical, Hollywood. As is well known, Carpenter has identified himself with the studio system of the 1940s and 1950s, where the guaranteed presence of a regular audience enabled films to be made which placed the primary emphasis on entertainment through plot- and character-driven narratives. The audience's desires and expectations were stimulated and managed through the familiarity of genre conventions, and filmmaking was conceived as something of a craft rather than anything more lofty. The role of the director was to render the technical and commercial processes involved as invisible as possible, so that the final result was a blend of the demands of the storytelling process and of the director's own style.

There is a view then that Carpenter is an anachronistic director, but such an unalloyed position is problematic. Carpenter's craft has not been just as a director; he has also been recognised for his highly effective screen music compositions, and has been a hired scriptwriter. Moreover, he is part of the group of filmmakers who emerged in the early to mid-1970s, the new wave or Hollywood renaissance of post-classical directors who were both self-taught and film-school educated. Crucially, such filmmakers were familiar with the work of their peers and of the saturated style of Hollywood's system of genre production. Working within a deregulated American movie industry, filmmakers such as Steven Spielberg, Martin Scorsese, Francis Ford Coppola and George Lucas have exploited the medium's commercial opportunities to make productions that have defined contemporary film and marked key transitions in American mainstream and art-house cinema. Others such as John Cassavettes, John Sayles and Robert Altman have been celebrated for their independence and heightened storytelling abilities. Carpenter, like Brian De Palma, is different; both being noted for their stylish re-interpretations of, and open homages to, directors of classical Hollywood (primarily Hawks and Hitchcock) as well as for their reliance on genre patterns of filmmaking. Both filmmakers have crafted astonishingly creative films, but in an age in which studios are increasingly driven towards high concept productions, there appears less of a desire for companies to accommodate the idiosyncratic nature of an independent director. Unlike filmmakers such as Sayles or Barry Levinson, who appear to move with some ease between independence and personal projects and the demands of the new Hollywood studios, Carpenter often has worked best when not under assignment.

As with De Palma, key early productions marked Carpenter as essentially a director of horror. But whereas De Palma moved beyond such films as *Carrie* (1976), *The Fury* (1978) and *Dressed to Kill* (1980) to make major action and gangster films such as *Scarface* (1983), *The Untouchables* (1987), *Carlito's Way* (1993) and *Mission Impossible* (1996), Carpenter continues to be regarded as a horror film director even though he has made as many science fiction movies, and the horror film makes up less than half his total output. Of course, Carpenter does continue to make horror films, such as *Vampires*, but it would perhaps seem that he has been enduring the legacy of his earlier productions – films such as *Halloween* (1978) and *The Thing*.

The seminal nature of these two films and the recognition accorded each within the pantheon of modern horror – *Halloween* as a principal slasher film and arguably the most sophisticated production within this subgenre; *The Thing* as the most strikingly original and visually explicit example of body horror – have helped to establish Carpenter as a filmmaker of invention and vision. This is part of the attraction that Carpenter's films have promised, but in noting the cultural reception for his work there needs to be a distinction made between an audience that has recognised the value of a film on its initial release and those who have become aware of it retrospectively. Here, films such as *Escape From New York* (1981), *They Live* (1988) and, most emphatically, *The Thing* were previously ignored but have gained new appreciation for the boldness of their fantasies.

Perhaps Carpenter is best viewed as a director of a generation; not just as one of the directors of the Hollywood renaissance emerging in the 1970s, but as one of a group of key filmmakers who came to be associated with the horror new wave of the late 1970s and early 1980s. From this generation, Carpenter is also perhaps most acknowledged by the audience that grew up with his films at the dawn of the video age. For such an audience Carpenter is often seen as a director of cult films. As Danny Peary writes, 'cultists believe that they are among the blessed few who have discovered something in particular films that the average moviegoer and critic have missed' (1981: xiii). For it is not just that certain Carpenter films underperformed or were dismissed on initial release, nor that their content has been viewed as remarkable, that has led to their 'discovery' and cult status. The fact that Carpenter has been overlooked as a filmmaker is a central factor. Amongst horror new wave directors Carpenter is, however, not alone in this regard.

Of those North American filmmakers most associated with the horror new wave – David Cronenberg, Tobe Hooper, John Landis, Joe Dante, George A. Romero – Carpenter is arguably the one who has persisted most successfully in making mainstream horror or fantasy and science fiction films. Since the 1980s, Romero has made few films and struggled to fund his own productions, Hooper has become a director of enervated direct-to-video horror features, whilst Dante and Landis have been lost to a mix of television productions, family fare and music videos. Cronenberg has distanced himself from mainstream filmmaking, but like Romero remains an esteemed figure within the horror genre whose work has received much critical attention. Similarly, Carpenter is regarded as a filmmaker of significant movies made within Hollywood's post-classical period but, considering the large body of films that he has made, there is a relative dearth of analytical and academic research, amounting only to a small number of books and scholarly articles.[1]

Since the horror new wave, the production of horror and horror/science fiction films has stuttered. Despite this, Carpenter has managed to continue working within the Hollywood system, through cleverly adapting and recombining genres. A B-movie aesthetic of sensationalistic, uninhibited and confident genre filmmaking has continually been a mark of Carpenter's productions, but this may explain why his movies have been both applauded and dismissed, and why he has received little academic attention. As Brooks Landon writes of *The Thing*, for example, 'it deserves our careful consideration rather than the careless condemnation that has thus far marked its reception' (1992: 44). Carpenter's B-movie aesthetic remains in later productions such as *Ghosts of Mars*, a film which although poorly received is characteristic of Carpenter's approach to genre filmmaking, with its deceptive simplicity.

Carpenter as a director of genre films forms the thread that unites the first five chapters of this book. The consequences of remaining faithful to genres are taken up by Grant, Woods and Smith, who focus principally on the issue of how genre conventions shape the representation of the social in Carpenter's films. Carpenter has often cited Hawks in particular as his ideal director, an observation which Grant develops in a wide-ranging survey of Carpenter's output. Grant argues for a consistent directorial vision across his films, which, apart from the spareness and moments of pictorially narrated 'pure cinema' that the adherence to genre brings, is characterised by a particular world view. Although superficially similar to Hawks in the appearance of some recurring themes, Grant finds that these films contain significant variations from Hawks's. Most notably, they depict worlds where the utter contingency of the characters' moral choices is made plain. In contrast to Hawks's heroes, who are usually temporarily cut off from normal society, Carpenter's characters often find that normal social structures and institutions themselves are the source of corruption, and indeed can be so corrosive that group solidarity is as likely to waver as to harden when confronted by them. This, Grant argues, gives Carpenter's films a more critical outlook than Hawks's; as a result, the dominant view of him as espousing some variety of a right-wing perspective is only a partial reading, and Grant sets out the necessary corrective. That the films have led to the dominant view is not accidental, but is, rather, the outcome of the demands that genres place upon their subject matter, and if the result is a certain incoherence, Grant observes, Carpenter is hardly unique in this regard.

If Carpenter's films are thus beset by certain structural tensions, readings of them which look for a unified narrative are unlikely to succeed. The next two chapters each follow through a different motif which recurs in a number of the films. They highlight through close textual analysis the surprising complexity to which each motif gives rise as the films are obliged to deal with such tensions, this complexity itself being an index of the cultural and political forces which shape popular film. Woods focuses on the depiction of secular authorities, which, as already noted, appear in many of Carpenter's films and are almost invariably shown to be suspect in some way. Since Carpenter consistently portrays the individual as the locus of moral superiority, in an examination of *They Live, Memoirs of an Invisible Man* and *Village of the Damned* (1995), attention is focused upon the way the protagonists are distinguished from the authorities against which they are pitched. In each case the developmental logic of the narrative is traced to show that, despite apparently well-established moral distinctions between the opposed parties, at key junctures the protagonist takes on characteristics which supposedly define the opponent, or, to state it otherwise, the cause for which they are fighting becomes unclear. Woods argues that this comes about once again not by chance but because the universalising underpinnings of the individualism to which Carpenter has recourse are unable to maintain the critical stance which the films promise.

Smith examines another notable motif, that of the siege (also found in Hawks), which forms a unifying thread between four early films, *Assault on Precinct 13*, *Halloween*, *The Fog* (1979) and *The Thing*. The aim is to interrogate the critical consensus, mentioned above, that Carpenter belongs to the 'reactionary' wing of horror directors, according to Robin Wood's influential definition of the term. While this view is conceded in some cases to be broadly justified, Smith undertakes a detailed analysis of the first of the quartet to demonstrate that it does not so easily fit into this category. Rather, he argues, the conventional criterion that has been used as the measure of a film's socio-political outlook, namely its representation of the 'other' whom the protagonists face, is particularly inadequate in this case. Smith amasses apparently incidental details of plot and setting, and shows how, working against the film's overarching generic imperatives, they resonate in a remarkably insistent and coherent manner with contemporary social anxieties, in ways which problematise the founding assumptions of the dominant consensus.

While the identification of a personal vision in Carpenter's films turns out to be more complex than at first seems the case, other aspects of his work as a genre-based director are more easily illustrated. While a desire for overall control links all directors who aspire to authorial status, Carpenter goes further than most in his participation in the more specialised aspects of film production. Perhaps rarest among these is his consistent appearance on the credits as composer or co-composer of the music for his films. Burnand and Mera show how Carpenter's distinctive style initially (and perhaps inevitably) draws on the science fiction films of the 1950s, and they go on to give detailed analyses of how music functions in some of his most famous films, including *Assault on Precinct 13*, *Halloween*, *Escape From New York* and *Escape From L.A.* (1996). The music is shown not to be particularly sophisticated, though it does develop over time, but is above all effective and in keeping with Carpenter's film style, in which lean presentation aimed at the manipulation of the audience's emotions is the prime concern. In particular, Burnand and Mera point to Carpenter's early and continuing experimentation with the borderline between music and sound effect, a subject which has only recently received more widespread attention from film music practitioners. Carpenter's ability to manipulate the audience is also foregrounded in Hall's account of another facet of the director's style: his attachment to the widescreen format. Hall charts the variety of responses which CinemaScope provoked on its arrival in Hollywood in 1953, not the least significant of which in the present context was its rejection by Hawks. Hall thus goes on to identify another dimension of Carpenter's style, namely a tendency to formalism (against Hawks's self-effacing narrative-driven style) which allies him more with a Hitchcockian approach to filmmaking. Hall shows this sensibility at work in a detailed account of the techniques Carpenter develops in *Halloween* to exploit the manipulative potential of the full widescreen ratio (a format which even Hitchcock avoided), and he pinpoints how the tension between the very different methods of his forbears proved to be productive for Carpenter, and one which well equipped him for his position on the margins of the new Hollywood.

Questions of the relationship between director and audience are taken up in very different ways in the next two chapters. They emerge in Mulvey-Roberts's discussion of the substantial number of Gothic themes and sensibility shared by many of Carpenter's films. In particular, Mulvey-Roberts highlights the depiction of the monstrous, especially as it figures in *Prince of Darkness* (1987), *The Thing* and *In the Mouth of Madness* (1995), as a threat to stable identity in the way that it plays on fears of the relationship between self and body. Indeed, this monstrosity threatens to dissolve the boundaries of the body, and analogously, the author argues, Carpenter's work stages the blurring of the boundaries between fantasy and reality, between the audience and the fiction, in a way which is fully in keeping with the Gothic fascination with feelings of terror and paranoia the genre was intended to provoke. The relationship between filmmaker and audience is approached from the opposite perspective by Conrich, who uses contemporary material to reconstruct the ways in which fans of horror films related to Carpenter's output in, primarily, the period 1978–82, during which time *Halloween, The Fog, Escape From New York* and *The Thing* appeared, and the American horror new wave was in ascendancy. Drawing largely upon the American fanzine *Fangoria*, Conrich establishes the esteem in which Carpenter was held, with the fans clearly being able to move beyond the immediate critical dismissals of the time and to respond to the new aesthetic which these directors were striving to create. He also shows how the characters from the films were given life beyond the screen by the creative efforts of the fans themselves. This rather different blurring of the boundaries between fiction and reality is demonstrated to be thriving in fan gatherings and in the medium of the Internet over twenty years after the films were released, an indication of their enduring status amongst a segment of the population.

Three chapters examining the treatment of gender in Carpenter's films follow. Writing from different perspectives on the collaborations between Carpenter and Kurt Russell, Shail and Williams agree that Russell's performances are the result of close interplay between actor and director, and indeed show a good deal of self-awareness in their parodies of traditional versions of masculine heroism. The authors diverge, however, over the consequences which they hold to follow from this. Focusing principally on the *Escape* films, Shail argues that while Snake Plissken's particular brand of anti-heroism is a result of the rather different political outlook of Carpenter and Russell, the ambivalence he thus embodies provides an outlet for the domestic audience's similarly conflicted feelings regarding ideals of masculinity in their contemporary socio-political context. Shail also finds significant differences between the treatment of Plissken in the two films, in a shift which parallels wider reconfigurations both of notions of masculinity and of postmodern cinematic practice more generally. In an argument which provides an alternative view of the sort of individualistic solutions typical of Carpenter discussed earlier by Woods, Shail suggests the overall result is a sort of compound and distanced depiction of rebelliousness which, sensitive to its times, reworks long-standing American notions of masculinity. For Williams, in contrast, the work of Carpenter and Russell produces representations of masculinity which, whilst satirical of older models, are only superficially critical. Though Plissken or Jack Burton (in *Big Trouble in Little China*) may parody Clint Eastwood's or John Wayne's portrayals of masculinity, their anti-authoritarianism is combined with a demonised portrayal of the alternatives, and the result is unacceptable nihilism. However, Williams also observes that there are exceptions to this pattern. He finds the fleeting outlines of an alternative masculinity towards the conclusion of *Escape From L.A.*, but his most sustained example is that of the pair's first collaboration, *Elvis*. Williams argues that, in a parallel with *Citizen Kane* (1941), Carpenter produces a film genuinely subversive of contemporary norms of masculinity, with a subtle and powerful depiction of a riven and vulnerable Elvis who, after a difficult childhood, flees his emotions and finally takes refuge in self-annihilating spectacle and excess.

One of the key aspects of the failure of masculinity in *Elvis* is the protagonist's inability to come to terms with his relationship with his mother. The complex, often critically overlooked interrelations in Carpenter's films between mothers and sons, both literal and metaphorical, form the basis of Young's chapter. She suggests that the pessimistic portrayal of social institutions in Carpenter's films is one of the recurring sources of the pleasure they offer the audience, exposing as they do their ineffectualness or hypocrisy. But where Williams finds that the films offer no alternative, Young argues that they often look to a mother-figure to deliver the protagonists from a failure of homosociality. The portrayal of this mother-figure is, however, deeply ambivalent. Discussing a wide range of films, Young shows how it moves from straightforward depictions of a mother saving her son (in, for example, *Village of the Damned*) or humankind (in *Starman*), to versions of the psychoanalytically-inspired notion of the 'monstrous feminine' in films such as *Christine* (1983) and *Prince of Darkness*, where the mother combines extremes of attraction and repulsion. While there may thus be some sense of subversiveness in the representation of the paternal Law across these films, Young concludes, it is nonetheless a limited one, underpinned by a naturalised understanding of gender and a nostalgia for the regenerative mother.

Films in which the monstrous feminine appears also figure non-coincidentally in Powell's account of Carpenter's horror/science fiction. In discussions of *In the Mouth of Madness*, *Prince of Darkness* and *Christine*, she demonstrates how these films re-work the theme of the occult, which in turn is part of European folkloric tradition. Such adaptation is shown in some detail to share a number of traits with the work of H. P. Lovecraft, from a sense of metaphysics, to narrative elements, to the creation of atmosphere, though of course utilising techniques which are appropriate to Carpenter's medium. Sutter Cane's novels in *In the Mouth of Madness*, for example, function much as Lovecraft's *Necronomicon*, a grimoire which summons an ancient evil that threatens madness and the destruction of humanity. Carpenter is most faithful to Lovecraft, Powell suggests, in his consistent portrayal of the helplessness of the protagonists in the face of these horrors.

The final critical contribution, before the interview with the director, draws together several of the elements noted above. Some authors have highlighted Carpenter's attachment to genre, others the degree of self-reflexivity to be found in his work. Some films have been argued to be critical of mass culture while as a whole Carpenter's output is at least in some senses an unapologetic part of it. Guins and Cruz argue that while Carpenter is obviously a seminal figure in modern horror, it is possible to identify in his work in the 1990s an ongoing engagement with questions of the nature of genre and reflexivity, and, moreover, an implicit critical commentary on the mainstream development of the horror genre during the decade. Focusing on *Body Bags* (1993), *In the Mouth of Madness* and *Vampires*, they identify a movement from a playful acceptance that horror will plunder its own conventions (a point also made by Mulvey-Roberts in relation to the Gothic) to a more qualified perspective. If repetition is (self-reflexively) seen to be a source of oppressiveness in *In the Mouth of Madness*, as Guins and Cruz show, by the time of *Vampires* Carpenter has developed his response: *Vampires* acknowledges the inevitability of repetition, but embraces it in a creative way which distances it both from the postmodern horror film and from the dismissal of mass culture articulated by the likes of Horkheimer and Adorno.

This necessarily brief sketch of the approaches the contributors have taken to the films has highlighted some points of agreement and some differences between them, while others have been left implicit. Further examples of both are to be found in the text as a whole, and this is of course as it should be in the assessment of a creative and prolific director whose career began in the mid-1970s and who has worked both within and outside the major studios. If, as the editors hope, this book gives the reader cause to re-examine his or her understanding of Carpenter's work, it will have served its purpose.

*Notes*

1   See, for instance, Williams (1979), Neale (1981), Telotte (1982), Prince (1988), Cumbow (1990), Loderhose (1990), Dietrich (1991), Billson (1997), Lagier & Thoret (1998) and Muir (2000).

*References*

Billson, A. (1997) *The Thing*. London: British Film Institute.
Cumbow, R. C. (1990) *Order in the Universe: The Films of John Carpenter*. Metuchen, NJ: Scarecrow Press (2nd edn., 2000).
Dietrich, B. (1991) '*Prince of Darkness*, Prince of Light: From Faust to Physicist', *Journal of Popular Film and Television*, 19, 2, 91–6.
Lagier, L. and Thoret, J-B. (1998) *Mythes et Masques: Les Fantômes de John Carpenter*. Paris: Dreamland éditeur.
Landon, B. (1992) *The Aesthetics of Ambivalence: Rethinking Science Fiction Film in the Age of Electronic (Re)production*. Westport, CT and London: Greenwood Press.
Loderhose, W. (1990) *John Carpenter: Das Grosse Filmbuch*. Hamburg: Bastei Lubbe.
Muir, J. K. (2000) *The Films of John Carpenter*. Jefferson, NC and London: McFarland.
Neale, S. (1981) '*Halloween*: Suspense, Aggression and the Look', *Framework*, 14, 25–9. [Reprinted in B. K. Grant (ed.) (1984) *Planks of Reason: Essays on the Horror Film*. Metuchen, NJ and London: Scarecrow Press, 331–45.]
Newman, K. (2001) *Sight and Sound*, 11, 12, 51–2.
Peary, D. (1981) *Cult Movies: The Classics, the Sleepers, the Weird, and the Wonderful*.

New York: Dell Publishing.

Prince, S. (1988) 'Dread, Taboo and *The Thing*: Toward a Social Theory of the Horror Film', *Wide Angle*, 10, 3, 19–29. [Reprinted in S. Prince (ed.) (2004) *The Horror Film*. New Brunswick, NJ and London: Rutgers University Press, 118–30.]

Telotte, J. P. (1982) 'Through a Pumpkin's Eye: The Reflexive Nature of Horror', *Literature/Film Quarterly*, 10, 139–49. [Reprinted in G. A. Waller (ed.) (1987) *American Horrors: Essays on the Modern American Horror Film*. Urbana and Chicago: University of Illinois Press, 114–28.]

Williams, T. (1979) '*Assault on Precinct 13*: The Mechanics of Repression', in R. Wood and R. Lippe (eds) *The American Nightmare: Essays on the Horror Film*. Toronto: Festival of Festivals, 67–73.

# CHAPTER ONE

# Disorder in the Universe: John Carpenter and the Question of Genre

## Barry Keith Grant

According to Andrew Sarris's classic formulation of the 'auteur theory', the auteur's vision is 'extrapolated from the tension between a director's personality and his material' (1979: 663). If we understand the 'material' to mean the constraints of genre (Sarris vaguely describes it as 'the stuff of the cinema' (ibid.)), then a generic approach to John Carpenter's films is particularly appropriate, for in his best films Carpenter astutely employs the conventions and iconography of his preferred genres to express a consistent vision. Carpenter, who also often works on the scripts, editing and electronic music for his films, is clearly an auteur in the classic sense of the term. This chapter will examine how Carpenter's feature films, from *Dark Star* (1974) to *Vampires* (1998), mobilise and mix the conventions of those genres he has mined most often – science fiction and horror, the western and action film – to depict a dark world tainted with evil and corruption in which morality is severely tested and social cohesion crumbles.

Carpenter is one of the few contemporary American directors, if not the only one, to work consistently and comfortably within established genres. All of his films are firmly rooted in genre, even when, as in the case of *Memoirs of an Invisible Man* (1992), which was publicised as a 'suspense-filled adventure with romance and comedy' (Brown 1992: 48), they seek to disturb generic expectations or to play with conventions. Frequently Carpenter has stated his appreciation for Hollywood's old studio system and for genre films, the mainstay of studio production. He has a particular fondness for the genres of the fantastic (as a youth Carpenter wrote and published several horror fanzines),[1] and largely because of the phenomenal success of *Halloween* in 1978, one of the most profitable independent productions ever made, Carpenter found a niche with horror and science fiction (Billson 1997: 18).

From the beginning Carpenter's work has incorporated the generic elements of science fiction, horror and action like his alien in *Starman* (1984) who absorbs the cultural artefacts sent into space by NASA's Voyager probe. Some of Carpenter's films are clearly generic 'product'. So, for example, *Starman* was intended to capitalise on the huge success of Steven Spielberg's two blockbuster hits about benevolent aliens, *Close Encounters of the Third Kind* (1977) and *E.T.: The Extra-Terrestrial* (1982); *Big Trouble in Little China* (1986) is an homage to Asian martial arts films; and *In the Mouth of Madness* (1995) an entry in the cycle of self-reflexive postmodern horror movies. Two of Carpenter's films – *The Thing* (1982) and *Village of the Damned* (1995) – are remakes of horror/science fiction movie classics, and most of his productions contain references to other movies in these genres. Critics have often noted Carpenter's reliance on genre conventions; Anne Billson, for example, praises *The Thing* for being 'a mighty convergence of all the horror and science fiction trends of several decades' (1997: 13), while Kent Jones sees Carpenter's films as lean genre machines (he describes *Assault on Precinct 13* (1976) as having 'the undiluted force of a terse, savage two-note guitar break' (1999: 29)). Even Robin Wood, who has attacked Carpenter's movies as ideologically suspect pastiches (a point to which I shall return shortly), concedes that the director has a special skill at bringing together a multitude of generic influences (1979: 24–6).

In turn, Carpenter has had a profound effect upon the genres from which he borrows. In the 1980s, along with Walter Hill, he was instrumental in the development of the new action film, as distinct from the traditional adventure or disaster film. The trend in Hollywood movies of the 1980s and 1990s towards minimally drawn characters in fast-paced narratives featuring much violent action can be traced back to Carpenter's early work. Most obviously, *Halloween* spawned the low-budget slasher films that dominated the horror genre from the early to mid-1980s and established many of its conventions: 'the shock-horror prologue, the subjective camerawork standing in for the killer's point of view, the dead bogeyman who keeps coming back to life' (Billson 1997: 20).[2] Less dramatically, variations on images from Carpenter films seem to turn up regularly in other genre movies, such as the gathering street people from *Prince of Darkness* (1987) who reappear in *End of Days* (1999) and *Bless the Child* (2000).

Indeed, Carpenter's allegiance to the pleasures of genre has been unwavering. He began making films in the 1970s, the decade of American cinema during which, as John Cawelti (2003) has noted, the various genres were undergoing a significant 'transformation' as many movies set about demythologising the classic conventions and debunking or subverting their traditional ideological meanings. For Cawelti, this development was the result of the convergence of several historical factors, including the demise of the Hayes Office in 1967, the continuing breakup of the traditional studio system of production, the popularisation of the auteur theory, and the rise of the 'new Hollywood', featuring a generation of brash young directors (Spielberg, Martin Scorsese, Paul Schrader, Brian De Palma, George Lucas and Francis Ford Coppola, among others) known collectively as the 'movie brats'. Like the French *nouvelle vague*, the films of these directors were stylistically heterogenous, but movies such as Coppola's *The Godfather* (1972) and Scorsese's *Mean Streets* (1973) shared a new, hip awareness of generic traditions. Once the movie brats successfully integrated into the industry, they tended to move away from a consistent identification with genre filmmaking. Carpenter, however, has steadfastly continued to make genre movies. Unlike most of the other directors redefining the horror film in the 1970s – George A. Romero, Larry Cohen, Tobe Hooper, David Cronenberg, De Palma – Carpenter has remained consistently devoted to the genre. Kent Jones has even suggested that 'Carpenter stands completely and utterly alone as the last genre filmmaker in America', comparable to directors such as Edgar G. Ulmer, Robert Siodmak, Sam Fuller and Robert Aldrich during the studio era, 'whose artistry is focused on satisfying genre conventions and the demands of narrative, and whose loftier preoccupations are filtered through said conventions' (1999: 26).

Carpenter uses genre to provide a kind of narrative 'shorthand' that contributes to the impressive narrative economy of his films. Just as Carpenter observes, regarding samurai films, that 'each time you make one, you don't have to go back and establish the legend of the samurai. He *is*' (Fox 1980: 42), so his films often eliminate exposition or delay it until the action is well underway, knowing the audience will be carried along by their familiarity with the conventions invoked. We do not know exactly what happened to Snake Plissken (Kurt Russell) before the plot of *Escape From New York* (1981) begins, although all the other characters do, but it does not matter anyway; his familiar dialogue, body language and attire tell us all we need to know about him. This approach allows the director to concentrate on an uncluttered depiction of action that exploits all the elements of the cinematic image: frame, depth of field, composition and movement, as well as the rhythms of editing. Genre theorist Steve Neale (1981) has devoted an entire essay to the deft manner in which Carpenter creates suspense in *Halloween* through his canny control of the camera's point of view in relation to characters within the narrative. Sequences such as the famous lengthy point-of-view sequence shot that opens *Halloween*, Pinback's adventure with the alien beachball-like creature in the lift shaft in *Dark Star*, and the long take depicting the gradual destruction of a room by gunfire in *Assault on Precinct 13* are moments in Carpenter's work that aspire to nothing less than pure cinema as experimental filmmakers conceive it.

This lean approach to narrative explains in part Carpenter's oft-stated admiration for the films of Howard Hawks. From this perspective, Hawks is the ideal auteur; not only did he work across a broad range of genres, from musicals to comedies to action films, but, more importantly, he was adept at expressing his personal vision subtly, within efficiently constructed genre narratives (he once remarked that a good director is 'someone who does not annoy you' (quoted in Wood 1968: 11)). Like Walter Hill (see, for example, *The Driver* (1978); *Last Man Standing* (1996)) and Romero (*Dawn of the Dead* (1978); *Knightriders* (1981)), Carpenter admires Hawks's ability to express a personal philosophy through genre rather than pretentious 'artiness', especially through his use of action as a physical index of moral value and his reliance on gesture to express professionalism in action in such films as *Only Angels Have Wings* (1939), *Red River* (1948) and *Rio Bravo* (1959).[3] Hawks's movies in this regard continue the tradition of American fiction begun by James Fenimore Cooper, in whose novels, as literary critic Marius Bewley has observed, 'an action is the intensified motion of life in which the spiritual and moral faculties of men are no less engaged than their physical selves' (1963: 73). Like Hawks, Carpenter relies on action as a primary means of developing character and assessing moral worth. Carpenter has often acknowledged Hawks as the major influence on his work, and his movies frequently contain homages to Hawks's films. *Assault on Precinct 13*, as many critics have observed, is structured as a combination of Romero's *Night of the Living Dead* (1968) and Hawks's *Rio Bravo*, while the children in *Halloween* watch *The Thing from Another World* (1951) on television – the very Hawks film Carpenter would remake four years later.

Yet Carpenter's vision is fundamentally different from that of Hawks, whose films frequently establish a narrative situation in which a group of individuals, mostly men, are faced with an important and difficult job while isolated from the rest of the world. In Carpenter's films, the threat just as often isolates the members of the group rather than brings them together. As Billson notes, in Carpenter's version of *The Thing*, which is more faithful to John W. Campbell Jr.'s source novella, 'Who Goes There?', the members of the group are set against each other by the monster rather than become united in order to defeat it: 'Here it's every man for himself. Survival of the fittest. Natural selection on the hoof' (1997: 61). For Stephen Prince, 'boredom and isolation have eroded Hawksian camaraderie' even before the appearance of the Thing (1988: 25). Similarly, in *Dark Star* the men have grown apart from each other, both physically and emotionally, precisely because they have been together for so long in the depths of space. The end of the film, when the men on the ship are blown out into space in different directions after the ship explodes (a reference perhaps to Ray Bradbury's 1949 short story 'Kaleidoscope'), literalises in physical space what already had happened to them psychologically. In a world in which, as MacReady says in Carpenter's version of *The Thing*, 'trust is a difficult thing to come by these days', Hawksian group solidarity is rarely achieved.

Equally important, Carpenter's films have a more critical political edge than Hawks's. As some have argued, Hawks's characters may live briefly on an existential precipice, but the safety net of dominant ideology always is stretched underneath. Hawks's cowboys may be cut off from the law while on the cattle drive in *Red River*, but ultimately the film endorses entrepreneurial capitalism. In Carpenter's films, however, often his characters are not only distanced from normal legal and social structures, but the films show those very structures as the locus of corruption, as in *Escape From L.A.* (1996) where the president of the USA is of the extreme right-wing and is committed to removing the 'undesireables' from his society: 'prostitutes, atheists, runaways – we're cleaning out the trash'. In *The Thing from Another World* Hawks initially pokes fun at the bureaucracy of the postwar American military, but when push comes to shove the members of the group work together to cook the

*Dark Star*: the claustrophobic depths of outer space

'supercarrot', defeating it through traditional American know-how. By contrast, in Carpenter's version where the men have turned on each other, the film ends not with the injunction to 'keep watching the skies' – that is, to be on guard against the alien Other – but with the image of MacReady (Kurt Russell) and Childs (Keith David), a black man and a white man, armed and eyeing each other warily across the icy expanse of the widescreen frame. This is an extremely loaded image, one that fails to resolve its narrative dilemmas (has the Thing been defeated? is either or both of the men a Thing?) and that consequently arouses rather than assuages anxiety about race relations in the US. Unlike Hawks's film, Carpenter's lacks satisfying closure in the manner of classic genre movies. Carpenter's view here, and typically, is much bleaker than that of Hawks, because in his world when danger threatens and social order is stripped away, men often regress to a primitive Hobbesian brutality. This dark tone is set immediately at the outset of *Dark Star*, Carpenter's first feature, which begins with an imperfect transmission from Mission Control on Earth informing the ship's crew that they lack both the political will and government funding to properly maintain their aging and malfunctioning ship – that, in other words, the men are completely on their own. With a total collapse of professionalism, the crew now blow up planets merely to relieve boredom.

In an influential essay on *Assault on Precinct 13*, Tony Williams argues that while the film is a very cleverly constructed genre piece, densely intertextual, ultimately it is reactionary because it 'cannot advance beyond the level of homage and probe into the nature of the materials it uses' (1979: 67). Williams claims that with its combination of horror and western genre conventions, the film represents the gang members who attack the police station as monstrously Other, similar to the way classic horror movies depict the monster and classic westerns depict Native Americans. The combined gangs include a horde of racial others (blacks, Latinos and Orientals), while the white gang members are interpreted by Williams as representative of hippies or the counter-culture (Robin Wood similarly sees them as 'revolutionaries' (1979: 24–6)). According to Williams, Carpenter's style makes identification with any of this undifferentiated evil mass impossible, so that ultimately the film offers only a choice between 'anarchic violence and arbitrary legality', thus situating it 'in the tradition of American right-wing movies where conservative individualism is opposed to unindividualised, violent totalitarianism' (1979: 70). Robert C. Cumbow has argued otherwise, accusing Williams of reading too much into the film ('Williams, it seems, wants Woodstock, and can't forgive Carpenter for giving him Altamont'), countering that *Assault on Precinct 13* instead articulates a politics of individual heroism (1990: 38). But it is Williams' interpretation of Carpenter's work as belonging to what Wood calls horror's 'reactionary wing' that has dominated the critical assessment of Carpenter.

Certainly the director's frequent statements about artistic pretentiousness in the cinema and that film is an emotional rather than intellectual medium (McCarthy 1980: 23) have not encouraged critics to look more carefully at Carpenter's films (one such comment is used by Williams as an epigraph for his essay). But these remarks should not be understood to mean that, for Carpenter, films are incapable of conveying ideas; rather, what he is saying is that by the nature of the medium they communicate to viewers in the first instance on an emotional, experiential level. Like Susan Sontag, to whom he refers, Carpenter believes that 'in place of a hermeneutics we need an erotics of art' (1966: 14).[4] Carpenter acknowledges the affective power of good storytelling in the opening scene of *The Fog* (1979): in the hands of an adept director who does not annoy you, we are held in thrall by a good story, like the boys listening in rapt attention to John Houseman's ghost tale; watching movies, we huddle together, like children around the campfire in the dark of night. Sontag claims that 'it is possible to elude the interpreters … by making works of art whose surface is so unified and clean, whose momentum is so rapid, whose address is so direct that the work can be … just what it is. Is this possible now? It does happen in films, I believe' (1966: 11). Her description would seem to apply perfectly to Carpenter's genre movies.

Robin Wood defines Carpenter's horror films as 'reactionary' rather than 'progressive' – that is, they endorse dominant ideology rather than challenge it – because of the ways they represent the monster (1979: 23–8). But according to Wood's own influential terms for understanding horror as a genre, much of Carpenter's work may just as easily be understood as belonging to the opposite camp. Carpenter's images of evil may be amorphous – a vile liquid in a tube, a dense evening mist, a shape-shifting alien – but they are never simply 'true' or 'pure'. Yes, Michael Meyers in *Halloween* is given no real psychological motivation and, as Wood points out, his apparent invulnerability makes him seem like the 'bogeyman' his psychiatrist, Dr Loomis (Donald Pleasence), asserts he is (1979: 26). However, Loomis's dismissive diagnosis may merely underscore the limitations of conventional psychiatry – as Wood himself suggests elsewhere about the considerably more detailed account of Norman Bates's condition at the end of Hitchcock's *Psycho* (1960) (1965: 121–2).

Ultimately, in many of Carpenter's films it is in fact the normal that is shown to be monstrous. In these films, as Robert E. Zeigler has perceived, 'the darkest side of one's own conscience wears not a mask but a familiar face' (1983: 786).

*Christine* (1983), for example, based on the novel by Stephen King, deflects its horror from the car (referred to as 'she' throughout the film) to normative hetero-sexual masculinity. In a narrative about a high school nerd, Arnie Cunningham (Keith Gordon), who acquires and becomes possessed by a supernaturally empow-ered 1958 Plymouth Fury and as a result transforms from a mild to wild teenager, Arnie's personality changes are little more than horrifying exaggerations of mas-culine potency as conventionally represented in Western culture. Arnie becomes exactly the kind of man that so many advertisements for automobiles, which feature male drivers with adoring women draped over the body work, construct consumers to be. For much of the film Carpenter leaves ambiguous the question of whether the car alone is killing people by itself or whether Arnie is in fact responsible. But despite Christine's ability to control the dashboard radio and to regenerate its exterior (a horrifying thought indeed to Detroit's skilled purveyors of planned obsolescence), in the climactic showdown in the garage Carpenter reveals that Arnie is behind the wheel after all. Thus, in contrast to such superficially similar horror films as *The Car* (1977) and King's own *Maximum Overdrive* (1986), in which the vehicles themselves take on a supernatural malevolent force, *Christine* makes it clear that Arnie's psyche is in control.

The theme of *They Live* (1988), similarly, is the necessity to see through the obfuscating haze of dominant ideology. In the story, aliens have infiltrated human society and control the media, literally creating what Frankfurt School theorists would call its 'false consciousness' encoded in television signals that create, accord-ing to a subversive hacker, 'an artificially induced state of consciousness that resem-bles sleep'. People must wear special sunglasses to become aware of the subtextual messages of the media that exhort us to be be happy, reproduce and consume. The film offers an Althusserian critique of the mass media as Ideological State Apparatus (Althusser 1971) ('they live; we sleep'), and the aliens are monstrous only insofar as we recognise them as smart capitalists – they are, as one human collaborator explains, free enterprisers for whom the Earth is 'just another developing planet. We're their Third World.' That the aliens pass for human and live among us, as our wives and husbands, is a particularly trenchant comment about the thorough inhumanity of American capitalism.

The distortion, as well as the potential, of the media – how its pervasive power manufactures consent – is a theme that informs much of Carpenter's work. *Assault on Precinct 13*, for example, begins with the police viciously shooting a group of gang members in an alley, like fish in a barrel, but the event is later described on the radio with obvious bias as 'a shootout with police'. In *The Fog*, disc jockey Stevie Wayne (Adrienne Barbeau) uses her radio to warn others about the deadly mist, while *In the Mouth of Madness*, about a horror writer who has gained terrible powers through the sheer magnitude of his popularity, similarly shows how popular entertainment, as in *They Live*, can distract us from the real world with unhealthy fantasies. The film's opening images of paperbacks being mass produced recalls the

*They Live*: we sleep ... a state of false consciousness

opening Detroit assembly line scene in *Christine* (as well as the similar beginning of Max Ophuls' *La Signora di Tutti* (1934), a satire about mass marketing).

But Carpenter's most common target of institutional horror is the Church. The Church has not got a prayer against the aliens in *They Live*, for example, and even its more pragmatic value as a front for the video hackers quickly disappears when it is raided by police. More explicitly, in *Prince of Darkness* (1987), evil is given literal shape, metaphysics becomes microbiology, and faith is forced to defer to science in order to deal with evil (Dietrich 1991). *Vampires* is 'Hawksian' in its focus on the procedural details employed by a group of vampire hunters hired by the Church. Kim Newman sees this focus as marking 'a significant shift of emphasis in the vampire sub-genre' (1999: 60), with all but two of the initial group of slayers quickly slaughtered by the master vampire, Valek (Thomas Ian Griffith). Jack Crow (James Woods) explains to Father Guiteau (Tom Guinee), the new priest assigned to him by the Church, that vampires are not 'a bunch of fuckin' fags hopping around in rented formal wear and seducing everybody in sight with cheesy Eurotrash accents … forget whatever you've seen in the movies'. So crucifixes fail to work as a defense against vampires – a violation of one of the genre's classic conventions that comments on the Church's emptiness as much as the literally empty police station in *Assault on Precinct 13* expresses the collapse of authority in the inner city (Cumbow 1990: 37).

Indeed, the Church is seen not merely as impotent but as the very source of corruption, responsible (through a vaguely explained 'inverse exorcism') for the creation of vampires in the first place, as represented by an old black crucifix that has the potential to give vampires the ability to walk unharmed in the light of day. Hawksian professionalism in *Vampires* is associated explicitly with the resistance to church ideology, embodied in the opposition of Crow and Guiteau in a conflict between pragmatism and faith. But as they pursue Valek, the priest finds himself forced to take up arms in a just cause, thus enacting a kind of radical liberation theology. Tellingly, Guiteau cauterises his neck wound with the smoking barrel of his machine gun, not with the balm of prayer, as his Christian creed is supplanted by the morality of violent action. In the climactic battle with Valek, the priest tosses a stake to Crow, reminiscent of the way Walter Brennan tosses a knife in one scene and a rifle in another to John Wayne in Hawks's *Red River*.[5] In the final scene, Crow accepts a rosary from Father Guiteau as they walk together into the darkness of the vampire stronghold to slay those that remain. But this gesture is less a suggestion that Crow is born again than a Hawksian gesture of respect for a comrade with whom he has experienced battle ('Time to slay some vampires … just the two of us', he says). There is still a job to be done for which professionalism is required.

My intention has not been to suggest that Carpenter's films are unproblematic – quite the contrary, some are seriously flawed indeed. *They Live*, for example, abandons its cultural critique halfway through to concentrate on the improbable heroics of its solitary hero Nada (Roddy Piper). Ironically, the film becomes exactly the kind of formulaic escapist entertainment it begins by critiquing as the opiate of the people, when Nada single-handedly destroys the alien's sole (!) broadcasting station, apparently saving the world. Also, despite all the Carol Clover-influenced talk about empowered 'final girls' inspired by *Halloween*, Carpenter's treatment of women (not unlike Hawks's) is often questionable. In *Vampires*, the only women we see are hookers and bloodsuckers, and the fatal bite the prostitute Katrina (Sheryl Lee) receives from Valek provides a thin pretext for including gratuitous scenes of semi-nudity and bondage.

Yet at the same time *Christine* exposes male anxiety as an attempt to possess women and position them as objects of circulation within a male economy (in both senses of the word), and the character of Carjack/Hershe (Pam Grier) in *Escape From L.A.* is a transsexual whose role is a striking example of the new hardbody action heroine touted as progressive in such movies as *Aliens* (1986) and *Terminator 2: Judgment Day* (1991) (see, for example, Tasker 1993). At best we could say that Carpenter's *ouevre* is deeply ambivalent, his work constituting what Robin Wood might more generously call a series of 'incoherent texts' – works in which a failure 'toward the ordering of experience' exposes dominant ideology (1986: 47). So if *Escape From New York* seizes upon the contemporary fear of growing crime and violence in America's inner cities, *Escape From L.A.* blames the situation on right-wingers and their approach to what the fascist president (Cliff Robertson) refers to as 'a final solution'. But we might note that Hawks himself was no less 'incoherent', his comedies, as Wood also noted, expressing the opposite view of professionalism from that depicted in the action films (1968: 68). Carpenter's first film, the short *The Resurrection of Bronco Billy* (1970), tells the story of a contemporary urbanite who survives modern life by retreating into western fantasies in which he is the classic cowboy hero, succumbing to what Wood, discussing Hawks's comedies, calls 'the lure of irresponsibility'. Carpenter's films, similarly, shuttle tellingly between, on the one hand, the popular pleasures of genre and, on the other, its progressive potential.

*Notes*

1    These fanzines had titles such as *King Kong Journal, Phantasm – Terror Thrills of the Films* and *Fantastic Films Illustrated*.
2    The slasher imitations of *Halloween* were in fact so numerous that they generated a critical debate involving such work as, most influentially, Clover (1992). See also Conrich (1995: 48–9).
3    For a discussion of the Hawksian qualities of Romero's horror films, see Grant (1996).
4    Carpenter discusses Sontag in Fox (1980: 42).
5    In 1978 Carpenter cited the rifle scene in *Red River* as his one conscious Hawksian reference in *Assault on Precinct 13* (Milne & Combs 1978: 95).

*References*

Althusser, L. (1971) *Lenin and Philosophy and Other Essays*. Harmondsworth: Penguin.
Bewley, M. (1963) *The Eccentric Design: Form in the Classic American Novel*. New York and London: Columbia University Press.
Billson, A. (1997) *The Thing*. London: British Film Institute.
Brown, G. (1992) 'Memoirs of an Invisible Man', *Sight and Sound*, 2, 2, 48.
Cawelti, J. (2003) '*Chinatown* and Generic Transformation in Recent American Films', in B. Grant (ed.) *Film Genre Reader III*. Austin: University of Texas Press, 243–61.
Clover, C. J. (1992) *Men, Women, and Chain Saws: Gender in the Modern Horror Film*. Princeton, NJ: Princeton University Press.
Conrich, I. (1995) 'How to Make a "Slasher" Film', *Invasion*, 11, 48–9.
Cumbow, R. C. (1990) *Order in the Universe: The Films of John Carpenter*. Metuchen, NJ: Scarecrow Press.
Dietrich, B. (1991) '*Prince of Darkness*, Prince of Light: From Faust to Physicist', *Journal of Popular Film and Television*, 19, 2, 91–6.
Fox, J. R. (1980) 'Riding High on Horror', *Cinefantastique*, 10, 1, 5–10, 40, 42–4.
Grant, B. K. (1996) 'Taking Back the *Night of the Living Dead*: George Romero, Feminism and the Horror Film', in B. K. Grant (ed.) *The Dread of Difference: Gender and the Horror Film*. Austin: University of Texas Press, 200–12.
Jones, K. (1999) 'John Carpenter: american movie classic', *Film Comment*, 35, 1, 26–31.
McCarthy, T. (1980) 'Trick and Treat', *Film Comment*, 16, 1, 17–24.
Milne, T. and Combs, R. (1978) 'The Man in the Cryogenic Freezer', *Sight and Sound*, 47, 2, 94–8.
Neale, S. (1981) '*Halloween*: Suspense, Aggression and the Look', *Framework*, 14, 25–9. [Reprinted in B. K. Grant (ed.) (1984) *Planks of Reason: Essays on the Horror Film*. Metuchen, NJ and London: Scarecrow Press, 331–45.]
Newman, K. (1999) 'Vampires', *Sight and Sound*, 9, 12, 60.
Prince, S. (1988) 'Dread, Taboo and *The Thing*: Toward a Social Theory of the Horror Film', *Wide Angle*, 10, 3, 19–29.

Sarris, A. (1979) 'Notes on the Auteur Theory in 1962', in G. Mast and M. Cohen (eds) *Film Theory and Criticism: Introductory Readings*, 2nd edn. Oxford and New York: Oxford University Press, 650–65.

Sontag, S. (1966) 'Against Interpretation', in *Against Interpretation and Other Essays*. New York: Delta, 3–14.

Tasker, Y. (1993) *Spectacular Bodies: Gender, Genre and the Action Cinema*. London and New York: Routledge.

Williams, T. (1979) '*Assault on Precinct 13*: The Mechanics of Repression', in R. Wood and R. Lippe (eds) *The American Nightmare: Essays on the Horror Film*. Toronto: Festival of Festivals, 67–73.

Wood, R. (1965) *Hitchcock's Films*. London: Zwemmer/New York: A. S. Barnes.

_____ (1968) *Howard Hawks*. London: Secker & Warburg/British Film Institute.

_____ (1979) 'An Introduction to the American Horror Film', in R. Wood and R. Lippe (eds) *The American Nightmare: Essays on the Horror Film*. Toronto: Festival of Festivals, 7–28.

_____ (1986) *Hollywood from Vietnam to Reagan*. New York: Columbia University Press.

Ziegler, R. E. (1983) 'Killing Space: The Dialectic in John Carpenter's Films', *Georgia Review*, 37, 4, 770–86.

# CHAPTER TWO

# Us and Them: Authority and Identity in Carpenter's Films

## David Woods

The importance that John Carpenter places upon having control over his films is well known. His name appears as part of his film titles, he contributes to multiple aspects of the filmmaking process, from directing to editing and scoring (and even piloting the often-present helicopter), and over time he has built up a regular team of actors and technical personnel with whom he knows he can work to produce what is often referred to as his 'personal vision'. As his reputation as a director was starting to grow, he stated that the only criterion for choosing which projects to make was 'that I get control of the film. Creative control. For a certain amount of money, you see, at this point in my career they will give me control *if* it's done cheaply enough. For a $10 million project they wouldn't give me that control. Not now' (Wells 1980: 220, emphasis in original). While the confidence on display here could barely hint at the complex and sometimes difficult relationships he was to have with the studios in the coming decades,[1] this conception of what constitutes the ideal form of filmmaking has remained one of the constants which character-ises Carpenter's outlook. At the same time, Carpenter also faithfully works within genres, to the extent that Kent Jones calls him the last genre filmmaker in America (1999: 26). Whatever vision he brings is thus expressed within the relatively close confines dictated by his chosen genres, which themselves range quite widely but often involve an amalgam of the western, horror and/or science fiction combined with action. Hand in hand with this deliberate self-restriction is his intention to make popular films, that is to say, films which primarily evoke an emotional response in the audience or, as John Muir puts it, 'to entertain and manipulate the masses in the manner of the Hitchcock or Hawks blockbusters he remembers from his own youth' (2000: 2). This disavowal of intellectualism defines his own filmmaking practices which, as is also widely acknowledged, marks him out from directors with more 'postmodern' sensibilities:

> I fight against becoming self-conscious. It's the death of a filmmaker, when he starts parodying himself. You can't; you've got to go by feelings. Later on you might say, 'I think I did that because of this'. But at the time, the minute you intellectualise something, it's cold, it's dead. (McCarthy 1980: 23)

And yet, of course, this emphasis on both the production and consumption of film as an affective practice can only be a partial account of the filmmaking process. Particularly during Carpenter's ascendancy critics were quick to identify what they found to be right-wing political subtexts in his films, starting with *Assault on Precinct 13* (1976) (Williams 1979; Wood 1979). True to his lights, Carpenter's immediate response to criticisms of the depiction of the youth gangs in *Assault on Precinct 13* as simply irredeemably evil was that the film was dealing with 'the good guys versus the bad guys. I had no intention of making a political or social statement. If I ever do make a political or social statement in a film, I'll either do it unconsciously or else I'll have to be taken away, because I don't believe in that sort of thing' (Appelbaum 1979: 13). While declarations of this sort are not likely to cut much ice with critics who detect such undercurrents, it is important to note both the intention as well as the fact that, insofar as Carpenter ever expresses a political opinion, he seems far removed from a right-wing agenda. Muir identifies a 'strong anti-authoritarian, laconic bent' in his films, which arises from his 'total displeasure with authority, and the establishment as a whole' (2000: 2). What is at stake in these differences between directorial vision and critical response is the complex relationship between on the one hand a directing style which seeks spontaneity, affect and the avoidance of 'messages', and on the other the demands which genres make of their material. More generally, the tension is between contemporary social and political issues and the transmuted forms they take in their cinematic representation. The intricacies of these transformations show themselves indirectly in Carpenter's films in the logic of their narratives which, if given close attention, belie their deceptively simple appearance.

One recurring theme in Carpenter's work is that of a divide between an 'us' and a 'them', between those who, representing the ordinary citizen, are 'good enough' in a Hawksian sense, beyond any recognisable social or political allegiance, and the forces which threaten them. While in some cases these forces are identified with the supernatural, in others 'they' often amount to, or at least include, an officially sanctioned authority (though aliens may also figure). It is films of the second type which will form the focus of interest here, affording as they do the most direct consideration of issues of the political. If the motif is examined in detail as it works itself out in particular films in this category, the apparent clarity and stability of the divide between 'us' and 'them' can be seen to waver, and with it the significance of the debates over Carpenter's world view is brought into sharper focus.

Invariably, authorities are painted in Carpenter's films in ways which amply support Muir's conclusion that they indicate a consistently anti-authoritarian sensibility at work. The crew in *Dark Star* (1974), for instance, wander the galaxy in a state of anomie, blowing up 'unstable' planets seemingly at random, and certainly without regard for any intelligent life they might contain. Technical support from Earth has been reduced due to government cutbacks and all sense of their mission being a meaningful one has broken down. The police provoke the siege in *Assault on Precinct 13* by murdering members of the street gang in cold blood, while the government in the two *Escape* films is presented as fascist and Christian fundamentalist respectively, and its eventual downfall at the hands of Snake Plissken (Kurt Russell) in *Escape From L.A.* (1996) seems to be depicted approvingly. Turning to films with aliens (as opposed to supernatural beings) as central figures, the official chain of command is rapidly shown to be unworkable in the face of alien infiltration and extreme threat in *The Thing* (1982), while the (friendly) alien visitor in *Starman* (1984) who takes the message of peace contained in a space probe at face value soon finds that Earth is 'hostile' and, far from being able to make peaceful contact at an official level, is forced to go on the run, hunted by a relentless scientific-military organisation. In each case, then, authorities which are directly or indirectly identified with the State turn out to be far from worthy of the people's trust.

Set against this backdrop, the films often follow the efforts of the protagonists to overcome the threats and hazards which the authorities more or less directly thrust upon them, and it is this pattern which has led to a widespread recognition of their individualistic outlook. 'Moral meaning', according to Robert C. Cumbow, 'must be on the level of individual heroism and humane treatment of one's fellows' (1990: 104). And indeed, in scenarios where little can be expected from the crooked authorities, Carpenter is at his most Hawksian because of his 'sense of an underlying code of behaviour – one sharp enough to distinguish bad guys from good, yet broad enough to redefine the very notion of goodness in terms of skill and responsibility, not social or political alliance' (1990: 110). Muir goes further, stating that even supposedly nihilistic heroes such as Plissken, and John Nada (Roddy Piper) in *They Live* (1988), embody Carpenter's romanticism, or more specifically 'a belief in American ideals and in man himself … [Carpenter] believes that man can do better, and his heroes consistently prove that worthy goals … can be accomplished, but only through individuality' (2000: 3). But as suggested earlier, the significance of these conflicts only becomes clear if the narrative logic is traced in detail, and what follows will consider some of Carpenter's least discussed films: *Memoirs of an Invisible Man* (1992), *Village of the Damned* (1995) and *They Live*.

*Memoirs of an Invisible Man*

In *Memoirs of an Invisible Man* the authority in question is in the first instance the CIA. When Nick Halloway (Chevy Chase) becomes invisible in an accident, his existence is soon detected, and most of the film is paced around Nick's efforts to outrun the Agency, whose intention is, he overhears, to keep him in a laboratory to find out the secrets behind his transformation. From the outset the Agency is shown to behave unreasonably, though the extent of its culpability is left ambiguous. Leading the hunt is David Jenkins (Sam Neill), whose first scene shows him before an unspecified government committee which is trying to expose him as a station chief and hitman paid by the CIA. The regard in which the Agency holds governmental proceedings is made clear when Jenkins cuts short the interrogation to investigate the accident. Though Jenkins had performed smoothly under questioning, he admits to his boss, Warren Singleton (Stephen Tobolowski), that he had been rattled by the information the committee had managed to piece together, but Singleton dismisses it as a 'dog and pony show'. Jenkins' marginal status – not quite an official employee but wielding apparently unbridled power, and something of a maverick whose tactics had previously caused a 'fiasco' in Iran – could be read as a device the film employs to distance the Agency from blame for the ruthless methods he adopts, or alternatively could be seen as a sign of its devious efforts to avoid accountability. Further plot details, however, may incline the viewer to the latter conclusion. Jenkins manipulates Singleton easily by appealing to his empire-building ambitions, with the latter only deciding to abandon Jenkins near the end of the film when it becomes clear that Jenkins' plans to 'own the Agency' are going to be uncovered. The question becomes how far this motivation through self-interest extends up the hierarchy. How far down it extends, however, is made clear. The agents and SWAT teams who pursue Nick seem to enjoy their work rather too much, taking against him with an inexplicable hatred, calling him an 'asshole' and, in their eagerness to catch him, indiscriminately shooting a bystander with a tranquilliser dart. As they wait for Nick to contact the head of the laboratory, Dr Wachs (Jim Norton), one of them stares leeringly at a woman doing a work-

An invisible Nick Halloway breaks free from Jenkins and the ruthless CIA in *Memoirs of an Invisible Man*

out in the park, almost missing Nick as a result. Wachs helps Nick escape by taking another poorly-aimed dart for him, and again the apparently unseemly job of interrogating a distinguished academic, who indeed has ties with the CIA, is undertaken with relish. We later learn Wachs has been killed for his pains. Ruthless self-interest, whether it be ambition for wealth or power or a more immediate satisfaction of impulses, is rife in the organisation. While this seems to leave open the possibility that the government itself is free of corruption, Nick is not inclined to think so. When Alice (Daryl Hannah) encourages him to go to Washington for help, he retorts acidly, 'you expect me to trust a politician?' The significance of this conflation will be revisited later.

Against this familiar backdrop of untrustworthy authority, Nick seems in some respects to be a fair representative of Carpenter's heroes. He is propelled through no fault of his own into an extraordinary situation which is beyond his control and, using his own resources, he finally vanquishes 'the bad guy'. Yet the sort of individualism which he embodies is a curiously fraught one. He too is driven by self interest. He has no commitments, and is more assiduous in chasing women (though it is clear he only wants one-night-stands) than he is in his job, in which he is depicted as a dilettante. We find he has offered to cover for someone for the visit to the laboratory where the accident happens, but only because he was drunk at the time. He is a member of a private men's club but only avails himself of the bar, and prefers to gamble on sporting events rather than use the sports facilities it offers. Of course it is only because he has a hangover that he is asleep in the laboratory when it blows up and he becomes invisible. However, as the film progresses it becomes clear that, as so often in science fiction, the motif of invisibility has a metaphorical as well as a literal meaning. We discover he used to dream of being invisible as a child since it would allow him to do whatever he wanted, but when it becomes a reality he is unable to act since to do so would give himself away. Fundamentally, however, his invisibility robs him of his agency because it prevents him from being recognised by others: 'I never realised how important it is to be seen, you know, acknowledged. You start questioning whether you exist at all.' And of course there are numerous suggestions that this was the condition of Nick's life before the accident. His boss asks him about a woman he saw just once six months previously, and his friends discuss him in rather uncomplimentary ways as he listens in, saying he is 'too narcissistic to kill himself'. ('So much for my good friends', he sighs.) Jenkins makes it explicit: with 'no strong emotional ties, no political beliefs, no particular interests', he has the perfect profile: 'he was invisible before he was invisible'.

At one level, then, the film seems to follow a pattern often found in Carpenter's work, with someone who is marginalised by society nonetheless making a meaningful intervention in the world. In this case, Nick struggles to become visible, rapidly passing from the literal sense of the word (his adult dreams in response to his plight consist of seeing himself as extremely visible, as a famous jazz musician or sporting star) to a seemingly more morally and emotionally meaningful one, as he comes to seek responsibility in the form of having a family with Alice. The film having firmly planted this vision in the viewer's mind, Nick finally manages to dispatch Jenkins and start a new life in what we are led to believe is Switzerland. And yet, for reasons

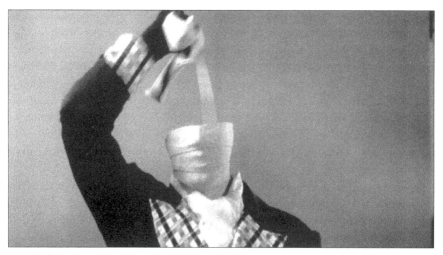

*Memoirs of an Invisible Man*: 'I never realised how important it is to be seen … You start questioning whether you exist at all'

beyond their cloying quality, the closing scenes of the couple's marital bliss, with baby on the way, seem unsatisfactory.

Perhaps the most obvious aspect of this comes with the striking similarities between Nick and Jenkins. Jenkins himself calls attention to this pattern, observing in one of his many appeals to Nick to give himself up that they are not so different, that they are both 'iconoclasts'. While this may not be the first description that they both invite, when they are in the lift heading for the roof in the final action sequence Jenkins comes up with the more plausible description of Nick as 'a natural' and 'cool, imaginative, elegant'. Indeed it is the case that Nick has only survived because he is as resourceful as Jenkins, and is finally as willing as he is to resort to murder. Some of the parallels may be explained by the Oedipal thread which is sustained throughout the film. Jenkins is presented as a man driven by a base love of power, in which his proclivity for violence is central. The latter, however, is consistently identified with a castration threat. When Singleton (perhaps rather unconvincingly) threatens Jenkins that he will be the next to disappear if things go wrong, Jenkins suddenly turns the tables on him, reminding him that 'I'm the one that kills people' and threatening to cut off Singleton's testicles and serve them up to one of his, Jenkins', henchmen. Nick's dream about being famous ends rather abruptly when, about to realise his conquest of Alice, he opens his dressing gown to reveal a transparent patch where his penis should be. Alice screams, and Jenkins, standing behind her, says 'Looking for something, Nick?' When Jenkins has him cornered, Nick says that whatever he is to become is his own choice, to which Jenkins responds that that is the reason he cannot let him live. Even George, Nick's friend and the owner of the beach house where Nick stays to avoid Jenkins, gets caught up in the general castration anxiety, unable to perform adequately with his wife during a night-time tryst on the beach. In the climactic scene where Nick kills Jenkins, he holds out his now-visible coat toreador-style and says 'olé' as Jenkins, in a mad lunge, pitches headlong off the roof; Nick's path to Alice is now unimpeded, and the Switzerland scenes follow.

If this reading is followed, then clearly the relation between the two main male characters becomes one of substitution rather than of some moral difference, as Nick comes to assume the role of the father. Indeed, for all the emphasis the film places on recognition as a desirable end, whatever resonances of a kinder social order this may suggest are swept away as Nick's self-interest is safely contained in marriage. If invisibility is the condition for both Nick's and Jenkins' pursuit of their immediate desires, the alternative on offer seems designed only to reproduce it.

Beyond this, however, Nick's supposedly virtuous stand against the system is further complicated by another facet of his existence: his job. The opening scenes convey a rather disenchanted view of the workings of big business. Apart from the fact that Nick makes a good living from apparently doing nothing, he too is quick to highlight its faults. The club which he attends is, he tells us in voiceover, also patronised by 'railroad tycoons and robber barons' who go there to discuss 'how much they have stolen that day'. And as we have seen, it is to some degree Nick's job, with its tendency to encourage greed and therefore alienation, which has allowed or perhaps encouraged his invisibility. To the extent that he starts to work against these tendencies, capitalism can be seen to function in the film as another 'them', another corrupt institution against which it is his fate to struggle. Yet here the similarities between the protagonist and what he fights against are even closer than his similarities with Jenkins. The film reaches a happy ending only because Nick is able to mobilise the forces of global capitalism. Again in voiceover, he tell us that once he has a line of communication established he can make money through speculative deals done over the telephone (in a telling parallel with his earlier betting on sporting events), and he observes that invisibility is no disadvantage in the financial world. As he languishes in the beach house he vows to 'make them pay' for what has befallen him, but it is never made clear just who 'they' are. It cannot plausibly be the agency which is tracking him down, so it seems the only other target of his resentment can be the cause of his metaphorical invisibility. Indeed on a literal level the only sources for his profits from speculation are the existing financial institutions, and thus it turns out that Nick can only take his revenge upon the invisible robber barons at the price of becoming one of them. This also helps to suggest the corruption in the CIA does not stop with Singleton; whatever the motivations of the apparently ethical Dr Wachs, Nick was only present in the doomed laboratory because it had dealings with the (tainted) wider world of finance. It is, perhaps, no coincidence that Nick paints the government more generally with the same brush as the devious CIA despite there being no evidence to distrust it given within the film; for, in the end, he is equally identifiable with both.

*Village of the Damned*

In *Village of the Damned* the interplay between untrustworthy authorities and individuals who take a stand against them is if anything more complex. Initially the camps between which the struggle will be fought seem clearly delineated. Much of the opening of the film works to establish the organic nature of the thriving small community which is the location for the action, where everyone knows everyone else and life has a familiar, predictable pace. The alien invaders arrive in the midst of this community in the form of babies, who will rely on the humans to support them until they are powerful enough to supplant all human life. We quickly discover they are able to affect an individual's behaviour through mind control, and take murderous action if they are threatened in the least. Once again a secular institution makes an appearance, in this case in the shape of a scientific team, and it receives the familiar Carpenter treatment.

When the scientists first arrive to investigate the mass blackout in the town, during which women of childbearing age become pregnant, their mission seems benign. When the multiple pregnancies are discovered, the scientists' leader, Dr Susan Verner (Kirstie Alley), announces an allowance of $3,000 a year for those who choose to have the babies. The offer is presented to the townsfolk as a humanitarian act on the part of the government; the scientists simply want to study such an unusual phenomenon. Declarations of beneficence on the part of authorities are of course always a bad sign in Carpenter's work, and as the film progresses it becomes evident that the scientists have known all along (if not beforehand) something of the nature of the alien children. Dr Verner in particular is shown to act in bad faith. She takes on the role of a doctor in the delivery room when all the children are born simultaneously, but she breaches this position of trust by removing the alien form of one of them who is stillborn without letting any of the townspeople know what they are dealing with. Later, whilst still portraying herself to the townspeople as a caring scientist, she goes before a shadowy committee to ask for further funds on the grounds that monitoring the children's growing powers is of interest to national security, dismissing the deaths and maimings which they have caused. In terms of the 'us and them' divide which the film establishes, then, the pattern seems a little more complex than in *Memoirs of an Invisible Man* and yet still quite straightforward: the organic community is the site with which the audience is encouraged to identify, and it is faced by two rather different 'thems', one of which is the familiar treacherous secular institution whilst the other is a malevolent alien force. And yet as the narrative develops, questions of identity and of how the lines should be drawn between these three broad sets of interests become rather more intricate than it would at first seem necessary for them to be.

The figure who takes responsibility in the face of this array of threats is someone who would have to be called a pillar of the community (which straight away sets him apart from Carpenter's usual heroes): Alan Chaffee (Christopher Reeve), the town doctor. Representing the community as he does, rather than being a marginal figure within it, the transformations which he undergoes make the issue of the differences between the three groups particularly striking. In the main confrontations of the film, those between the townspeople and the aliens, much is made of the moral superiority of the humans because they have emotions, most notably compassion. Though this is left more or less implicit for most of the film, Chaffee eventually tells the children that 'without feelings you're a second-rate mimic of a higher organism'. And of course it is this human trait which the aliens have had to count on, with numerous instances being shown of the adults protecting them even though their final goal is to destroy humanity, these being set in sharp contrast against the dispassionate violence which the aliens mete out for the slightest accidental physical harm the humans cause them. The motive for their actions is underlined by the leader of the aliens, Mara (Lyndsey Haun), Chaffee's own daughter. They do not act out of hate – 'emotion is irrelevant. It is not in our nature' – but out of 'a biological obligation'. The lack of emotion on the part of the aliens is perhaps predictably mirrored in the actions of that other 'them', the government scientists. It is because of their focus on national security, and presumably the military potential of the aliens' powers, that the scientists stand by and allow the townspeople to be killed. Late in the film, we are told that in those other countries where colonies survived the governments have destroyed the entire community without warning because any evacuation would alert the children, and this action is indeed presented as the only – reasonable – option.

But if this distinction between a compassionate us and a rational them is a prominent theme in the film, it develops in unexpected ways, the most obvious example being the actions of Chaffee himself. For it is an unavoidable implication of the narrative that he is only able to defeat the children insofar as he becomes like them. In the first instance he realises that killing them is the only way for humanity to survive (he tells Jill McGowan (Linda Koslowski), the school principal, that it is 'the only thing we can do'), but beyond that it is precisely only by suppressing his emotions that he is able to resist the children's mental probing and bring the bomb in amongst them. Mara was mistaken to assume that the adults' attitudes which had protected them so well were invariable; Chaffee is in the end far from being 'the prisoner of [his] own values' but rather joins 'them', blocking his feelings and making the sort of rational calculation of species survival odds that would be familiar to the aliens (and, of course, to the scientists). Indeed, rationality is consistently identified with successfully perpetrated violence throughout the film. Chaffee's actions contrast with the only substantial display of emotionally-charged violence in the film. The angry mob, led by one of the mothers suddenly given to a pseudo-Old Testament style of speechifying, march by torchlight to the barn where the children have isolated themselves, but the rabble is easily defeated by the children's mind control, their leader burning herself to death with her own torch. It seems, then, that the film endorses the view that emotion, the distinguishing feature of humanity, leads to defeat, which in the final analysis is to be avoided at all costs. Mara sums it up thus: 'we are all creatures of the life force. Now it has set us at one another to see who will survive … Life is cruelty. We all feed on each other … in some way to survive.' A rather different 'we' than Chaffee wants to admit to, but one which he finally has to embrace.

Mara's view is supported by the film in other, less direct ways. The notion that life is essentially a matter of survival is echoed in the various references to reproduction found throughout. The opening shots are of deer roaming the sweeping hills, with livestock then falling unconscious at the same time as the humans, highlighting their biological similarity and shared place in the environment. These as well as the early shots of the school barbecue, of a young couple buying a house and McGowan's discussion of pregnancy with her husband, all promote a sense of the importance of birth and growth: humans in a natural cycle. Excluded from this cycle, the (virgin) mother of the stillborn child takes to the bottle saying she 'can't hack it', and eventually kills herself.

Reproduction as the ultimate imperative of course determines the invaders as well. The alien children were supposed to be paired off with each other, but one of them, David (Thomas Dekker), is alone because the stillborn one was to be his partner. Unsurprisingly, Mara tells him 'without a mate you are of less importance to us'. David, however, is the alien who comes to feel emotion, but his sub-plot, which is absent from the original novel and the screenplay for the 1960 film, further complicates the play of identity. In a community where religion is evidently central to the way of life, there is something vaguely scandalous about the fact that it was the virgin who did not give birth and that as a result David is, in a word, saved. His physical rescue is carried out by his mother, McGowan, but more metaphorically he is saved from being an alien, and indeed meets Chaffee's criterion for counting as human, because he does not have a 'mate'. It is because he is faced with this lack that he comes to feel empathy for others, as in the graveside scene where Chaffee looks at his wife's headstone. He also experiences emotions more generally: he takes no part in the violence but rather hides in fear, and knocks Mara over when the group turns on McGowan, who then manages to rescue him just before the bomb explodes. This is, then, a strange sort of salvation, in which death and absence are the condition of becoming human. The surprisingly existentialist character of this plot-line works markedly against the more obvious and comforting meaning of Chaffee's actions, whereby, as a man whose religious faith is clearly signalled in the film, he follows his beliefs and sacrifices himself affirmatively for the sake of others. On the contrary, the alternative to understanding his actions as being based on a rational calculation seems to be that, rather than a higher power, it is death which, beyond biological differences, is the source of love and compassion. The question of who 'we' are has become tangled indeed by the end of the film.

*They Live*

Complexity also lies just beneath the surface in Carpenter's only film in which he dispenses with his own norm of avoiding explicit political commentary: *They Live*. This film, produced towards the end of the Reagan era, has been held up as 'a vehicle for [Carpenter's] own ... radical political beliefs. It's a full-out attack on con-temporary America as a heartless consumer society, dominated by money and the media' (Goodman 1989: 21). Since the story depicts an America with rising poverty levels where those in power collaborate with aliens to make themselves wealthy at the expense of the general population, who are in turn kept passive by a welter of subliminal media messages, Joan Goodman's description seems accurate at least on some levels. Indeed, the film contains some genuinely radical moments. During the expositional scenes, Frank (Keith David) tells Nada about the economic depression in his home town, with the shutting down of manufacturing industries: 'We gave the steel companies a break when they needed it', he says. 'Do you know what they gave themselves? Raises. The golden rule: he who has the gold makes the rules.' Although he too is the victim of the depression, Nada's initial attitude, when Frank threatens

John Nada (Roddy Piper) finds the resistance movement's base, where he begins to discover the threat from the aliens in *They Live*

rather rhetorically that they should start smashing up the bosses' cars, is a moderate one: 'You ought to have a little more patience with life.' When Frank highlights the hyper-competitive nature of the system, he replies 'I believe in America. I follow the rules'. And yet as Nada gradually pieces together the alien plot against the people the positions reverse and it is he who starts to voice the radical view. Thus Frank later seems to have rather changed his opinion, saying he just wants to keep his job, 'walking a white line' and minding his own business. Nada retorts that 'the white line is in the middle of the road. That's the worst place to drive'. Between such dialogue, the depiction of the homeless surviving in a shanty town bitterly named 'Justiceville', the scenes of brutal police oppression, and the insistence on the shallowness of a media-driven consumerism amounting to a distinct 'false consciousness', the film is palpably critical of the dominant political climate of the time.

*They Live* has with some justification been criticised for abandoning these radical premises in favour of pursuing action-based generic formulae, with criticism usually settling in particular on the over-extended fight scene between the two protagonists. Nevertheless, the narrative is more complex than the 'Republicans as aliens' plot-line and the action-hero shootout at the end might suggest. As Cumbow notes, the aliens' plan, which is to turn Earth into a division of their wider business interests, is successful only because a large segment of the population is willing to go along with it. Comfort and complacency are the problem: 'In the world described in *They Live*, we are collaborators in our own subversion. The aliens are … a mirror of ourselves' (1990: 185). It might be added that while the narrative overtly places the blame for the divisions in society on the hypnotic effects of the doctored media transmissions, with their empty hymns to the goodness of fame and fashion, and seems to hint that false consciousness will evaporate thanks to Nada's destruction of the television station responsible for these soporific signals, it is noticeable that the aliens themselves are very happy to partake, in a presumably unhypnotised way, in the consumerist heaven which they have engineered. Moreover, Holly Thompson (Meg Foster), the reporter who betrays the protagonists, seems to have made her choice with the fullest insight of any of the characters into what both sides offer. As Cumbow also observes, the main problem with the aliens seems to be what they look like rather than what they do (1990: 187). He argues that Carpenter has deliberately blurred the distinctions between us and them in this case, with an implicit indictment which might prove uncomfortable for the audience. Once again the film promises a sense of social critique, and a rather more subtle one if this reading is followed.

Nevertheless, a number of elements work to counter any such meanings, some of which are familiar from the examples above. After their epic fight, Frank and Nada retire to a hotel to recover, and the conversation becomes reflective. 'Maybe they've always been with us, those things out there', muses Frank. 'Maybe they love it, watching us kill each other off, feeding on our own cold fucking hearts.' The feeding metaphor, foreshadowing Mara's account of the nature of things in *Village of the Damned*, of course serves to give the socio-political specifics of the film's critique of competitiveness a more mythical dimension. Curiously, Frank's observation is a response to a revelation by Nada, which at first sounds like an insight into the history of the aliens but turns out to be something rather different. 'A long time ago, things were different then', Nada begins, but goes on to describe how he ran away from home as a child because his father suddenly began treating him with extreme cruelty. Although only a brief detail in *They Live*, Nada's conclusion would not be out of place in *Memoirs of an Invisible Man*: 'I've got news for him', he announces (even though the ostensible topic of conversation is the alien threat), 'there's going to be hell to pay, because I ain't Daddy's little boy no more.' The blind street preacher who talks of revolution knows what the aliens are up to because 'this world may have blinded me, but the Lord has let me see'. The universalising cast of these incidents as diagnoses of the causes of competitiveness extend to the description of its ills. While it would perhaps be expecting too much for the film to avoid the clichéd representation of trades unions as a racket, the issue of just who is impoverished by the economic system veers between the omnipresent iconography of the working man, which indeed sits rather poignantly with that of the homeless, and the insistent message of the hacker that it is the middle classes who are under attack. In his speech celebrating the Earth-alien alliance, the alien leader identifies the human beneficiaries of the pact as being the 'power elite', yet Drifter (George 'Buck' Flower), a former inhabitant of Justiceville, seems to have little difficulty in joining their ranks by means of the vaguely-defined act of 'selling out'. Nada defiantly dies to save the world, but exactly what he is fighting against and what might come next are finally questions the film cannot answer.

Here, then, is the pattern which unites *Memoirs of an Invisible Man*, *Village of the Damned* and *They Live*. In each case, a pursuit of the logic of the narrative shows that the identity of the protagonists often shades into that of the forces against which they are fighting, or at least what they are fighting for to some extent remains indeterminate. Why this might be the case is of course hardly a matter of an individual quirk or failing on the part of Carpenter. The first two films are based on pre-existing texts and produced within the large studios, and so as Carpenter himself indicates are subject to more constraints than his independent films. As an example of the latter, and one where the embargo on explicit political comment is lifted, *They Live* gives Carpenter the freest hand to communicate his own political perspective. The wider point is rather that, whether a film is held to originate with a single auteur or not, certain patterns repeat themselves because of the effects of wider influences in the filmmaking process, the most important of which in this case is arguably genre. The exact balance between the director's intentions and the extent to which genre characteristics shape the final result could of course only ever be a matter of speculation, and is ultimately beside the point. Michael Ryan and Douglas Kellner argue that 'the political stakes of film are ... very high because film is part of a broader system of cultural representations which create psychological dispositions that result in a particular construction of social reality, a commonly held sense of what the world *is and ought to be that sustains social institutions*' (1990: 14, emphasis added). In this case it is the emphasis on individual responsibility and action that these films share which needs to be highlighted. It seems that the apparently clear-cut distinctions which structure the films start to blur because they are, finally, not clear enough, and as a result the stories they tell of independence, responsibility and freedom unravel in the ways indicated. In this sense, Ryan and Kellner would argue that the films, in producing resolutions which work only so long as they are not examined too closely, function to 'placate social tensions and to respond to social forces in such a way that they cease to be dangerous to the social system' (ibid.). In Carpenter's case this process is more ambiguous than usual, however, for his films are often marked out by their seamless conveying of quite densely plotted narratives in which the disciplines imposed by their genres are scrupulously followed through no matter where they will lead. In this way, Carpenter's films allow a particular insight into something of the complexity involved in popular film's re-staging of the social tensions which shape its audience.

*Notes*

1 From the vantage point of another ten years' experience Carpenter is willing to make distinctions: 'I have different standards. I always look at the independent films and say, "My God, I can't believe we *did* that" ... But, in terms of the big studio films, I usually think, "I can't believe I *survived* that" (Cumbow 1990: 194, emphasis in original).

*References*

Appelbaum, R. (1979) 'From Cult Homage to Creative Control', *Films and Filming*, 25, 9, 10–16.
Cumbow, R. C. (1990) *Order in the Universe: The Films of John Carpenter*. Metuchen,

NJ: Scarecrow Press.

Goodman, J. (1989) 'The sharp shooter', *Guardian*, 22 June, 21.

Jones, K. (1999) 'John Carpenter: american movie classic', *Film Comment*, 35, 1, 26–31.

McCarthy, T. (1980) 'Trick and Treat', *Film Comment*, 16, 1, 17–24.

Muir, J. K. (2000) *The Films of John Carpenter*. Jefferson, NC and London: McFarland.

Ryan, M. and D. Kellner (1990) *Camera Politica: The Politics and Ideology of Contemporary Hollywood Film*. Bloomington, IN: Indiana University Press.

Wells, J. (1980) 'New Fright Master John Carpenter', *Films in Review*, 31, 4, 218–24.

Williams, T. (1979) '*Assault on Precinct 13*: The Mechanics of Repression', in R. Wood and R. Lippe (eds) *The American Nightmare: Essays on the Horror Film*. Toronto: Festival of Festivals, 67–73.

Wood, R. (1979) 'Introduction', in R. Wood and R. Lippe (eds) *American Nightmare: Essays on the Horror Film*. Toronto: Festival of Festivals, 7–28.

# CHAPTER THREE

# A Siege Mentality? Form and Ideology in Carpenter's Early Siege Films

## Steve Smith

According to Robin Wood's influential thesis, the key to reading the political or ideological investments of the horror film is to be traced to the status of the monster, regardless of the question of the monster's real-world plausibility. For Wood, the reactionary or conservative version of horror characteristically presents the monster as the embodiment of some pure, inscrutable evil; as an essentially atavistic force which erupts within a technologically advanced world, and functions as a kind of reminder of a Manicheanism that is utterly indifferent and prior to the vicissitudes of human history. Progressive horror equally exploits the allegorical potential of the monster, but does so in a diametrically opposed sense. Here, the monster represents the vehicle or possibility of a critique that is irreducibly social in nature. 'Evil', in this sense, is always, despite the ideological temptation to believe otherwise, a phenomenon that is historically produced and therefore open to transformation. Wood's most forceful example of 'progressive' horror is to be found in his reading of Hitchcock's *Psycho* (1960) (1989; see also 1984), in which, he argues, the horror element derives directly from the realm of the social – that is, the patriarchal struc-ture of the family, viewed as a key social institution within contemporary American society – rather than from some abstract force of evil.

On the face of it, Carpenter's early quartet of siege films – *Assault on Precinct 13* (1976), *Halloween* (1978), *The Fog* (1979) and *The Thing* (1982) – lend themselves to Wood's definition of the reactionary horror film, in that each might be taken as a variation on the same theme: a small, enclosed community is pitted against a seemingly irresistible and relentless external force that is bent on its destruction for reasons that are largely beyond the comprehension of its members, and, indeed, of the viewer. Of the four films, *Halloween* might here function as a paradigm example. In several important respects a reworking of the Hitchcock film in which Wood finds so much to praise, it nevertheless marks a kind of transitional point between Hitchcock's film and the contemporary strain of increasingly self-referential Hollywood slasher movies for which it is often cited as a key influence. In particular, it bears Carpenter's hallmark paring down of his generic precursors. Even without going as far as Wood does in his reading of *Psycho* as familial psycho-drama, it is difficult to deny that in his juxtaposition of the psychologist's professional discourse on the reasons for Norman Bates's (Anthony Perkins) dysfunctionality and the lengthy closing sequence featuring the palpably incomprehensible and uncomprehending gaze of Bates, Hitchcock seems at least willing to pose the question of the source of Bates's madness. By contrast, Carpenter is noticeably less forthcoming on the question of an explanation for – and thus attribution of any meaning to – Michael Myers' actions. Two constructions are explicitly posited, but both point in the same direction. For the inhabitants of suburban Haddonfield, Myers is, of course, the very 'bogeyman' that the festival of Halloween ritually evokes; but further, unlike Hitchcock's psychologist, Carpenter's representative of the psychiatric community, Dr Sam Loomis (Donald Pleasence), has long given up on any attempt at understanding or rehabilitation. In the film's second scene, Loomis consistently refers to Myers as 'it', and his words upon learning of his escape – 'The evil has gone' – place him firmly on the side of Myers' victims. His culminating resort to gunfire is entirely in keeping with this attitude, while his position on Myers is implicitly given credence by Carpenter's closing shot of the empty space where a mortal body should lie.

On such a reading, the question of the tonality and purpose of Carpenter's opening scene becomes clearer. In its implicit reference to the incest taboo, it gestures at the problematic of dysfunctional family relations. Yet, the parents who are eventually seen standing either side of the young boy are silent, and never reappear subsequently in the film. Carpenter's procedure here is more akin to that of George A. Romero in another notably minimalist siege movie, *Night of the Living Dead* (1968), a film which Carpenter is known to admire and which also begins with a prefatory scene featuring brother and sister. As with Romero's film, Carpenter's opening sequence gestures toward the psycho-social matrices of the modern thriller that represents its most immediate cinematic precursor, but does so in such a cursory, overtly simplistic manner that it is difficult to escape the conclusion that its tone is simply dismissive or even parodic in intent. The break with the requirement of explanation, and thus of a certain empathy with the killer, signals a new take on the genre – which is arguably implicit in *Psycho* – in which the emphasis is firmly on violent spectacle and its accompanying evocation of terror. And Carpenter, like Romero, seems to know that the capacity to scare an audience and the characterisation of the killer as irrational and evil are in direct proportion.

Carpenter's characteristically reductionist approach to his acknowledged precursor films is similarly to the fore in his 'remake' of *The Thing from Another World*

(1951), generally acknowledged as the work of Howard Hawks, its accredited producer. Hawks's presentation, while focusing, as will Carpenter's rewriting, on the reaction of the victims of an apparently relentless aggressor, nevertheless draws attention to the allegorical dimension of the Thing – as the product of humanity's pretension to master nature through technology, and its accompanying contemporary resonance of nuclear apocalypse – largely through the artifice of the representative nature of the group's disparate composition. Even if Hawks's resolution is more than a little vulnerable to the accusation of oversimplification in proposing a compromise position between the diverse interests of the scientists, the military and the common American citizen, it at least allows the issue to be addressed. Carpenter's approach, in contrast, rather than, say, attempting to refine the terms of the issue, dispenses entirely with such concerns. In his hands, the Thing becomes just another avatar of The Shape (Michael Myers), all the more memorably for the viscerality of its special effects. Furthermore, unlike Hawks, Carpenter is little concerned to explore the possibility of collective resistance. Like Myers, the Thing individuates, picking off its lone victims one by one, and thereby, with startling efficiency, undermines the communitarian values through which both Haddonfield and the Antarctic research outpost nominally constitute themselves. Individual resistance fails, as might be expected, but Carpenter, like Romero, insists on the concomitant impossibility of any kind of effective collective action as well. In both films, then, Carpenter would appear to fail Wood's test of political progressiveness on two related counts: first, in his refusal or disinclination to engage with questions of the meaning and source of the monster-figures; and second, in his failure to countenance the possibility that the monster might effectively be combated, which is, of course, but another way of characterising its abnormal, quasi-supernatural power.

Among Carpenter's early siege movies, *The Fog* assumes something of an ambiguous status when viewed from Wood's perspective. On the one hand, it is structurally analogous to *Halloween* or *The Thing* insofar as the central narrative thread pits an enclosed community against an irresistible external force. In addition, it features Carpenter's hallmark evocation of claustrophobia, suspense and fear. On the other, if, like *Halloween*, it is set at a time of community celebration – the centenary of the founding of Antonio Bay – it exploits its temporal setting as more than simply an index of atmosphere. In fact, an important strand of Carpenter's film works to undermine the town's mythologised self-image as the very essence of American self-reliance and meritocratic values. In other words, Carpenter does engage with the allegorical meaning of the fog. If the film turns on something analogous to a Freudian 'return of the repressed' (Wood 1984), then what is repressed is precisely the material conditions that enabled the foundation of the coastal community, and the pretext for its return is precisely the town's complacent self-mythologising ethos as embodied in the Centenary celebrations that frame the film's narrative. The difference between this film and those discussed above is that the truth is available to one of the characters, a truth that mitigates the inexplicable nature of the fog, and introduces the possibility of a coherent reading at the level of allegory. That is, when the drunken priest, Malone (Hal Holbrook), learns of the leper colony and the fact that the town was established on the basis of stolen gold, the fog suddenly emerges

The return of the repressed: the ghostly ship sails back to the coastal community of Antonio Bay in *The Fog*

as a less irrational, inexplicable phenomenon than previously appeared the case. Not that Carpenter is particularly forthcoming on the allegorical meaning at stake, but given his predilection for notions of property and territory insofar as they are implicit in the siege movie as such, then it is difficult not to find here, in its broadest sense, a fictional analogue for the roots in territorial expropriation of the United States itself.

Such a possibility, of course, is suggestive and far-reaching, but its potential is mitigated by two factors: first, its evident subordination in the film to Carpenter's virtuoso handling of the elements of horror and suspense; second, the truth is clarified only near the film's end, upon Malone's discovery of his grandfather's diary. But the dramatically powerful realisation that the fog is thus an agent of historical revenge, and the accompanying realisation on Malone's part that he is to be the sixth and final victim complicates, and ultimately derails, the motif of the 'return of the repressed'. If the latter starts out by functioning classically as a traumatic element from the past that returns unexpectedly to disrupt the smooth-running everydayness of the present, then Malone's acceptance of his fate introduces a logic of sacrifice and redemption. Malone's assumption of the sins of his forefathers functions, that is, to close the circle, to pay the price demanded by the past, and thereby to free his fellow citizens from their own distant complicity. Rather than forcing a recognition of those iniquities, Malone's death prepares the ground for their continued collective avoidance. Despite the film's closing words, 'Look out for the fog' (an implicit reference to the final words of Hawks's *The Thing from Another World*), now that the ghosts of its past have been satisfied, it is difficult to imagine that the community of Antonio Bay might have anything further to fear from them.

Carpenter's earlier *Assault on Precinct 13* apparently has more in common with *The Thing* and *Halloween* than the albeit tentative and circumscribed historical resonance of *The Fog*. Widely seen by contemporary reviewers and audiences – and, indeed, marketed – as a suspenseful horror film set in Los Angeles, the film is easily amenable to a reading of the kind that Wood might readily characterise as 'conservative'. Such a reading would unerringly focus on Carpenter's representation of the multiracial street gang, whose 'assault' on the eponymous Precinct provides some of the film's most memorable set-pieces. Tony Williams, for example, forcefully argues that the mere fact of setting the film – albeit, primarily, for financial reasons – in the contemporary metropolis obliges Carpenter to offer some sort of position on the 'gang problem' that provides the storyline with its central impetus. As it is, in presenting gang culture as palpably 'other', anonymous, psychopathic and amoral, Carpenter reduces what is a pressing social problem, and, arguably, an important index of socio-racial exclusion, to the abstract status of evil villainy. The real core of Carpenter's film is in contrast provided by the reactions, and, ultimately, the resistance of those who stand in the gang's way, signaled by the culminating triumph of the film's heroic threesome of Bishop (Austin Stoker), the highway patrolman, Wilson (Darwin Joston), the prisoner and Leigh (Laurie Zimmer), the Precinct secretary. Politically, Williams argues, Carpenter's assumption that his raw material can simply be emptied of its social and ideological weight and reconfigured in accordance with aesthetic principles more normally associated with the rather less familiar settings of the pulp science fiction or horror genres that Carpenter so admires, comes down, at best, to a 'false innocence' on his part, the familiar refusal to engage ideologically with his material. At worst, it inscribes the film in a 'tradition of simplistic right-wing movies where conservative individualism is opposed to unindividualised violent totalitarianism' (1979: 70). On this reading, Carpenter would simply be reinforcing the popular conservative views of urban gangs as constituting a serious threat to social order. As Susan A. Phillips puts it, in their association with criminality and random violence, '[gangs] have been likened to some frightful organism – a cancer feeding off the body of society, spreading like a fungus to destroy itself and everything it touches' (1999: 63). In the way it locks onto such views of gang culture, Carpenter's film would, then, take its place alongside contemporary films such as *Death Wish* (1974) and the first three *Dirty Harry* films (1974–76) in their tendency to demonise liberal values of understanding and tolerance – not only as naïve and ineffective, but as part and parcel of the problem of urban criminality.

This is a serious charge, of course. In his riposte to Williams, Robert C. Cumbow dismisses the second objection, while only implicitly engaging with the first. Cumbow's argument relies on notions of artistic expression and imagination, and hence on the assumption that criticism is called upon merely to interpret the film 'on its own terms' (1990: 43). Thus, for Cumbow, Carpenter may legitimately take the gang element and its accompanying social context and employ it as an image of 'threat and terror with which to play out the age-old mythic battle between good and evil'. The film, for Cumbow, simply does not and need not 'make pretensions toward historical or cultural accuracy' (1990: 42). It is difficult, indeed, to locate any common ground between Cumbow and Williams, since to a large extent each argument depends on ultimately irreconcilable assumptions concerning the practices of both filmmaking and film criticism. What both are guilty of, though, is a failure to take into account the real textual complexity of what is Carpenter's most intricately woven and ambiguous film.

In what follows, contra Cumbow, it will be argued that Carpenter does, in fact, consistently engage with the socio-political dimension of his material in often quite subtle and unexpected ways. Williams, however, may well be correct in his characterisation of the film, at the very least, as non-progressive or conservative, but, in limiting his analysis to the level of its represented content, he seriously oversimplifies the kinds of problems – including, in particular, that of the film's generic identity – that Carpenter must resolve in order to achieve even the outlines of an overall coherence.

Perhaps the key moment for the 'conservative' reading of *Assault on Precinct 13* occurs during Carpenter's surprisingly lengthy and intricate expository section, in the scene of the ruthless murder of a little girl, Kathy (Kim Richards), by the nameless white gang member. Cumbow even describes this moment as 'the most horrifying ... in Carpenter' (1990: 27), partly because of its violation of the cinematic taboo on violence toward children, partly for the graphic, almost voyeuristic way in which it is portrayed. The sheer shock-value of the scene nevertheless harbours a more measured, ideological purpose: decisively to extinguish any lingering sympathy the viewer might have for the gang following the film's opening scene in which six of its members are gunned down by the police. The pointedly excessive nature of the gang's response (prefigured in the second scene of the film where vengeance is sworn) would then serve retrospectively to vindicate what Commissioner Davidson (Maynard Smith) at the news conference (the report of which Bishop listens to on his car radio) calls the 'deplorable extremes' to which the police must resort in order to tackle 'the juvenile gang problem'. It would also vindicate the palpable politically-motivated inaccuracy of the news report in which the deaths of the gang members – '*los seis*' – are said to be the result of a 'shoot-out' with police. Following Kathy's death, it is difficult not to identify with the actions of the traumatised, grieving Lawson (Martin West), Kathy's father, as he takes the dying man's gun and heads off vigilante-style in pursuit of vengeance.

Much, then, hangs on the Kathy episode. There is, however, more than a suspicion that the scene is not perhaps to be taken in quite the way that initial impres-

The demonised 'other'?: a gang member sworn to vengeance in *Assault on Precinct 13*

sions might suggest, and that its very extremity is to be read with more than a little irony, as a self-conscious comment on the very outrage Carpenter calculated it to provoke. Nothing can quite be stated conclusively, but one might legitimately ask whether there is not something a little excessive or clichéd in Kathy's slightly cloying sweetness and charm? Or whether the scene does not strive just a little too obviously, particularly at the moment of the bullet's impact, to out-do Sam Peckinpah's characteristic depiction of senseless violence – even without the slow motion? Might it also be significant that the actress cast in the role of Kathy was best known for her lead role in the 1975 Disney production, *Escape to Witch Mountain*? Might the scene be read as *too* overtly manipulative? That is, might Carpenter be attempting implicitly to signal a distance from the horror genre at the point in the film where it is most explicitly invoked? Such a suspicion, which obviously goes against the overt rhetoric of the scene, is moreover borne out when we widen our scope to consider the purely narrative logic of the chain of cause and effect that culminates in Kathy's shooting. What emerges from such an analysis is something more complex than the mere intervention of evil, social or otherwise.

In this connection, the apparently incidental question of the status of the ice cream seller assumes a crucial importance. In his chapter on *Assault on Precinct 13*, Cumbow poses an important question, while failing either adequately to answer it or even to see what might be at stake in such an answer: 'Carpenter continues to enhance the ominous tone of the film. An "ice cream man" readies his gun, and takes notes: is he an undercover surveillance man?' (1990: 27). Indeed, once the whole narrative context of the scene is taken into account, it is difficult to avoid the conclusion that the ice cream man is actually a police informant or paid stooge. This would explain his initial reluctance to serve Kathy when she first approaches him, as well as his distractedness and anxiety as he serves her whilst keeping one eye on the black Ford cruising back and forth. Crucially, though, it accounts for the fact that he gives her the wrong flavour of ice cream: it is on her return to the van to point out his mistake that she interrupts the gang's attack on the man. Is it conceivable that the gang might have waited until she has been served before they finally approach him, or use her as cover for their approach? Interestingly, in Carpenter's original storyboard for the scene,[1] the frame depicting Kathy's shooting is accompanied by a brief hand-written note: 'Startled, white warlord fires.' The fact that the warlord's surprise was excised from the finished film suggests that Carpenter not only hesitated over the precise narrative justification for the child's murder, but also that he realised its political stakes, given that, in the absence of any gesture of surprise, the warlord's actions cannot but be seen as cold-blooded and, to an extent, premeditated. Such a calculation, however, undoubtedly applies to the 'ice cream man' whose murder – following Kathy's – is intricately tied up with the killing of 'los seis' the previous evening.

The important ideological point to be made here is that a crucial factor in Kathy's death is the ongoing and ruthless struggle between gang members and authorities, in which she becomes unwittingly enmeshed. She is not the victim of some abstract force of evil in the same way, for example, as Myers' sister in the opening scene of *Halloween*. Such a reading of Carpenter's subtle insinuation of the determinant role of the social realm in what appears random and senseless is reinforced by a close analysis of the broader narrative sequence in which Kathy features. Clearly, the sequence is important insofar as Lawson's seeking sanctuary in Precinct 13 is essential to the setting up of the siege which is the film's central focus, but there is more at stake here than a mere narrative expedient. Let us pose, therefore, a simple question of causality: how is it that Kathy finds herself alone and exposed in what her father calls 'this horrible neighbourhood'? What is her father doing in such unfamiliar territory? The reason appears to be as follows: he wishes to persuade Kathy's nanny, Margaret, to move in with them, now that 'Fred', her husband (or possibly her father) is 'gone' (or, as Kathy indiscreetly puts it, 'dead'). Lawson is apparently expecting some resistance on Margaret's part – despite his incomprehension at the prospect of her refusal – and, in order to lend a little emotive weight to what is basically a job offer, has Kathy accompany him (hence the rehearsing of lines in the car). This brings to mind the contrasting socio-economic (and, perhaps, racial) status of Lawson and the nanny, and, in turn, the historic compartmentalisation of Los Angeles along lines of class and race. This situation was exacerbated by what became known as the 'white flight' to the wider county area in the wake of the accelerated ghettoisation of the city in the 1960s – a mainly white, bourgeois response to the civil rights movement and the not unconnected race riots that erupted in the South Central district of Watts in the summer of 1965. In other words, a key facet of the causal chain that culminates in the death of Kathy has a distinctly historical resonance deriving directly and irreducibly from two determinate social conditions of contemporary Los Angeles.

Cumbow describes the interweaved convergence on the police station of Lawson, Bishop and Wilson as a date 'with destiny' (ibid.), as if some inexorable force were at work underpinning the inner logic of what looks on the surface to be mere coincidence. Closer analysis suggests, however, that we may well be dealing with a more or less inexorable force, but that its status is irreducibly social. In this regard, the narrative sequence that brings Lieutenant Bishop to Anderson Precinct is particularly interesting, and there is ample evidence to suggest that Carpenter has elaborated it with particular care. Bishop is first encountered as he sets off to work on a Saturday evening shift. Things appear unremarkable enough, and an unmistakable sense of the everyday is evoked as he drives along the freeway, listening to the radio and appearing relaxed and enthusiastic. As in the Kathy narrative strand, however, the surprising insistency of the detail begins to tell another story. The major clue is found in the following exchange between Bishop and Lieutenant Gordon on their first meeting in the latter's office at Precinct 13. Ostensibly, Gordon is there simply to hand over control to Bishop until the following morning when the station will finally close. Gordon's attitude throughout the interchange is a little stand-offish; not quite aggressive, but not warm:

| Gordon: | All you do is answer the telephone and send over any strays. There may be some who still think this is a police station… |
| Bishop: | I don't understand why this place is still open. |
| Gordon: | Well, it is and it isn't, Lieutenant. The result of transition [Gordon starts to leave]. I really think someone in the central office wanted to give you something special on your first night out. |
| Bishop: | [alone now] That sure got around fast.[2] |

It is tempting, on first viewing, to regard the 'something special' Gordon refers to here as dramatic irony on Carpenter's part – to understand it as a reference forward to the unusual events that will ensue. But the perceptibly sarcastic tone of Gordon's parting words, the fact that he is no longer looking at Bishop as he utters them, suggests something different; that they betray a less subtle kind of irony, insofar as 'something special' means just the opposite: banal, menial. The hidden force behind this observation is strengthened by the knowing expression that accompanies Bishop's closing words. This expression, which Carpenter pointedly highlights, suggests that he now realises what is afoot. Bishop is black. This is his first shift since his promotion to the rank of lieutenant. What he realises is that he is being subjected to a kind of rite of initiation instigated by his white superiors in order to put him in his place. In a further twist, what looked (again) to be a coincidence – Bishop grew up four blocks from Precinct 13 – is part of the ruse. He is thus literally as well as symbolically back 'in his place'. His colour, furthermore, retrospectively explains a number of incidental details; the frosty reaction of desk-sergeant Chaney (Henry Brandon) on his arrival ('Yeah?', 'Lieutenant Bishop', 'Yes, *Sir*'),[3] as well as the reason Carpenter's script foregrounds the lieutenant's skin colour a moment later in the scene with Leigh ('Black?', 'For over thirty years') – even at the cost of a hackneyed joke. Most tellingly of all, it explains why, over the car radio, Bishop was greeted by his commanding officer, Collins, instead of the operative he was expecting ('surprised to hear your voice, sir'), and makes clear the irony – indeed, the double irony – of Collins' dampening down the new lieutenant's aspirations to heroism on his 'first night out' ('There are no heroes any more, Lieutenant'). The fact that what is involved is what Collins calls 'a temporary reassignment' to the larger, more prestigious LAPD (Bishop belongs to the California Highway Patrol, as indicated by his uniform) adds a further dimension to his later words to Gordon ('That sure got around fast'). The 'word' about his promotion has migrated across police departments, no less, and Bishop now realises what this means.

Why is it, then, that Bishop's promotion is such an issue? Once again, an apparently insignificant detail provides a clue. On his first appearance in the film, the onscreen byline states that we are in West Los Angeles. The block from which Bishop emerges is clearly situated in a prosperous suburb, and the implicit contrast with Anderson, where Bishop grew up, is visually stark. The block is conspicuously white in colour, as is his unmarked patrol car. Now, of course, Bishop must live somewhere, but why does Carpenter choose to highlight it? At the time Carpenter was writing his screenplay, the Mayor of Los Angeles was Tom Bradley. Bradley is noteworthy for being the first African American mayor of a city with a long history of racial inequality and segregation. His election in 1973, when he defeated the white conservative incumbent, Sam Yorty, was the culmination of an acrimonious campaign in which the issue of race had figured prominently. Bradley grew up in South Central Los Angeles (where Carpenter's film is set, and thus where Bishop grew up). As with Bishop, Bradley began his career as a cop – in the LAPD proper – and was ambitious and hard-working enough to rise to the rank of lieutenant, the first African American to do so, and he moved out of the ghetto as soon as he could afford to. Bishop's promotion thus has an unmistakable symbolic resonance, as do his words to Leigh, when the latter voices a characteristically white attitude to ghetto life: 'Your father or someone obviously got you out of Anderson early enough.' Bishop replies, as he makes to leave: 'By the way, no one took me out Anderson when I was a baby. I walked out myself when I was twenty.'

Although less thoroughly elaborated, the sequence featuring the prisoners' journey also carries a specific weight beyond its status as a mere narrative pretext to set up the besieged group that will be called upon to defend Anderson Precinct. The revealing moment here is the interchange between Starker (Charles Cyphers), who is responsible for the prisoners' transportation, and the prison warden; the former, seeing Caudell (Peter Frankland), one of the three prisoners coughing and in discomfort, asks, 'Is he alright?' The warden answers, 'Ah, he's just got a little cold', but it is, of course, because of the seriousness of his illness that they are obliged to stop off en route. Is the viewer, in other words, to discern in the warden's words an element of indifference or vindictiveness? If so – and the warden's brutal treatment of Wilson only reinforces the point – then a clear causal link would hold between such vindictiveness and the arrival of the prison bus at Anderson. In other words, more than mere coincidence is once again involved despite first appearances. In fact, all three narrative sequences constituting Carpenter's elaborate set-up of the siege involve what we might call the effect of a determinate displacement whose roots are decidedly social. That is, each of the three characters who find themselves in Anderson Precinct would, if such factors were not in play, be somewhere else: Bishop, on the road, patrolling the state highways; Wilson on his way to Sonora penitentiary; and Lawson back in his white enclave. In each case, moreover, this sense of out-of-placeness is directly linked to socio-historical factors pertaining to contemporary Los Angeles: respectively, institutionalised racism, prison brutality and racial and economic segregation. Nor are these simply neutral factors; they stem more or less directly from the exercise of economic and political power. If the rootedness of gang culture in urban exclusion and deprivation is further taken into account, then what is created is a heady mix with considerable scope for – at the very least – a critical engagement with pressing contemporary socio-political realities.

Yet such an engagement never quite happens. Once the siege proper begins – with the first attack, during which Carpenter dispenses with some peripheral characters in the Precinct – it is as if the ground suddenly shifts and a quite different film emerges. The carefully elaborated specificity of the three central male characters is completely forgotten: Bishop's colour or rank is no longer an issue; Wilson's status as condemned convict changes as he is released from the cells and handed a rifle; and Lawson is literally silenced. What happens, in fact, is that the explicit generic reference-point of the film alters dramatically, and a recognisably Hawksian problematic comes to the fore. Several factors attest to this. The gang as such fades into the background, and the focus of attention shifts to the dynamics of character interaction and development; Leigh emerges as a typically Hawksian woman (tough, engaged, worldly-wise, but not without a certain erotic charge) (see Wise 1996); the somewhat unheroic deaths of the convict, Wells, and Julie, the telephonist, also mark the disappearance of the two remaining characters who most closely resemble character-victims from horror (they are disoriented, scared, panicked). By contrast, we never have the impression that the remaining central threesome are quite as frightened or helpless as, perhaps, they should be. Rather, they exude an inner confidence and confront set-backs with casual stoicism. The values at stake, too, become the recognisably Hawksian ones of teamwork, resourcefulness and bravery. Moreover, Wilson's remark to Leigh when she is hit, 'you were good [in there]' (a direct quotation from *Rio Bravo* (1959)), alerts us to the primacy that Hawks accords to self- and mutual respect. No sentimentalism is countenanced; they accept that if, individually or collectively, they are not 'good enough' then they will perish.

Carpenter's shift to a concern with the particular qualities of the individual characters also seems, at first, characteristically Hawksian in a narrowly ideological sense. As is well known, Carpenter's film was conceived as homage to Hawks's *Rio Bravo*, and numerous incidental references are made to the film. But the most important borrowings bear upon Hawks's characteristic concern with the reconciliation of individual interests in the context of an enclosed community that requires common purpose in order to survive. As Wood notes, *Rio Bravo* is characteristically Hawksian in its 'relegating of society to the function of a *pretext*' (1996: 92, emphasis in original), and he further argues that it is the evolution of the characters and their interrelations which take centre-stage, rather than the classic western's concern with 'the defence of civilised values' (1996: 96). And yet, in *Rio Bravo*, Hawks provides a strong sense of resolution at the purely narrative level that is entirely consistent with the latter. For not only are the 'bad guys' – the ranching Burdett family and their hired hands – seen off in the film's only concession to spectacle (the final showdown to which Carpenter specifically alludes with the acetylene cylinder scene in *Assault on Precinct 13*), but it is not difficult to read the triumph of Hawks's three heroes, Chance (John Wayne), Dude (Dean Martin) and Colorado (Ricky Nelson), as the triumph of the 'civilised' values of respect for the individual and the rights of property, both of which are key issues for the classic western's take on the West. The precise modality of Carpenter's resolution, in contrast, is rather more difficult to gauge. In one sense, his ending mirrors that of Hawks: the 'lawless' attackers are defeated through a very Hawksian combination of resourcefulness, bravery and teamwork. As Lawson, the ostensible reason for their resistance, is taken away on a stretcher he mouths a gesture of gratitude. The newly-forged sense of comradeship is confirmed as Bishop recognises death-row prisoner Wilson as his equal with his penultimate line of the film, 'It would be a privilege if you'd walk outside with me', and they walk up the steps from the precinct basement together. The redemptive feel of Carpenter's ending is, furthermore, underscored by the contrast it establishes with Romero's *Night of the Living Dead*, where the heroic Ben leaves the cellar of the besieged house alone only to be mistaken for a zombie by the posse and shot. In fact, if Romero's film can be read as a bleak riposte to Hawks's redemptive solidarity, then it is tempting to view *Assault on Precinct 13*, in turn, as a simple restatement of Hawksian values.

And yet, it is difficult to take Carpenter's ending quite as unambiguously as this, and there are grounds to consider it in more self-conscious terms. The final stage of the siege is played out at great pace, and the coda that follows certainly gestures at the idea of order restored and justice done, but it is difficult not to be struck by its sheer brevity. There is none of the relaxed, light-hearted tone that marks Hawks's coda, as Carpenter cuts rather brutally to his blood-red end-titles – which, again, are markedly brief – as the menacing synthesiser theme earlier associated with the film's most harrowing sequences emerges in accompaniment. There is furthermore, perhaps, something revealing in Bishop's line. In *Rio Bravo*, Hawks uses his coda to signal a future for his characters beyond the timeframe of the film. By contrast, Bishop's reference to 'outside' necessarily implies that once they are returned to the world that lies beyond the now mythic space of the police station no further relationship will be possible between the survivors, since the differences they have transcended through their combined efforts – black/white, cop/criminal, insider/ outsider, male/female – can only reassert themselves once their adventure is over. We might even discern in Bishop's egalitarian gesture a studied, almost excessive, solemnity, and read in its stylised language a grand but ultimately empty gesture. The imminent reassertion of the outside world, in which things are a little more complex, is implicit in the attempt by the white-helmeted cop to take Wilson into custody before Bishop angrily repulses him. Similarly, we already have a sense of this moments earlier in the handling of Leigh's departure. Whereas *Rio Bravo* ends with the consummation of an attraction, *Assault on Precinct 13* ends in its frustration as Leigh, refusing the offer of a stretcher, exchanges a lingering, expressionless glance with Wilson and then walks off in silence.[4]

But it is tempting to go further and view the entire narrative resolution of the film as almost self-consciously phantasmatic. On the one hand, particularly if viewed with reference to the Hawks model of the 'happy', redemptive ending it cannot but be taken seriously as the authoritative voice of the film. On the other, its dissonant, almost uncanny elements point in quite another direction: that of seeing, in its very familiarity and straightforwardness, the patent inadequacy of the ending in the face of the situation in relation to which it stands as a putative answer. In addition, the apparently strong sense of resolution in *Assault on Precinct 13* is further undermined by the fact that its constituent elements (the victory of the besieged group, the redemption of Wilson through Bishop's gesture) are pointedly incongruous in view of the kinds of issue that the film sets up in its opening section. It is as if Carpenter stops short of a whole-hearted endorsement of the narrative resolution that he nevertheless explicitly proposes. Having first tried to acknowledge the historical weight of his materials, Carpenter abandons the attempt in order to satisfy the generic requirements of, first, horror, and later the Hawksian communitarian problematic. Interestingly, none of Carpenter's other early siege films is subjected to this kind of ambivalence, and it is tempting to link this directly with the fact that the generic framework within which they operate is adequate to master the material only as long as the material is already emptied of its historical dimension. In *Assault on Precinct 13*, recourse to genre would then function as a kind of path of least resistance when the ideological weight of the elements can only otherwise lead to impasse. In this sense, the film's ambivalence would function finally as a somewhat oblique argument in favour of Carpenter's professed preference for movies as escapist entertainment. *Assault on Precinct 13* may ultimately achieve this status, but it has at least the merit of not quite letting us forget what we are escaping from.

*Notes*

1 Available on the Special Edition DVD version of the film.
2 Interestingly, at the start of this scene Bishop breaks an awkward silence by referring to 'sunspots' and 'pressure on the atmosphere' (a possible reference to *The Texas Chainsaw Massacre* (1974)) as the cause of the wave of criminality Gordon complains of. Gordon completely ignores Bishop's comment. As if to add to the strange tonality of the whole scene, one of the crimes Gordon vociferously complains about ('We've had a 312 every fifteen minutes') turns out to relate to nothing more than obscene publications (according to the California Penal Code).
3 The racial undertones of this encounter are compounded when we recall that Henry Brandon, who plays Chaney, had played the role of Scar in Ford's *The Searchers* (1956), where he is the victim of the visceral racism of John Wayne's character, Edwards, with whom Bishop ironically shares his forename.
4 It is tempting, here too, to infer a somewhat critical take on Hawks's purportedly inclusive liberal individualism as an exclusively male preserve. Significantly, as the central threesome emerge from the smoke caused by the explosion of the gas cylinder, Leigh stands between the two men, and must therefore be brusquely disposed of for the Hawksian problematic to be seen to prevail.

*References*

Cumbow, R. C. (1990) *Order in the Universe: The Films of John Carpenter*. Metuchen, NJ: Scarecrow Press.

Phillips, S. (1999) *Wallbangin': Graffiti and Gangs in L.A.* Chicago: University of Chicago Press.

Williams, T. (1979) '*Assault on Precinct 13*: The Mechanics of Repression', in R. Wood and R. Lippe (eds) *The American Nightmare: Essays on the Horror Film*. Toronto: Festival of Festivals, 67–73.

Wise, N. (1996) 'The Hawksian Woman', in J. Hiller and P. Wollen (eds) *Howard Hawks: American Artist*. London: British Film Institute, 111–19.

Wood, R. (1984) 'An Introduction to the American Horror Film', in B. K. Grant (ed.) *Planks of Reason: Essays on the Horror Film*. Metuchen, NJ: Scarecrow Press, 164–200.

_____ (1989) *Hollywood from Vietnam to Reagan*. New York: Columbia University Press.

_____ (1996) '*Rio Bravo*', in J. Hiller and P. Wollen (eds) *Howard Hawks: American Artist*. London: British Film Institute, 87–102.

# CHAPTER FOUR

# Fast and Cheap? The Film Music of John Carpenter

## David Burnand and Miguel Mera

I usually score my own films because I'm the fastest and the cheapest ... and I love making music. My dad [Howard Carpenter] was a composer and a musician and a music teacher [Western Kentucky University], who earned his PhD in music at the Eastman School in Rochester, New York. I grew up around it and I grew up around movies and film scores. (John Carpenter, quoted in Cumbow 1990: 192)

Given his background and the experience of performing in a rock 'n' roll band, it is hardly surprising that Carpenter would eventually choose to write the music for his own movies. What is perhaps more surprising is the infrequency of film directors who are also film composers. Throughout the history of film very few have been able to approach both tasks; a select group that includes figures as diverse as Charlie Chaplin, Noel Coward, Mike Figgis and Tony Gatliff. Of the twenty films Carpenter has directed to date, seventeen of these have been scored or co-scored by him (see table overleaf).[1] In addition, he has even had occasion to write music for other films, for example the Academy Award-winning short, *The Resurrection of Bronco Billy* (1970). This not only highlights Carpenter's passion for music-making, but his whole attitude towards filmmaking. There is a clear ambition to be involved in every aspect of a film's production and to understand each process from the inside. This attitude is exemplified by Carpenter himself with particular reference to editing:

| Year | Film Title | Director | Composer(s) |
|------|-----------|----------|-------------|
| 1970 | *The Resurrection of Bronco Billy* | James R. Rokos | John Carpenter |
| 1974 | *Dark Star* | John Carpenter | John Carpenter |
| 1976 | *Assault on Precinct 13* | John Carpenter | John Carpenter |
| 1978 | *Halloween* | John Carpenter | John Carpenter |
| 1978 | *Someone's Watching Me* | John Carpenter | Harry Sukman |
| 1979 | *Elvis* | John Carpenter | Joe Renzetti |
| 1979 | *The Fog* | John Carpenter | John Carpenter. Electronic realisation by Dan Wyman |
| 1981 | *Escape From New York* | John Carpenter | John Carpenter, Alan Howarth* |
| 1981 | *Halloween II* | Rick Rosenthal | John Carpenter, Alan Howarth* |
| 1982 | *Halloween III: Season of the Witch* | Tommy Lee Wallace | John Carpenter, Alan Howarth |
| 1982 | *The Thing* | John Carpenter | Ennio Morricone |
| 1983 | *Christine* | John Carpenter | John Carpenter, Alan Howarth* |
| 1984 | *Starman* | John Carpenter | Jack Nitzsche |
| 1986 | *Big Trouble in Little China* | John Carpenter | John Carpenter, Alan Howarth* |
| 1987 | *Prince of Darkness* | John Carpenter | John Carpenter, Alan Howarth* |
| 1988 | *They Live* | John Carpenter | John Carpenter, Alan Howarth |
| 1992 | *Memoirs of an Invisible Man* | John Carpenter | Shirley Walker |
| 1993 | *Body Bags* | John Carpenter | John Carpenter, Jim Lang |
| 1995 | *In the Mouth of Madness* | John Carpenter | John Carpenter, Jim Lang |
| 1995 | *Village of the Damned* | John Carpenter | John Carpenter, Dave Davies |
| 1996 | *Escape From L.A.* | John Carpenter | Shirley Walker, John Carpenter |
| 1998 | *Vampires* | John Carpenter | John Carpenter |
| 2001 | *Ghosts of Mars* | John Carpenter | John Carpenter |

* credits specify 'in association with'

Editing movies gives you a lot of perspective on what you can get away with as a director – what you need to tell a story. I think any director who has ever edited a movie is helped enormously. I think it's like learning the camera. You have to be able to tell a story, at least from my point of view. If you understand the camera and how it works and what you can do with it, and then you understand editing – the process of editing is what you can do to manipulate the film you shot – and then you understand sound mixing, and so on, I think you become a more rounded director. (Cumbow 1990: 188)

It is only now, after thirty years in the business, that Carpenter is receiving critical recognition for his polymath approach to filmmaking. This chapter deals with Carpenter's musical contributions, with an emphasis on his early films, those which best illustrate his methods, leading to an examination of more recent musical developments in his work.

## Dark Star

The cult film *Dark Star* (1974) was begun whilst Carpenter was a student at the University of Southern California. Initially the fifty-minute film was 'too long to be a short, too short to be a feature' (Cumbow 1990: 10), and was consequently twice re-worked and expanded with financial assistance from producer Jack Murphy and distributor Jack H. Harris, finally receiving a limited theatrical release in 1974. As Carpenter's first feature length project, it contains a number of musical devices, techniques and ideas that begin to define the Carpenter sound. There are two main musical themes used in *Dark Star* (Fig. 1A and 1B overleaf).

What is immediately apparent from these two themes, as with so much of Carpenter's music, is the preponderance of semitonal movement. In fact, theme 1B is constructed entirely from a repetitive falling semitone motif, sounding like an echo and thus suggesting the vast emptiness of the universe through which the characters travel. The whole melodic pattern then rises harmonically bar on bar, again by a semitone. The most significant feature of theme 1A is that the dominant chord of C sharp major 'resolves' onto a C major chord a semitone lower, and not onto F sharp minor as might normally have been expected. This is noteworthy because C major does not naturally belong in the key of F sharp minor. The harmonic idiosyncrasy is not a jazz substitution, but rather a parallel-shifting, gothic horror cliché. The harmonic and melodic patterns outlined above all have the same purpose: they aim to destabilise the tonic, making the listening experience uncomfortable and edgy. These extremely simple and effective musical signifiers or 'unconsummated symbols' (Langer 1957: 240) are also frequently used to represent space and space travel and can be found in numerous films, including *Star Wars* (1977) and in some earlier episodes of the television series *Star Trek*.

The music for *Dark Star*, whilst containing some potentially engaging ideas, does not develop in a musically interesting way. Theme 1B in particular develops poorly, simply ascending *ad nauseam* in semitones until the cue ends. The melodic movement of the theme becomes so predictable (as when listening to an instrumentalist play-

Fig. 1A

Fig. 1B

ing scales) that any potential suspense that may have initially been created is quickly negated. If this music does not achieve its principal aim of creating tension and suspense, then its narrative contribution is questionable. Likewise, theme 1A's piquant harmonic shift does not take the composer into a new key or a different harmonic plane, but simply appears as a flash of colour. This is musically disappointing; clearly the composer has not been able or willing to develop the initial musical material.

However, Carpenter demonstrates a more creative approach to the use of diegetic music and to the musical treatment of sound. For example, the opening communication from Earth is punctuated with structured bleeps that are reminiscent of Bebe and Louis Barron's bold, electroacoustic score for *Forbidden Planet* (1956). In both films the abstract sounds take on metaphorical meanings within the context of their environments. For example, in *Dark Star*, an early discussion between Pinback (Dan O'Bannon) and Doolittle (Brian Narelle) about the latest planet they have destroyed is accompanied by the gently undulating timbres of the equipment in the cockpit.

| Pinback: | What are you gonna name it? |
| Doolittle: | What? |
| Pinback: | The new star, what are you gonna name it? |

| Doolittle: | Who cares, don't bother me. |
| Pinback: | Commander Powell would have named it. |
| Doolittle: | Commander Powell is dead. |

Doolittle's final statement is heightened by a dejected synthesiser droop, similar to those found in space-invader arcade games of the 1970s and 1980s. Underlining the dialogue with this 'musical' gesture gives it a humorous punchline. If it had not been for this sound, the audience may have read more pathos into this situation than Carpenter seems to have intended. Consequently, the relationship between characters on the ship becomes clearer; the emasculated Pinback and the masculine Doolittle bicker like an old married couple, rather than maintaining an efficient professional relationship. These men are tired of their environment and of each other, and need to find their own space, physical and emotional, within the confines of the ship. It is not surprising that the search for this space involves recreational, diegetic music. The mother figure for these men, and instigator of the recreational music, is the ship's computer: 'for your listening enjoyment, we now present the moonlight melodies of Martin Segundo and the scintilla strings. Our first selection is the perennial favourite *When Twilight Falls on NGC 891*.' The computer provides an example of what Michel Chion terms 'acousmachine' (1999: 45).[2] Music here is intended to provide relaxation and whilst the 'tacky', easy-listening, lounge jazz may help the characters find a temporary escape, it simply highlights for the audience the banality and boredom of their situation; the music is as cheap and unfulfilling as the lives of these men.

*Dark Star*'s Doolittle takes refuge in his music

Doolittle is perhaps the only character who finds a real escape in music. He creates his own musical instrument from water-filled glass bottles and tin cans, and he plays a meandering, improvisatory fantasia that finally enables him to engage with his humanity and creativity in a way that is otherwise impossible on the ship. The primitive instrument sounds like an out-of-tune music box, perhaps representing his regression to childhood. What is significant is that Carpenter chooses to stop the flow of the action at this point, in order to give us a deeper emotional insight into the characters via the use of this music.

Perhaps the most inspired use of diegetic music within the film is the Country and Western song, 'Benson, Arizona', used in the opening title sequence:

A million suns shine down
But I see only one
When I think I'm over you
I find I've just begun

The years go faster than the days
There's no warmth in the light
And how I miss those desert skies
Your cool touch in the night

(Chorus)

Benson Arizona, blew warm wind through your hair
My body flies the galaxies my heart longs to be there
Benson Arizona, the same stars in the sky
But they seem so much kinder when we watch them you and I

(Repeat Chorus)

Now the years pull us apart
I am young and now you're old
But you're still in my heart
And the memory won't grow cold

I dream of towns and spaces
I left far behind
Where we spent our last few days
Benson's on my mind

(Chorus)

The deliberate incongruity of Country and Western music is extremely effective. The song is part parody, but also a reverent 'nostalgia trip' for the characters. There is, in fact, an interesting dichotomy already present in much Country and Western music, as it tends to be firmly rooted in a major key with strong diatonic harmony, yet frequently has lyrics expressing negative emotions; a concept that is also witnessed in 'Benson, Arizona'. In stark contrast to Carpenter's underscore, this is music that belongs to a clear earthbound location, and time. Its effect is to dispel the customary sanitised iconography of cinematic space travel. These men are not emotionless, efficient, space beings surrounded by clinical, white walls; they are lonely, flawed individuals who long to return home. Country and Western music frequently deals with the themes of loneliness, loss and longing. In addition, Country and Western music belongs to its own desert frontier and the comparison between this and the frontier that the *Dark Star* explores is not an idle one.

### Assault on Precinct 13

Music opens *Assault on Precinct 13* (1976), introducing the stark red on black titles sequence. A drum machine is heard behind the obsessively repetitive titles theme, which is a pop synthesiser riff that builds only in texture, and not thematically (see Fig. 2A).

The influence of Carpenter's days in a rock 'n' roll band are clear. His melodies are rarely more than rock riffs, but no less effective for that. But Carpenter can also demonstrate a more ambitious approach with synthesisers, especially where this means taking minimalism to its limits. Early in the film a held, high synthesiser note, with no changes other than inner frequency modulations, accompanies a scene of gang members taking part in a blood-brotherhood ritual. Despite its emulation of a high violin section, this synthesised sound holds just long enough to go beyond a musical gesture. Instead, it becomes a sound effect, and it returns at moments of violence, such as the young girl's murder and her father's revenge killing of the gang leader. This creates an enclosed and uncomfortably intimate feeling, and adds to the sense that all the characters are trapped in some way, not just the prisoners in transit.

Dialogue is important to a low-budget film that has little opportunity for expensive cinematography or *mise-en-scène*. Carpenter's music tends to avoid underscoring dialogue, other than with held notes. He uses a small number of simple musical or sonic devices to represent characters and associated situations. For instance, the drum machine accompaniment from the titles theme is heard on its own later in the film, and becomes associated with the multi-racial gang. The synthesiser theme is added at the close-up of the gang members in a car. This music ends abruptly at the visual cut to police officer Bishop, deliberately avoiding the convention of using music to bind scenes, and thus matching Carpenter's stark montage exposition of characters and situations.

As Lt. Bishop (Austin Stoker) prepares to enter Precinct 13 for the first time since becoming a police officer, Carpenter introduces a plaintive electric piano theme (see Fig. 2B). We hear this several times later in the film. It returns at quiet moments during the siege, acting as musical articulation of the rhythm of the siege itself: attack, calm, attack, calm, etc., each attack becoming more violent, and each lull offering an opportunity for the besieged to bond. At first hearing, however,

Fig. 2A

Fig. 2B

this piano theme seems to link back to the fragment of a tune Bishop whistled earlier, as he began his journey to the ill-fated police station. The key signature is the same, and the relationship between the two melodies is that of a vague recollection. This piano music could be construed as a non-diegetic realisation of a diegetic source, but no particular attention is brought to the theme by Carpenter at this stage, other than this being the first time we hear an electric piano. Yet later in the film, shortly before the final assault, Lt. Bishop whistles the fragment of tune again in an extended form. Prisoner Wilson (Darwin Joston) (effectively characterised as a 'good guy' by now, despite his conviction for multiple murders) listens, and comments, 'kinda pretty'. But this fuller version of the whistled tune negates its apparent resemblance to the piano theme in appearing to be now more old-fashioned, and raises the question of whether Carpenter ever intended a connection. A more conventionally minded and educated film composer might have looked for opportunities such as this to make subtle thematic references, but such an approach is often more about musical structure than about film narrative, unless it is very carefully handled. We must conclude that the whistled tune and piano theme are similar only because of the limited melodic and harmonic palette of the film. Bishop's whistling is set up as a link between 'before' and 'after' the siege, as well as offering an opportunity for policeman and prisoner to share a small moment of contact beyond fighting for their lives. It also gives a sense of nostalgia to the characterisation of Lt. Bishop, who had grown up around the district served by Precinct 13 in the days before drum machines and synthesisers filled the airwaves. In addition, for film buffs it is clearly a reference to *Rio Bravo* (1959), which Carpenter admits as the model for *Assault on Precinct 13*. 'That's real pretty' is what Stumpy (Walter Brennan) says when Dude (Dean Martin) and Colorado (Ricky Nelson) finish singing a duet during a lull in the action. We hear this tune again after the final gunfight, when they whistle a fragment of it as they strut back through town together. Carpenter avoids quoting the original tune from *Rio Bravo*, but there are rhythmic similarities nonetheless.

Early in *Assault on Precinct 13* the drum machine and titles theme are associated with the gang, and with an increasing sense of jeopardy as a gun-sight point-of-view targets innocent members of the public. This is not high-adrenaline youth music, but a lethargic and rather indifferent expression of the repetitions and inevitabilities of raw urban life. Synthesisers and drum machines represent the city, and the music expresses the ordinariness of gang violence in Los Angeles, through a mechanical, brutal indifference. Shortly before the murder of the little girl, the solo drum machine overlaps and contrasts with the equally mechanical, yet innocent, ice cream van music. This contrast is heightened by the two musics and their associations being brought together in meta-diegetic space. The ice cream van is in the diegesis and calls upon happy memories of childhood, despite the bleak Los Angeles setting and the worried attitude of the driver who may owe protection money to the gang. The drum machine is purely in our minds, however. There is no attempt by Carpenter to suggest that this music is anything but understated underscore representing and characterising the gang. This brief and apparently unimportant meeting of two sound worlds pre-empts the significant proximity of the father/daughter characters and the gang.

Moments later, and away from the protection of her father, the little girl draws attention to the van's music, which for her represents the availability of ice cream. The driver quickly turns off the music, to emphasise that he is not working, but decides to serve the girl anyway, hoping to get rid of her quickly as the gang's car circles his position. Despite the typical minimalism of Carpenter's approach, there is a clear comparison to be made with earlier films and pre-cinematic drama. To take an apparently unlikely precursor from Restoration theatre, John Dryden's *An Evening Love* (1671) features two simultaneous serenades representing two rivals and their musicians, who eventually fight. Such musical opposition became a common device in the theatre and can also be found in opera (for example, Giacomo Meyerbeer's *Les Huguenots*, 1836), and even in concert music such as 'Fourth of July' from Charles Ives' *Holidays Symphony* (1913).

The simplistic adoption of this device can also be found in several films. At one point in *Casablanca* (1942), the uneasy coexistence of French and Germans is expressed in song by the *habitués* of Rick's bar, the 'Marseillaise' winning the day. But this only replicates a theatrical approach to the representation of opposition through music. The move from the theatrical stage to the recorded and edited form of cinema brings new technical possibilities and the potential for expanded dramatic function through sound design. In *Zulu* (1964), itself a siege movie, the dramatic purpose of the diegetic music becomes deeper than mere labelling of opposing camps. The two armies sing their emblematic anthems and these musical contrasts serve to enhance a scene in which the Zulu warriors prepare to attack Rorke's Drift once again. Chanting and rhythmic interjections are answered and counterpointed by the besieged British garrison of Welsh Guards singing 'Men of Harlech'. Aural point-of-view is used initially to contrast the musics still further, but their increasing aural proximity draws attention to the universality of music as a potent medium for human expression and group identification. Just as in *Assault on Precinct 13*, sonic juxtaposition mirrors the story. Carpenter does not handle these elements so subtly or powerfully as Cy Endfield does in *Zulu*, where the contrast and combination of sound provide a pre-emptive exposition of the noble dénouement of *Zulu*. Nevertheless, in *Assault on Precinct 13*, as relationships develop inside the police station, the drum machine's association changes from the gang to their besieged opposition. By introducing a synthesiser variation of the title music, this theme is transformed into the music of the police and their prisoner-allies. Given the opening scene of the film, where gang members are ambushed by the police, and given the trust that develops later between Lt. Bishop's people and his prisoners, there is some attempt to show the common denominators of human behaviour regardless of 'tribal' affiliations, and there is a clear attempt to represent this through simple musical devices.

*Halloween*

In his study, *The Voice in Cinema*, Michel Chion poses a fascinating question with regard to the structural significance of the scream, or 'screaming point' (1999: 76), in cinematic narrative:

> Why a woman's scream? Is this a phenomenon endemic to a cinema of sadists who get off on the spectacle of a woman as prey to terror? Yes, but: we might also speculate that for men, the woman's scream poses the question of the 'black hole' of the female orgasm, which cannot be spoken nor thought. (1999: 78)

In John Carpenter's most influential and famous exploitation movie, *Halloween* (1978), the female screams are not only structurally relevant, reinforcing Chion's psychoanalytic interpretation, but are powerfully personified by the piercing synthesiser score. If we take, for example, the opening steadicam point-of-view sequence, we can hear how the music is, in essence, nothing more than the extrapolation of a scream itself. Initially, there is no music as the camera 'floats' around a suburban household and looks in on a teenage couple kissing in the living room. The scopophilic similarities to *Peeping Tom* (1960) are obvious. The couple decides to progress to the bedroom and as the camera tilts upwards we see the bedroom light being switched off. It is at this point that Carpenter chooses to start his music cue, highlighting the fact that safety disappears as soon as the light is turned off.[3] We hear a high-pitched, three-note motif, the mimesis of a scream. This synthesiser outburst is continued by an oscillating, nauseating high G natural which eventually descends by semitones as it begins to be punctuated by repeated, descending piano figurations. These motifs respectively introduce the gulps and gasps that the victim is about to emit and the endless cry of the scream. We see the hand, from behind the camera's point-of-view, take a knife from the kitchen drawer and then the murderer ascends the stairs, finding a Halloween mask on the floor, which he puts on. It is here that the significance of the musical scream becomes apparent, because Carpenter uses the same high three-note motif for the moment when the murderer sees the naked girl. This aural calling card is an important psychological link for the whole film, because it highlights the reason why the murder is about to be committed. The girl about to be murdered is experiencing her sexual awakening (which could be viewed as morally reprehensible and therefore explains her punishment), and this is clearly linked to the moment that her bedroom light is turned out.

The film's most famous (and frequently parodied) musical theme is a driving piece in 5/4 time that contains Carpenter's hallmark musical language (see Fig. 3). The devices of simple, recognisable melodic fragments and 'Herrmannesque step-down modulation' (Brown 1994: 266) of a semitone, together with ostinato patterns, appear here as they do in much of Carpenter's work. The interesting feature about the score for *Halloween*, however, is that the time signature is deliberately chosen to disorientate the listener: '5/4 is nuts, you know, where does it end and what's going on? You can't find the start and stop of it; it's off.'[4] However, in itself a 5/4 time signature cannot create unease. The musical structure must also take advantage of the potential rhythmic possibilities. Carpenter achieves this by

Fig. 3

using unpredictable and uneven phrase lengths. For example, the music heard over the opening titles is in a mixture of three- and four-bar phrases, with the four-bar phrases usually including the main three-note rising motif. The overall result is that there is a combination of changeable rhythmic patterns. These features give the film an obsessive, ruthless grit. This is the music of the murderer, Michael Myers: cold, impersonal and relentless with an incessant semiquaver pedal note constantly driving the music forward.

Whilst many film scholars and critics have acknowledged the historical importance of this film in 'spawning a string of sequels and kicking off a row of teen slasher movies',[5] film *music* scholars tend to find little of note in Carpenter's scores. For example, Brown states:

> Though it is difficult to imagine music that would be more appropriate to Carpenter's primitivistic horror film, the creation of such a score as *Hallow-een*, or for that matter as the director's music for his other films, from the 1976 *Assault on Precinct 13* to the 1988 *They Live*, is at this point beyond the reach only of the tone deaf, and even there one wonders. (1994: 266)

This is harsh criticism, especially as Brown concedes that the music *is* appropriate for the film. Of course, John Carpenter's music does sound cheap, as if it has been put together very quickly and with little polish. This is unsurprising in the early low-budget films such as *Dark Star*, *Assault on Precinct 13* and *Halloween*. Indeed, it adds an endearing B-movie charm to these flawed yet fascinating films. However, one of the areas in which Carpenter's lack of sophistication as a composer is most apparent is in the predictability of the music. As a filmmaker, Carpenter is acutely aware of the limitations of the horror genre and seems to try and find ways of toying with the audience's expectations, or as he puts it, 'you know something is going to happen, the question is when'.[6] The problem with much of Carpenter's music is that the 'when' often seems to be exactly where the audience expects it. The music rarely takes the listener on a dramatic journey, it simply establishes a mood and continues as anticipated. There is usually very little development of musical material throughout his films and, as a consequence, the music does not grow with the characters or narrative themes. Film music can achieve much more than this. One need only listen to other 'horror' composers such as James Bernard, Elisabeth Lutyens or Howard Shore to appreciate the difference. Whilst Carpenter is an extremely *musical* director, not least in his innovative use of diegetic music, he is not an especially adventurous or sophisticated composer.

*Escape From New York*

*Escape From New York* (1981) demonstrates many of the features of a typical Carpenter soundtrack, not least the reliance on synthesisers, for which he was assisted by regular collaborator Alan Howarth. The 1970s analogue synthesiser sound emphasises low-pass filtering of rich electronic waveforms, and creates the distinctive sound of many early Carpenter movies. In this film there is much evocative use of

sound and music, with bass lines sounding like heartbeats, and with hypnotic osti-
nati and colouristic moments creating a sense of soundscape rather than traditional
underscore. Nevertheless, the titles music (see Fig. 4) is a synthesiser pop ballad,
similar in style and mood to the electric piano theme in *Assault on Precinct 13*. The
connotation is sadness, loss and perhaps a certain heroism, but certainly not high
adventure, despite the storyline.

Fig. 4

Much of the film blurs the distinction between music and sound effects: for
instance during the opening scene when a synthesised, rising glissando effect follows
the camera as it cranes up to look towards Manhattan Island from above a parapet.
This sound then cross-fades with that of an approaching helicopter. Clearly the
glissando is a synthesiser making a potentially musical sound, but equally clearly
it is not music. Later, an iterated synthesiser pulse acts as both rhythmic accompaniment and additional helicopter sound effect. These two unassuming examples
illustrate the absence of conceit in Carpenter's approach to music and sound. He is
not attempting to impress the audience as a composer or sound designer, but merely
wishes to use sound in all its forms to assist in the telling of the story.

There can be, however, a downside to this non-specialisation, as illustrated by
the bizarre choice and performance of music as Snake Plissken (Kurt Russell) prepares to fly into Manhattan. An unexpected version of Claude Debussy's piano pre-
lude *La cathédrale engloutie* (Book I, No. 10, 1910) is heard on synthesiser. This is
different in musical character from anything else we hear in the film, and is entirely
at odds with the tense mood of the flight. Had it been played on piano, as originally
intended by Debussy, this might have conveyed a paradoxical sense of calm in the
mind of Snake and, thus, an approach to scoring in keeping with Carpenter's ironic
treatment of action adventures. With this stilted and uncharming version, however,
it can only be presumed that Carpenter felt there was some symbolic significance to
the music's title, though precisely what, is open to speculation. After all, New York
is only surrounded by water, and not submerged by it. For all of its supposed clever-
ness, this is the weakest musical moment in the film.

On safer ground, Carpenter creates some effective synth sounds and proto-
music as Snake walks through the prison-city searching for the President (Donald
Pleasence): for instance high-pitched synthesiser effects imitating part-human, part-
machine screeches, accompany the 'crazies' emerging from the sewers. Continuing
this music-sound fusion, we hear the rhythmic 'helicopter' effect again, together with
unworldly synthesised cries created by the same internal pitch modulations heard in
*Assault on Precinct 13*. Later, there are machine noises reminiscent of electric arcing.
When Snake leaves the train with the President, the synthesised 'cry' heard earlier is
choreographed to the action, as Snake is attacked, whilst heavily reverberated drum
machine hi-hat cymbals continue to sound like electric cicadas.

A more conventional approach to scoring occurs as Snake and Cabbie (Ernest Borgnine) look for Brain (Harry Dean Stanton). This is straightforward anticipation music featuring rhythmic octaves, but such conventions are rare in Carpenter's earlier films, in terms of both content and the placing of cues. Carpenter's music rarely mediates between scenes in order to ease the visual edits and thereby create continuity. The audience is expected to be film literate, and in need of no such comforting, and so the lack of dramatic underscoring supports Carpenter's ironic approach to the action movie in a way that the synthesiser version of *La cathédrale engloutie* does not.

The 1996 sequel, *Escape From L.A.*, provides an interesting comparison, and composer Shirley Walker has shed some light on the nature of her work with John Carpenter. This was her second collaboration with Carpenter, the first being *Memoirs of an Invisible Man* (1992):

> For *Escape From L.A.*, John wrote certain scenes with synth guides that I then reworked with different electronic colours, but I also got to create synth cues of my own. John knew he wanted the orchestra for the big final confrontation because the sound FX would be so huge. (Blumenthal 1999: 16)

It is clear that we are in different musical territory from the outset, though the real differences increase as the film progresses. The title music is an updated arrangement of that from *Escape From New York*, but more dramatic in its articulation of the visuals. Compared with the earlier film, the electronic sounds are more modern. There are fewer filtered analogue waveforms and more samples. In addition, the musical styles are more eclectic, producing a postmodern hotch-potch of rock, Middle Eastern, Spaghetti western, mock-Gothic choral, surf and quasi-James Bond music. Whilst the orchestral music achieves the objectives Walker states, it goes against the intimate character of Carpenter's own music. In general, it seems that the higher budget ($50 million as opposed to $7 million for *Escape From New York*) resulted in more music, more conventionally used and placed in the film.

These musical tendencies started earlier, however. *In the Mouth of Madness* (1995), for which Carpenter collaborated with Jim Lang, also contains a great deal of music, suggesting that they felt the need to lift the drama of certain scenes. In this film, sound and music tend to distance the audience from the characters, and a wide range of musical styles is used, often gratuitously. The typical synth opening for the titles turns into a heavy-rock guitar track, of no thematic significance to the rest of the film, though it certainly establishes a high-energy mood. This was a pragmatic decision, following from the preview audience's appreciation of the temp track, which featured music by Metallica. For the rest of the film there are 'doomy' choirs with didjeridu, 'groovy' electric piano cues, Chinese music, Penderecki-like strings, electroacoustic sounds and harp chords, most of which detract from an otherwise entertaining film.

Some of Carpenter's earlier approach to sound and music remains, such as the fusing of sound effects with music (the gate noises as the children run out onto the street). There are also some attempts to play with confusions of diegetic and non-diegetic sound, such as the muzak and blues guitar. The soundtrack, however, falls between two stools, failing to offer either the idiosyncrasy and intimacy of Carpenter's earlier work, or the full-on sound design and dramatic scoring of a conventional horror movie.

*Vampires*

The concept of a vampire-western movie is nothing new. Take for example *Curse of the Undead* (1959), *Near Dark* (1987), *Sundown: The Vampire in Retreat* (1991) and *From Dusk 'Till Dawn* (1996), but Carpenter's approach to this cross-genre movie is entirely individual. Despite a series of bad reviews and a poor showing at the box office, *Vampires* (1998) shows a 'surprising energy and vigour coming from a director who has in the past decade seemed not very far from being a member of the walking dead himself' (Bond 1998: 26). One comment in particular, made by the chief vampire slayer Jack Crow (James Woods) to Father Adam (Tim Guinee), graphically illustrates the film's ethos: 'forget whatever you've seen in the movies, they don't turn into bats, crosses don't work ... you wanna' kill one you drive a stake right through its fuckin' heart.' This film attempts to be serious about the subject matter, it is not a parody, and it aims to convince us that vampires, or rather the evil they represent, does exist in society.

One of the film's most impressive features is its score, which marks a significant turning point in Carpenter's musical career. Gone is the slavish reliance on synthesisers, as Carpenter assembles a rock band named *The Texas Toad Lickers* to play the music. The ensemble consists of drums, percussion, bass, rhythm and lead guitars, pedal steel and Dobro guitars, synthesisers, Hammond organ and saxophone; Carpenter himself plays the synthesisers and rhythm guitar. The other performers are amongst the finest musicians available. For example, Donald 'Duck' Dunn (bass) and Steve Cropper (lead guitar) both played in Booker T. & the MGs, the legendary Stax House Band, and with artists such as Otis Redding, Eric Clapton, Muddy Waters, Bob Dylan, Elvis Presley and Wilson Pickett, as well as appearing in *The Blues Brothers* (1980). The significance of this ensemble is that there is a clear attempt to represent the film's geographical location with instruments such as the Dobro and pedal steel guitars, as opposed to the geographically non-specific synthesiser score more typical of Carpenter's movies.

There are two main musical themes in *Vampires* and these represent, respectively, the evil master vampire, Valek (Thomas Ian Griffith), and the vampire slayers (especially the chief slayer, Jack Crow). Valek's theme is a four-note synthesiser pattern (Fig. 5A) that is usually accompanied by drums and percussion, and the slayers' theme (Fig. 5B) is a blues/rock piece for steel guitar and band. There is also a third theme (Fig. 5C), but it is more difficult to define what this may or may not represent and it is this ambiguity which makes the score stand out from many of Carpenter's others. The music does not always attempt to tell the audience what to think, but allows them to draw their own conclusions.

Theme 5C undergoes a number of transformations throughout the film. It is first heard over the opening titles on gentle synthesised bells, presumably to represent innocence. It is also developed on the guitar at various points in order to give a feeling of distance, solitude, melancholy and the passing of time. In addition, the theme forms the basis of a religious plainchant that is used extensively in the exorcism re-enactment ceremony. Aside from the varying orchestrations of these themes, Carpenter seems uncharacteristically keen to develop and expand the material rather than simply repeat it. When Crow, Montoya (Daniel Baldwin) and Katrina (Sheryl Lee) arrive in Santiago, for example, the basic harmonic and melodic material of the theme is expanded into a piece that sounds similar to the Moody Blues' 'Nights in White Satin' (1973), and highlights the increasing importance of their heroism. Therefore, Carpenter maintains his customary minimalist approach, but also manages to exploit this simple melody for a great deal of organic musical and psychological material.

Fig. 5A

Fig. 5B

Fig. 5C

The choice of a rock score is itself significant. Previously Carpenter had not composed music exclusively in this style, although films such as *Christine* (1983) and *Body Bags* (1993) show an obvious passion for this type of music. Rock characterises the rebellious nature of Jack Crow, though clearly Carpenter is aware that this is a nostalgic view of the music:

> I love certain kinds of rock 'n' roll, but the *idea* of rock 'n' roll can often be very destructive. I mean, you've seen a lot of people who've died from it, just from the lifestyle of it. And often, rock 'n' roll's meaning has changed over the years to where now it has nothing to do with rebellion anymore. (Cumbow 1990: 127)

Whilst *Vampires* includes more sophisticated music and musical development than usual, it is hardly representative of Carpenter's film scores. It suggests, at least, that his attitude to music may at last be catching up with the potential offered by larger budgets.

What is clear from films such as *In the Mouth of Madness* and *Escape From L.A.* is that they lack the degree of personal involvement and intuition that are amongst the most interesting features of Carpenter's earlier, low-budget films. It is clear that his direct involvement in composing scores is not merely a cheap or fast option, but offers the director greater control of an element that is often farmed out to composers who have had little involvement in production and post-production decisions. The obvious features of Carpenter's scores are obsessive repetition, primitivism and minimalism, and an improvisational approach that works at the most basic level of musical communication. The favouring of synthesisers over fully orchestral scores supports this personalised style, whilst also allowing music to be better absorbed into the soundscape. This has enabled Carpenter to blur the boundaries of sound effects and music. That this has become the aspiration of a growing number of filmmakers in recent years suggests that there is much to be learnt from studying Carpenter's treatment of sound and music, despite the obvious lack of sophistication in his approach.

*Notes*

1   Carpenter is credited for co-scoring *Halloween II* and *Halloween III: Season of the Witch*, films which he did not direct. A music credit is also given to Carpenter for all of the subsequent *Halloween* films, but these are merely references to the re-use of the original theme.
2   'Acousmachine', or 'Acousmêtre', is a term Chion uses for the computer HAL in *2001: A Space Odyssey* (1968), referring to a screen character that can be heard but not seen by the audience.
3   See *The Night He Came Home: John Carpenter's Halloween* (television documentary presented by Mark Kermode) tx BBC 2, 30 October 1999.
4   Carpenter in *The Night He Came Home*: 1999. Carpenter was taught how to play this rhythm on bongos by his father.
5   *The Night He Came Home*, 1999.
6   *The Night He Came Home*, 1999.

*References*

Blumenthal, P. (1999) 'The Shirley Walker Interview', *Legend*, 28, 15–17.
Bond, J. (1998) 'John Carpenter's *Vampires*', *Film Score Monthly*, 3, 10, 26.
Brown, R. S. (1994) *Overtones and Undertones: Reading Film Music*. Berkeley: University of California Press.
Chion, M. (1999) *The Voice in Cinema*. Trans. Claudia Gorbman. New York: Columbia University Press.
Cumbow, R. C. (1990) *Order in the Universe: The Films of John Carpenter*. Metuchen, NJ: Scarecrow Press.
Langer, S. K. (1957) *Philosophy in a New Key: A Study in the Symbolism of Reason, Rite and Art*. Cambridge, MA: Harvard University Press.

# CHAPTER FIVE

# Carpenter's Widescreen Style

## Sheldon Hall

I just love Panavision. It's a cinematic ratio, and I don't think you can see it anywhere but the movie house. On television, you see squares and that's fine for television. (John Carpenter, in Appelbaum 1979a: 11)[1]

Carpenter's preference for the anamorphic widescreen frame (2.35:1 aspect ratio) can partly be attributed to his being a child of the 1950s. His recollections of early filmgoing, as reported in interviews, fix 1953, the year CinemaScope was introduced, as the beginning of his love of cinema. Though he cites the initiating film as the non-widescreen 3-D *It Came from Outer Space* (1953), he has also described the impact made on him by a performance of *The Robe* (1953) – the first CinemaScope release – recalling the unveiling of the immense 'Scope screen as its curtains slowly parted.[2] Carpenter has used Panavision (the successor format to CinemaScope as the industry's standard anamorphic widescreen process) for every one of his theatrical features since *Assault on Precinct 13* (1976).

It is well known that spectacle, rather than suspense, was the original cause for the introduction of CinemaScope to the American film industry in the mid-1950s. Earlier experiments in adopting widescreen formats, in 1929–31, failed because – coming too soon after the introduction of one new technology in the form of synchronised sound, and during a box-office boom period – the market was not yet ready for further novelty.[3] Following the successful launch in 1952, by independent operators, of Cinerama (involving three synchronised film strips projected on a single, deeply curved screen), a number of new processes were introduced by the major studios. All had aspect ratios (the proportion of width to height) wider than the almost square Academy format (1.37:1), which in the early 1930s had replaced the standard silent ratio of 1.33:1. These were subsequently successfully diffused throughout the industry, more or less widely in direct relation to the ease with which they could be incorporated into prevailing production and exhibition structures. The best-known format, CinemaScope, involved a wide image being optically 'squeezed' (a process known as anamorphosis) onto a standard 35mm film strip, which was then unsqueezed in projection to achieve a ratio between 2.55:1 and 2.35:1. The non-anamorphic alternative is to crop the upper and lower edges of the film frame in projection, blowing up the remainder to achieve a larger and slightly wider picture, though not as wide as that of 'Scope (the most common ratio being 1.85:1, though the exact proportions vary somewhat from theatre to theatre). A measure of their success is that the Academy ratio soon disappeared from commercial cinemas in the West.

Enlisted in the war against television and other leisure pursuits competing for the consumer's attention, the various big-screen formats significantly altered patterns of *mise-en-scène*, shot composition and *découpage* which had largely remained stable since the silent era. Though embraced by the studios' marketing departments, they nonetheless often met with strong resistance or only grudging acceptance from key creative personnel. CinemaScope, VistaVision, Todd-AO and others, might have been particularly advantageous in the presentation of large-scale action scenes, opulent sets and sprawling outdoor locations, but they also had to be used for more intimate scenes, for which they seemed less obviously suited. Many veteran filmmakers expressed dissatisfaction at the burdens the new formats seemed to impose. Thus, John Ford said of CinemaScope: 'I hated it. You've never seen a painter use that kind of composition – even in the great murals it still wasn't this huge tennis court. Your eyes pop back and forth, and it's very difficult to get a close-up' (Bogdanovich 1978: 92).[4] Fritz Lang's famous remarks about the anamorphic aspect ratio only being suitable for snakes and funerals may have been scripted for his appearance in Godard's *Le Mépris* (1963), but the difficulties he experienced in filming *Moonfleet* (1955) in CinemaScope are surely representative of those which most of his contemporaries would have faced:

> It was very hard to show somebody standing at a table, because either you couldn't show the table or the person had to be back too far. And you had empty spaces on both sides which you had to fill with something. When you have two people you can fill it up with walking around, taking something someplace, so on. But when you have only one person, there's a big head and right and left you have nothing. (Bogdanovich 1997: 224)[5]

Despite these drawbacks, the period which I term the 'widescreen era' – roughly 1953–70 – saw the development of a sophisticated widescreen aesthetic, in which the various apparent shortcomings of the new technologies were triumphantly overcome. The subtle and complex arrangement of action within the anamorphic frame, by directors such as Otto Preminger, Nicholas Ray, Anthony Mann and Vincente Minnelli, represents a substantial development of Hollywood's classical art. In their work, and that of others, the close-up became much rarer than previously or since (though it was used far less frequently in classical Hollywood practice than is often assumed, or than is common today); the medium-to-long shot, often coupled with the long take, with action staged in breadth and depth, came to predominate. Some filmmakers who found themselves unable to utilise the entire picture area took to 'masking off' portions, through the placement of objects or shadows around the significant action, to produce an artificial frame within the frame.

Other directors found adjusting to widescreen more immediately congenial. Even before the introduction of CinemaScope, Preminger's characteristic style already lent itself to methods which were consciously distanced, discreet and unobtrusive, allowing the spectator a Bazinian freedom of choice in selecting where to concentrate his attention.[6] Asked by Peter Bogdanovich if he welcomed 'Scope, Preminger replied:

> Yes. But it really didn't make that much difference. It is actually more difficult to compose in CinemaScope and Panavision. I mean, when you go to a museum, you find that very few painters choose these proportions. But somehow it embraces more – you see more. So I've been doing all my recent pictures in Panavision, which I think is a better lens than CinemaScope.
>
> [Bogdanovich] *It would seem to fit your long-take technique better.*
>
> It's true that on a very wide screen, cuts shock you more. I don't believe in cutting too much or doing too many reaction shots. (Bogdanovich 1997: 627)[7]

It might seem odd, given his particular attachment to anamorphic cinematography, that John Carpenter has so often expressed a desire to be part of that Hollywood which existed before CinemaScope: 'If I had three wishes, one of them would be "Send me back to the 1940s and the studio system and let me direct movies". Because I would have been happiest there. I feel I am a little bit out of time' (Milne and Combs 1978: 95).[8] It is ironic, also, that Carpenter should be so drawn to two directors – Alfred Hitchcock and Howard Hawks – noted for their disdain of anamorphic photography. Hitchcock never used it, though five of his films were shot in VistaVision (a non-anamorphic process which offered a variable aspect ratio, with a recommended optimum framing of 1.85:1). Hawks used 'Scope only once, to his dissatisfaction, on *Land of the Pharaohs* (1955). His comments to Peter Bogdanovich are worth quoting at length:

> I don't think that CinemaScope is a good medium. It's good only for showing great masses of movement. For other things, it's distracting, it's hard to focus attention, and it's very difficult to cut. Some people just go ahead and cut it and let people's eyes jump around and find what they want to find. It's very hard for an audience to focus – they have too much to look at – they

can't see the whole thing. If you are going to cut to a close-up, you should have a man speaking in the same relative position on screen. It's hard to form those compositions. I like the 1.85:1 ratio better than any other – the one we used on *Rio Bravo* and *Hatari* – it gives you just a little more space at the sides. If the CinemaScope size had been any good painters would have used it many years ago – and they've been at it a lot longer than we have. (Bogdanovich 1962: 17)[9]

One guesses that Hitchcock concurred with Hawks in the latter's view that the very wide frame made control of the spectator's gaze difficult (particularly important for an arch manipulator like Hitchcock), and in his preference for the 1.85:1 ratio for its balance of height against width (it matches closely the 'Golden Mean' of classical aesthetics – roughly 1.6:1). Carpenter, however, is on record as disliking the ratio his idols preferred:

> I love Panavision as a composing rectangle. There seems to be two really good visual ways of composing. One is the old-fashioned format which they never use any more [1.33:1/1.37:1]. It's a square. Beautiful to compose. And then there's Panavision, which is also beautiful to compose. It's perfect for the two-shot. 1.85:1 is a bastard ratio because you can't compose anything in it. It's not wide enough or tall enough ... And it really doesn't lend itself to pretty pictures. You have a close-up and there's a little space off to the side. Well, in Panavision, you've got background and foreground objects to play with ... When you have a person standing in a Panavision frame, there's a lot of space on either side, and if you cast [a] bunch of shadows and you have some doors and darkness back there, you can have something jump out. (Appelbaum 1979a: 11)

There is a further oddity about Carpenter's cited influences. Even putting to one side questions of thematic preoccupations and ideological disposition, Hitchcock and Hawks may be seen to represent divergent and arguably antithetical tendencies within classical cinema: the former flaunting his technical and stylistic resources, with a rigorously precise control and self-conscious virtuosity which often approach the extremes of abstract formalism; the latter concealing 'style' and the signs of directorial presence in favour of an impression of direct, unmediated access to the narrative world, its inhabitants and their relationships. The difference is ultimately, as Robin Wood has suggested, one of a 'broad distinction ... between actor-centred cinema and image-centred cinema' (1989: 213–14).

Put that way, it is Hitchcock rather than Hawks with whom Carpenter belongs, spiritually and aesthetically. Indeed, though it is Hawks whom Carpenter has most often acknowledged as a role model – to the extent that his regular producer/collaborator, Debra Hill, has said that 'John would like to pattern himself after Howard Hawks's career'[10] – it seems to me that any similarities between their work are few and generally superficial. If Carpenter and Hawks share anything it is perhaps the desire for the kind of stylistic self-effacement the Hollywood system has usually tended to encourage – though even this is variable in Carpenter's case, due partly to the Hitchcock counter-influence.

Hitchcock is often, of course, identified with the notion of (in his own phrase) 'pure cinema': that is, purely cinematic storytelling, visual (and sonic) narration rather than 'photographs of people talking'. All his technical and stylistic inno- vations follow from a formalist interest in film-as-film, which often exceeds the requirements of film-as-narrative. Carpenter seems to share some aspects of this view of cinema's potential, and the deliberate exclusion of thematic and 'human' interest from his work is surely in pursuit of some such common goal. Nonetheless, the Hitchcock influence, if considered purely at the level of style, has produced in Carpenter's best work a formal economy and fluidity which would certainly justify claims for his accomplishment as a specialised generic storyteller. These qualities are seen most clearly in his handling of the one formal/technical facility whose possibili- ties Hitchcock chose not to explore: the anamorphic frame.

Carpenter makes particularly effective use of the anamorphic frame in *Halloween* (1978). This film has often been compared to *Psycho* (1960) in that they are both progenitors of the 'stalk and slash' cycle of horror movies which proliferated in the late 1970s and early 1980s. But it is Carpenter's style, his use of patterns of camera movement and editing most often associated with Hitchcock, especially in the con- struction of point-of-view and 'identification', which clearly marks *Halloween* as the most consciously Hitchcockian of his theatrical features. The film's minimal narra- tive is seemingly designed to facilitate the kind of formal exploration of the potenti- alities of Panavision as Hitchcock undertook with the long take in *Rope* (1948), the point-of-view structure in *Rear Window* (1954), 3D in *Dial M for Murder* (1954), and confined spaces in all three of these films as well as in *Lifeboat* (1944).

*Halloween*'s refusal to develop the psychology of its characters concentrates our attention on their role as components in a design or machine. Richard Combs has described the film as 'one of the cinema's most perfectly engineered devices for saying "Boo!"' (1979: 27). The desired audience response, of fear and apprehension leading to prolonged suspense climaxed by sudden shock, derives precisely from the spectator's eye being allowed to wander across the breadth and into the depths of the frame. Areas of shadow and darkness are purposefully arranged to invite and tease the gaze, rather than to deflect it to a principal point of interest. But the use of Panavision cannot be considered apart from its employment in conjunction with a range of other rhetorical devices: the alternation of long takes and reverse-field cut- ting, objective and subjective camera, static and moving shots. Carpenter's use of the horizontal frame, in combination with the depth afforded by wide-angle lenses and deep-field staging, enables a systematic exploration of the formal possibilities inherent in his minimal narrative.

We might begin by considering the use of the point-of-view structure which many spectators may assume obliges us to 'identify' with Michael and his lethal gaze. On the contrary, the temporary placement of the camera in Michael's opti- cal or physical position, while it ensures that we see what he sees, does not identify us with him emotionally but precisely distances us from him, while enhancing our sympathetic concern for the objects of his gaze.[11] The celebrated subjective opening shot is striking first as a stunt, and as a device which prevents our recognition of the bearer of the look, before it impresses us as a representation of emotional experience. In later sequences where Michael stalks Laurie (Jamie Lee Curtis) and her friends, we are often positioned behind or alongside Michael but are denied the reverse-angle cut which would show us his reaction if he were not wearing his mask: the necessary precondition for empathy, as both Carpenter and Hitchcock have noted in interviews.

We are, however, given just such a reaction shot when positioned with Laurie at those several points where she becomes aware of being followed. At these moments – such as when Laurie watches as the car Michael is driving passes her and Annie (Nancy Loomis) and comes to a momentary halt, or when she looks out from her bedroom window at Michael standing below – suspense derives in part from the fixed distance between Laurie/the camera/us and Michael: she is not close enough to identify him clearly, to recognise or dispel the threat, and the camera does not close the gap. A variation of this device is Carpenter's manipulation of the distance of the camera from Laurie and her friends. It does not always stay with them as they traverse the sidewalks of Haddonfield, but will sometimes hold a fixed position as they walk into the shot's depth. In refusing to be prompted into movement, to be motivated by the action happening before it (as is customary in classical cinema), the camera's objective autonomy suggests Michael's subjectivity even in his absence, and again increases our anxiety for Laurie.

In those shots where Michael does appear as onlooker, he is invariably positioned at the extreme edges of the Panavision frame. These include, for example: his first appearance in Laurie's presence, albeit unseen by her, when she peers in through the door of the deserted Myers house, and Michael appears from the shadowy area at screen right and is silhouetted against the light streaming in from outside; his reappearance moments later, as we see a shoulder occupying the same position on the screen, watching as Laurie walks away down the street (the beginning, presumably of *his* 'identification' with *her*); and Michael's appearance to Tommy's (Brian Andrews) schoolyard tormentor (who *does* see him clearly after running into him, though again we are denied the reverse angle) outside the yard, where he is at screen left, with the boy at screen right. These and other similar shots both reiterate Michael's position as community outsider – he is from Haddonfield but not of it – and prepare us for his possible reappearance at the edges of the screen, which the audience will later tend to scrutinise anxiously for signs of his presence. When he does appear there we receive a momentary shock; when he does not, or when his appearance there is delayed, we endure prolonged suspense. The possibility is also established of the spectator's expectations of his appearance being cheated, realised in those moments when a hand or figure other than Michael's takes 'his' place and surprises us and/or one of the characters: Sheriff Brackett (played by Carpenter regular Charles Cyphers) is twice used in this way, abruptly tapping the shoulders of both Laurie and Dr Loomis from behind.[12]

In addition to his exploitation of the breadth of the anamorphic image, Carpenter also makes unusually extensive use of its depth. As already noted, the spatial separation of Laurie and Michael is strongly marked in those shots where they appear together, or where their proximity is suggested. In the daylight scenes set in under-populated suburban streets, Carpenter stresses the contrast between the apparently endless space and the limitations of the camera's field of view: the possibility that something might still be hidden from view despite the clear light and the wide frame. This is achieved by his placement of the camera in relation to objects which both suggest deep space and offer a hiding place: trees, bushes, fences, hedges, placed in the foreground or at the edges of shots, which frame or come between Laurie and her friends, the camera and – possibly – Michael.

The motif is developed, with variations, in the nighttime scenes of the film's second half, in which the significantly pregnant spaces are concealed by darkness. Here, too, the width of the frame permits the multiplication of hiding places, and the darkness increases the possibility of Michael's appearance from any one of them. This is most conspicuous in, for example, the scene where Lynda's (P. J. Soles) boyfriend Bob (John Michael Graham) goes to the kitchen for a snack after they have made love, and Michael emerges from the shadows to pin him to the wall; and in the complementary scene of Laurie's discovery of Lynda, Bob and Annie's bodies in the bedroom. Elsewhere, Carpenter employs frames within the frame – in the form of doors and windows – to block vision and separate characters from one another, or the camera from the action. Examples include Michael's first appearance beside Laurie in the Myers house, separated from her by the front door; his (and our) observation of Annie through the windows of the washing-machine outhouse; and his eventual killing of Annie in the garage, seen from two different angles through misted-up car windows.

Many of the film's most famous moments of fright or anxiety involve not Michael's sudden eruption into the frame from areas of darkness, but his gradual appearance in the background, a shadowy figure standing or sitting up behind Lau-

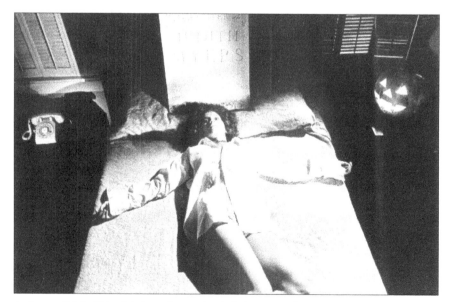

Annie, one of Michael Myers' victims, is discovered in the bedroom in *Halloween*

rie's shoulder, as her complacent assumption of safety is countered by yet another awakening. At these moments, Carpenter employs deep staging without deep focus, with one plane – the foreground – in focus and the other intentionally blurred. The obvious point of this is that Laurie is unconscious of Michael's continuing threat; its subliminal effect may be the spectator's sense of having noticed something that the camera has not yet adjusted to (and hence the spectator may anticipate, or *will*, the delayed rack-focus).[13] The climactic use of both deep space and off-screen space is the closing montage of 'empty' spaces, cued by Dr Loomis's (Donald Pleasence) glances off camera and reprised from their earlier function as locations for the action. They confirm Michael's invincibility and suggest his ubiquity: he must be *somewhere* even if he is not immediately visible, and we are invited to imagine for ourselves his threatening gaze directed at us.

Carpenter employs three basic kinds of camera movement in *Halloween*: tracking (dolly) shots, handheld camera and the Panaglide (an early form of Steadicam). The last, which combines some of the flexibility and versatility of handheld cameras with the smoother movement of tracks, is used most famously in the virtuoso opening subjective sequence, which gives the appearance of being a single shot, though there are several disguised cuts.[14] Tracking shots (or what appear to be tracking shots; some may use the Panaglide) are featured most extensively, and serve a number of distinct purposes. One of them is the gradual disclosure of off-screen space, to reveal something of which we were not previously aware. For example, after Dr Loomis finds the matchbook beside the abandoned pick-up truck, the camera tracks right to show us the driver's dead body, still undiscovered, in the bushes. As Lynda and Bob settle down for sex on the couch, the camera tracks backwards through the living room to find Michael watching (only his back and shoulder visible at screen left).

In these scenes the camera's movements are autonomous, dictated by their function as omniscient narration. In the scenes centred on Laurie, camera movement and placement are more strictly motivated by her own movements. For example, the early street scenes feature extensive tracking along and around the suburban sidewalks, the camera usually moving backwards (presumably with the use of the Panaglide) as Laurie and her friends advance towards it. Here and elsewhere, Carpenter uses extended two-shots or group shots, keeping all the action within and spread across the frame, rather than breaking the dialogue up into separate close-ups for each successive speaker (these were done for reasons of economy and a short shooting schedule, but Carpenter's later, more generously budgeted films employ similar methods). Reverse-field cutting is usually avoided except for those point-of-view structures which stress the camera's position as being fixed in relation to the subject of the gaze.

The inclusion on Criterion's laserdisc of several additional sequences filmed by Carpenter to pad out the running time of the US network television edition of the film – and therefore shot in Academy ratio rather than Panavision – conveniently demonstrate by default the extent to which the film's *mise-en-scène* and lateral shot composition specifically exploit the properties of the anamorphic frame and its suggestion of infinitely extendable space. In one of the extra scenes, Dr Loomis addresses a panel of medics across a lecture theatre; rather than using a 'horizontal'

Dr Sam Loomis searches for the evanescent Michael Myers

long shot, the scene is filmed with reverse-field edits along the axis between Loomis and his interlocutors. In another, a telephone rings and is followed not by a camera movement but by a straight cut to a close-up of it from Laurie and Lynda's point-of-view.[15]

In the climactic scenes of Laurie's pursuit by Michael, Carpenter borrows most extensively Hitchcock's characteristic use of moving point-of-view: complementary forward- and backward-tracking movements centred on Laurie's viewpoint (compare, from among many possible examples, Vera Miles' approach to the Bates house in *Psycho*). Here, more rigorously and exclusively than in the earlier, daylight section, the camera remains close to Laurie, keeping the same distance from Michael as she does (though, as noted, it sometimes sees what she does not). Carpenter also follows Hitchcock's strictures on keeping the 'size' of the image, as much as its vantage point, constant so as to reinforce identification with the protagonist (constructed, of course, by means other than just point-of-view, including Curtis's sympathetic performance).[16] An exception to this, noted by Curtis herself in her audio commentary on the Criterion laserdisc, is when the camera cuts to a high angle of Laurie as she sits on the couch and drops the knife which she has just used to stab Michael. Curtis comments that the greater distance from Laurie makes her foolish action of dropping the knife less plausible, more artificially contrived, than if the camera had remained close enough to find motivation in her facial expressions. As a result, she claims, theatrical audiences invariably groan aloud at this point, having been 'thrown out' of identification with both Laurie and the film. This reinforces the point made here about camera proximity and graphic composition determining the spectator's emotional and psychological relationship to a character or situation.[17]

What I have tried to show here is the operation of Carpenter's style, in this one picture, in terms both of its narrational functions (its control of spectator response and the construction of identification), and in the element of formalism which seems to underpin it. *Halloween* seems to me the Carpenter film in which narrative and style are most successfully matched, and in which the suppression of thematic complexity works in its favour rather than making one wish for further elaboration. The opposition, as I have defined it – it could reasonably be redefined as an interplay rather than a conflict – between the Hawksian and Hitchcockian tendencies of Carpenter's work, can perhaps be seen to embody a wider contradiction to do with a clash of the conventions inherited by the contemporary post-classical Hollywood cinema. Combs has described Carpenter's achievement in *Halloween* as a precarious 'balancing act ... an aesthetic high-wire routine' which embodies his position as an old-fashioned craftsman in the self-conscious, self-aware new Hollywood:

> There is a contradiction, and a fine line, here – and one which Carpenter treads with unerring skill: the first tenet of classic Hollywood storytelling, which Carpenter takes as his model, is its invisibility; yet in order to touch the nerves of an audience which has seen it all so many times before, Carpenter must employ the style in a manner which allows them to recognise the manipulation and still willingly submit to its spell. (1979: 27)[18]

Carpenter's reconciliation of these opposites can be seen (may indeed be seen as embodied) in his use of Panavision. Though his anamorphic images, in *Halloween* and elsewhere, do not display the complexity of some of those in the work of Preminger, Ray or Minnelli, nor the baroque manipulations of scale and perspective characteristic of a Sergio Leone, they are rarely less than elegant and intelligent in their arrangement of space and action.

*Notes*

1   Carpenter was speaking before the introduction of 'letterboxed' videos and widescreen televisions.
2   *Moving Pictures*, BBC2, tx 9 January 1993.
3   See Belton (1992) for the most thorough critical account to date of the history of widescreen technologies and aesthetics.
4   See also Bogdanovich (1978: 102–4) for Ford's views on the even wider three-strip Cinerama format ('It's worse than CinemaScope').
5   Of the six directors questioned about CinemaScope in Bogdanovich's book, only one – Otto Preminger – speaks of it positively.
6   For André Bazin's views on the possible contribution widescreen formats might make to his conception of cinematic realism, see Bazin (1985).
7   Panavision replaced CinemaScope as the anamorphic format of choice from the early 1960s onwards, and continues to be in regular use. The classic analysis of Preminger's use of CinemaScope in *River of No Return* (1954) is in Barr (1963); for a dissenting view see Bordwell (1985).
8   The authors' title for this interview article – a reference to *Dark Star* (1974) – also suggests someone preserved beyond his proper time.
9   This passage was substantially edited for its reprinting in Bogdanovich (1997).

10 In the audio commentary to the Criterion Collection laserdisc of *Halloween* (The Voyager Company).

11 See Neale (1981) for a sophisticated analysis of the pattern of 'aggressive looks' in the film.

12 Carpenter tries variations of this device in *The Fog* (1979), in which the *mise-en-scène* and shot composition trick the audience into giving its attention to one part of the Panavision frame, and a figure appears instead from the 'wrong' part of the image. See, for example, the scene in which Cyphers' character ('Dan O'Bannon') is killed.

13 Compare William Wyler's staging of Horace's (Herbert Marshall) death scene in *The Little Foxes* (1941): in the one sequence in the film which refuses deep focus when it seems most obviously called for, Regina (Bette Davis) remains in clear focus in the foreground, indifferent to her husband's sufferings as he staggers, out of focus, up the staircase in the far distance of the shot.

14 In his Criterion laserdisc commentary, Carpenter claims this opening shot was inspired by the extended boom shot which opens Orson Welles' *Touch of Evil* (1958). For his comments on the use of Panaglide in *Halloween*, see Appelbaum (1979a: 12).

15 The use of telephone calls to induce suspense is expanded with Laurie's phone conversations with Annie and Lynda, both of which immediately precede (and in the latter's case, coincide with) their murder. As Carpenter himself has pointed out, the clear inspiration for this is Hitchcock's *Dial M for Murder*; variations on it in are presented in *Someone's Watching Me!* (1978) and *The Fog*.

16 See, for example, his remarks on *The Birds* (1963) in Truffaut (1984: 290).

17 This example would also seem to contradict Debra Hill's claim that 'we start out by using very wide shots and as the suspense builds, we get closer and closer, so that the last fifteen or twenty minutes of the film is all done in medium close-up [sic]' Appelbaum (1979b: 22).

18 In his subsequent review of *Big Trouble in Little China* (1986), Combs describes Carpenter's early work (*Dark Star, Assault on Precinct 13* and *Halloween*) as a 'cinema of great negative capability', constituting 'acts of criticism in themselves [which] defined themselves by what they were not, looking for irreducible components of form and style that would actually become the films' (1986: 365).

*References*

Appelbaum, R. (1979a) 'From Cult Homage to Creative Control', *Films and Filming*, 25, 9, 10–16.

_____ (1979b) 'Working with numbers', *Films and Filming*, 25, 12, 20–4.

Barr, C. (1963) 'CinemaScope: Before and After', *Film Quarterly*, 16, 4 , 4–24.

Bazin, A. (1985) 'Three Essays on Widescreen', *The Velvet Light Trap*, 21, 8–16.

Belton, J. (1992) *Widescreen Cinema*. Cambridge, MA and London: Harvard University Press.

Bogdanovich, P. (1962) 'Interview with Howard Hawks', *Movie*, 5, 8–18.

_____ (1978) *John Ford* (revised edition). Berkeley, CA and London: University of

California Press.

____ (1997) *Who the Devil Made It*. New York: Alfred A. Knopf.

Bordwell, D. (1985) 'Widescreen Aesthetics and Mise en Scène Criticism', *The Velvet Light Trap*, 21, 18–25.

Combs, R. (1979) '*Halloween*', *Monthly Film Bulletin*, 46, 541, 27.

____ (1986) '*Big Trouble in Little China*', *Monthly Film Bulletin*, 53, 635, 364–6.

Milne, T. and R. Combs (1978) 'The Man in the Cryogenic Freezer', *Sight and Sound*, 47, 2, 94–8.

Neale, S. (1981) '*Halloween*: Suspense, Aggression and the Look', *Framework*, 14, 25–9.

Truffaut, F. (1984) *Hitchcock* (revised edition). New York: Simon and Schuster.

Wood, R. (1989) *Hitchcock's Films Revisited*. New York and Oxford: Columbia University Press.

CHAPTER SIX

# 'A Spook Ride on Film': Carpenter and the Gothic

Marie Mulvey-Roberts

The fog descended on John Carpenter while he was driving to Stonehenge during a trip to England for a film festival in 1977.[1] What threatened to envelop him was so elusive that he wanted to capture it on film. To make the ephemeral solid, immutable and permanent is the filmmaker's perennial challenge. Yet to frame within the cinema screen that which is both nebulous and amorphous is to subvert a fog's true nature. The same can be argued for the Gothic whose terrors are ushered in by Carpenter's film *The Fog* (1979). Plotted as a mariner's ghost story, peopled with nautical killer lepers, a female disc jockey and a dipsomaniac Catholic priest, its hybridity conjures up the difficulties of classifying the Gothic caught in the act of endlessly deconstructing itself.

Carpenter felt that he was in the middle of nowhere as he watched the fog approach the stones, which are believed to be the remains of an ancient solar temple. 'Nowhere' is a place of Gothic interest frequently located in the shadowlands of borders, transgressive spaces or in the interstitial states that are a leitmotif of so many Carpenter films. His eponymous cinematic fog functions as a formless time machine transporting from the past diseased phantoms intent on revenge. It is from the future that Carpenter's film *Prince of Darkness* (1987) draws on the menace of an infernal other world in its crossings between the boundaries of dreams and reality. In Carpenter's *In the Mouth of Madness* (1995), the interface between real life and fiction becomes the film itself. One of its final scenes is of the hero being filmed watching the film in an act of solitary, almost incestuous, spectatorship. By doing so, he becomes witness to his own performance in the making.

The observed becoming the observer is part of the diabolical cunning of the film-maker who manipulates the cinema screen as a membrane between realities. Another is the looking glass, which appears in *Prince of Darkness* as a surface for reflection that is inter-penetrable with another dimension. Then there are the characters in *Vampires* (1998), who inhabit the twilight zone between life and death. For them, human skin is the membrane dividing the living from the undead. In *The Thing* (1982) the invasion of form by formlessness transgresses the boundaries between the human and the non-human, while in *Christine* (1983) the borders between the animate and inanimate are broken down by a fetishisation of the feminine.

Such crossings bring about a disruption of human identity. This combined with the terror of assimilation into a collective Gothic otherness suggests the notion of the Thing as a category for the non-human, the nameless and the unidentifiable. This 'it' resembles the Gothic in that both burst out of a restrictive taxonomy or an existing definition in a series of endless rebirths of the monstrous. The matrix of terror in Carpenter's films resides in the fear of being taken over by alien entities, which obliterate the individual's sense of personal identity. These range across a malevolent fog, a satanic awakening, a monstrous growth, a race of vampires, a rei-fied Plymouth Fury car and a horror novel, through to the very films of Carpenter himself. Possession by cinema whether for a character, viewer or filmmaker, is the arch danger for a director of the Gothic.

Carpenter expressed his intentions as a Gothic filmmaker in regard to *The Fog* by saying that he wanted to create 'a spook ride on film, taking the audience through twists and turns and having things jump out at them' (Scanlon 1979). For him, the fog had initially evoked the mistiness in Dracula films, though it was to be his memory of the fairground haunted-house attraction that turned him towards the vehicle for the film.[2] Ironically, he dressed the fog in the garb of a ghost story in order to make the spook ride appear more substantial. Not only was the fog to be a character in a film, but also its leading player. How could Carpenter direct the fog so as to imbue it with charisma and star-quality? Was it sufficient for fog in perfor-mance to be merely a pulsating and glowing mass?[3] In regard to the viewer, the fog can be read not just as a conductor of miasma but also of metaphor. Penetrating, invasive and yet without boundary, this shape-shifter remains the proverbial out-sider. Like the Gothic it can conceal that which is already there, at the same time as accentuating the hidden. Both facilitate 'the return of the repressed' whose only release appears to be through terror (see Wood 1984). Carpenter's fog is a phan-tasmagoric fabric of fear heralded by the female disc jockey in the lighthouse. Her voice over the radio waves is similar to the fog in that it too can penetrate walls and barriers. The fog creeping inland is spectral since it contains the vengeful phantoms whose ship, the *Elizabeth Dane*, had many years ago been lured onto rocks by the greed of the townsfolk wanting to purloin their cargo of gold. The ghostly mariners are returning to reclaim their gold and to retrieve, in particular, a golden crucifix. Against these grisly revenants, unlike vampires, the cross affords no protection. The priest who clutches it to his breast unknowingly embraces his death warrant in the final scene. The inevitability of death is offset by the conflation between dreaming and reality in a rhyming couplet written by Edgar Allan Poe, which appears at the start of the film:

Is all that we see or seem
But a dream within a dream?

Clutching the crucifix, Father Malone (Hal Holbrook) approaches the ghostly mariners with their stolen gold in *The Fog*

*Prince of Darkness*

The boundaries between sleep, dream and reality collapse in *Prince of Darkness*, which centres around the Brotherhood of Sleep, a cryptic religious sect that has been kept secret even from the Vatican for 2,000 years. Father Carlton (Donald Pleasence) reads the prophetically entitled text 'The Sleeper Awakes' and whilst the Prince of Darkness is in the process of awakening, those who fall under his power become somnambulists. According to Father Carlton, everyone in close proximity to the Brotherhood of Sleep has the same dream, which had also been dreamed by the sect's ancient guardian priests. Likewise, the cinema audience shares the same cinematic dream or nightmare. In order to try and diffuse the tension of being cornered by two zombified women, Walter (Dennis Dun) asks them if they have liked any movies they have seen. Their deadpan response to his metafilmic question is further confirmation of their dehumanised state.

The moral chiaroscuro of the Gothic with its play on darkness and light is a trope for the cinema. In *Prince of Darkness*, the prophesied 'Father' is being brought from the dark side directly through the luminosity of a looking glass. Kelly, the female acolyte delivering the deliverer is, at the same time, the actress Susan Blanchard, who is facilitating the film director's vision and its materialisation via the cinema screen. A related Gothic trajectory, which is evident from Mary Shelley's *Frankenstein* (1818) to Anne Rice's Vampire Chronicles starting with *Interview with the Vampire* (1976), is the search for origins which can open up levels of rebirthing. Such a nascent level of meaning may be viewed in *Prince of Darkness* where the acolyte becomes a midwife delivering the avatar from the meniscus of the mirror that has the viscosity of amniotic fluid. Taking place in a church, this rebirth is being investigated by a group of scientists. In common with the members of the scientific community in Carpenter's *The Thing*, the observers are being taken over by that which they are observing.

In *Prince of Darkness*, where science is being utilised by religion, the scientific researcher Kelly has been aptly 'chosen' by the Father. Her subsequent mysterious and accelerated pregnancy is inflected with incest. In turn, she becomes a spectacle monitored by another watcher reporting back to those who are resisting domination by the Father. This satanic impregnation is the unholy Immaculate Conception of the Anti-Christ. Her swollen belly not only signifies the birth of the Prince of Darkness but also her developing abjectness.

In her book, *Powers of Horror*, Julia Kristeva identifies abjection as an in-between state, which simultaneously evokes repulsion and attraction (1982: 1–2). In *The Thing* the internal undifferentiated monstrosity breaking out of human form awakens primal fears of the cannibalising and all-consuming figure. And in a film in which there are no women, the Thing is the embodiment of the absent mother. Its grotesque and growing protuberances are evocative of the Cronenbergian image of birthing as in the external womb in *The Brood* (1979), where the inside is placed outside. What remains outside Kelly in *Prince of Darkness* after her swollen stomach has subsided is blood on her face, which represents a displacement of the afterbirth. Father Carlton invokes such lustrations as the ritual of churching, the purpose of

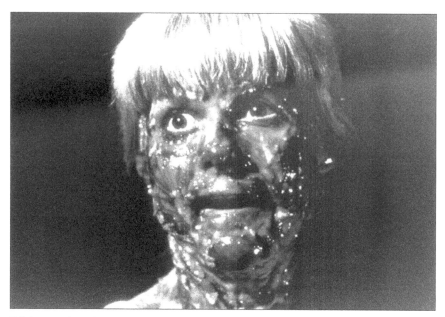

Kelly's ruptured and bloodied face marks her abjectness in *Prince of Darkness*

which was to purify a woman after she has given birth by praying for help against this 'unholy spirit'. Furthermore, Walter enacts his own symbolic passage through the birth canal when he is pulled through a hole in the wall out of the reach of two zombified women who would otherwise have 'midwived' his rebirth into the Brotherhood of Sleep. Even those who have been taken over by the evil force in the church retain glimmers of recognition of their own individuality such as Calder (Jessie Lawrence Ferguson) and Kelly, who demonically laugh at their own reflections. Nevertheless, the characters actually penetrating the mirror relinquish their individuality for a collective Gothic darkness into which they are reborn. The looking glass acts metaphorically for the magic mirror of the cinema screen onto which is projected a phantasmagorical illusion of light and shade.

Another version of the Prince of Darkness, who upholds the polarisations between light and dark and the living and the dead, is the master vampire Valek (Thomas Ian Griffith) who appears in *Vampires*. The action centres on preventing him from completing the ceremony of the forbidden exorcism, which would enable vampires to walk in the sunlight. If he succeeds, those hunting him and his kind would lose their most effective weapon. Led by Jack Crow (James Woods), a band of vigilante vampire-busters breaks up nests of vampires by dragging them into the daylight where they spontaneously combust. The theme of the sun is repeated throughout the film. The Sun God Motel serves as a brothel for Crow's men, while the astronomical symbol of the sun appears in a picture of the master vampire revealing that he had been a priest during the fourteenth century. A Cardinal, who at first assists Jack in tracking Valek down, eventually betrays him by turning him over to the master vampire who needs his participation in the forbidden exorcism. This involves hanging Jack from a blazing cross from where his blood will be shed in a chalice, in a perverse parody of the Crucifixion and the Catholic rite of tran-substantiation. Jack is chosen to be the sacrifice because he had killed his father who had turned into a vampire and infected his mother. In a vampiric variation of the Oedipal and Frankenstein myths, Jack eventually destroys the master vampire by impaling him on the cross in the sunlight. This act of penetration is also an exorcism of the vampire legacy that Jack had inherited from his father.

## The Thing

Familial perversity is explored further in *The Thing* where men 'give birth' to an entity able to replicate itself as any living creature. The proliferation of *The Thing* is a variation on the solitary male propagation brought about by Victor Frankenstein. The action of *The Thing* takes place in and around an American research station in Antarctica, which is invaded by an alien creature, which had been long-buried in ice after a crash landing from outer space. Once thawed it takes the shape of other living beings, thereby creating a breakdown of trust within the community since no one can be sure of who is actually human. The self-appointed leader, J. R. Mac-Ready (Kurt Russell), devises a blood test in order to determine who has already been infected by the alien. He has realised that since each piece of the Thing is an individual organism, every drop of blood will become autonomous.[4] In *Vampires*, the shedding of blood leads to a loss of humanity whereas in *The Thing* it confirms who is human and who is not. The Thing, by voraciously consuming living beings and then imitating them, may be associated with Sigmund Freud's notion of the uncanny (1985). In arousing 'dread and creeping horror', the uncanny object is both *heimlich* (literally homely or familiar) and *unheimlich* (literally unhomely or unfamiliar). *Heimlich* is indicative of that which is concealed while its lexical opposite signifies a repression generating anxiety and fear.

Kelly Hurley's reading of the Gothic body as a 'horrific re-making of the human subject' (1996: 5), which she applies to the *fin de siècle* revival of the Gothic, is applicable to *The Thing*. She regards the abhuman subject as a 'not-quite-human subject, characterised by its morphic variability, continually in danger of becoming not-itself, becoming other' (1996: 3). This ensuing monstrous becoming is intrinsic to the transformations taking place in *The Thing*. It is also indicative of the difficulty in stabilising human identity once it has been polluted by the Gothic subject. By straddling borders, the horror for the spectator is the realisation that the familiarity of the human is lost to a nauseating and abominable liminality (1996: 24).[5] As a manifestation of both the uncanny and the abject, the monstrous body represents a horror of the indifferentiation of the now defamiliarised human. Monstrosity is also a fear of oneself, particularly of the alienation within the self. As Hurley points out, the human body at a fundamental level is 'a quasi-differentiated mass, pulsating and viscous' (1996: 34). In regard to the Thing, the men who have been assimilated by the alien become that which has absorbed them and vice versa.

Mikhail Bakhtin's account of the grotesque captures this dialectical reversal and dissolution of boundaries when he points out, 'the body swallows the world and is itself swallowed by the world' (Morris 1994: 233). He goes on to note:

the grotesque ignores the impenetrable surface that closes and limits the body as a separate and completed phenomenon. The grotesque image displays not only the outward but also the inner features of the body: blood, bowels, heart and other organs. The outward and inward features are often merged into one.

We have already sufficiently stressed the fact that grotesque imagery constructs what we might call a double body. In the endless chain of bodily life it retains the parts in which one link joins the other, in which the life of one body is born from the death of the preceding, older one. (Morris 1994: 234)

The oozing viscosity of the Thing is what Hurley calls the 'gothicity of matter' (1996: 33). Its mimetic horrors arise from its being an undifferentiated body or interstitial creature. In *The Thing* matter rises up and consumes the bounded world and then reconfigures it in the original image of its host. Hurley suggests that the Gothic can be a conserving genre in that through depicting the abhuman, it reaffirms and reconstructs human identity at the point at which it is dissolved. Otherness, liminality and monstrosity serve to reaffirm categories such as the specificity of the human subject. In *The Thing* MacReady's endeavour to retain the bodily integrity of the workers at the station depends on his ability to isolate the human from the non-human. Once all the men have been shot or become assimilated into the Thing, MacReady is left alone with Childs (Keith David). Both men wait to see who has been dehumanised by the invader. The film ends with this stark image of the protagonist waiting to discover the monster within.

Hurley suggests that 'in its obsession with abominations, the Gothic may be said to manifest a certain gleefulness at the prospect of a world in which no fixity remains, only an endless series of monstrous becomings' (1996: 28). According to Bakhtin, 'the grotesque body, as we have often stressed, is a body in the act of becoming. It is never finished, never completed; it is continually built, created, and builds and creates another body' (Morris 1994: 233). Likewise the Thing, the alien entity as grotesque body, threatens to burst out of its restraints and engulf the whole world. Blair (A. Wilford Brimley) uses a computer to calculate that 'if [the] intruder organism reaches civilised areas [then the] entire world population [will be] infected 27,000 hours from first contact'.

*Christine*

The destructive alien body takes on a different form in *Christine*, which is based on one of Stephen King's novels. The eponymous Gothic heroine is a 1958 Plymouth Fury, which turns out to be a killer car, whose 'make' is evocative of the mythological female Furies of Ancient Greece. The beginning of the film showing Christine nearing the end of construction on an assembly line can be read as a reminder of the way in which femininity is socially constructed. Men's fears of the *femme fatale* protesting against the intrusion of the male gaze peering at the female genitals may be seen in the way she slams down her hood on the hand of a line inspector who peers at her from underneath. He screams and is seen later cradling his hand, which is swathed heavily in bandages.

Later, in 1978, Christine is purchased by the anti-heroic Arnie (Keith Gordon) who compensates for his lack of a girlfriend and status-symbol car (invariably co-dependents) by falling in love with this 'old banger'. Arnie transforms himself into a hero by humanising his automobile through fetishism; a process which normally dehumanises the human. A remark directed towards serial killer Michael Myers in *Halloween* (1978) by one of the teenage girls – 'I hate a guy with a car and no sense of humour' – could also be extended to the seriousness of Arnie's fetishistic relationship with Christine. After he has restored Christine to her former glamour, this assembly-line built *femme fatale*, decked out in red paint and silver chrome, makes an ironic commentary upon the hazards of teenage courtship as well as on America's love-affair with the car. Arnie is mockingly called 'Cuntingham' by his best friend Buddy Repperton (William Ostrander). Christine the car is more than an icon of male sexual prowess, she is also a sex symbol in her own right, even behaving like a jealous woman by trying to choke her female rival. As a variation on the Gothic body which lies at the polar end from the pulsating, growing, indefinable mass of *The Thing*, her metallic rigidity of form signalled by her steely curves is a perversity of over-definition and a parody of feminine overkill. By turning into the embodiment of the scarlet lady, she eventually becomes the reality of her own representation as fleshless dominatrix.

## In the Mouth of Madness

The perplexing relationship between fiction and reality permeates *In the Mouth of Madness*. Through the use of metafilmic strategies, Carpenter explores the relationship between the film and the text along with that of the viewer and the viewed in their disturbing negotiations with Gothic horror. The film opens with John Trent (Sam Neill) being forcibly committed to a mental hospital. He insists that he is sane until confronted by an investigator to whom he declares himself to be suffering from insanity.

Trent has been an insurance investigator looking into the mysterious disappearance of the best-selling novelist Sutter Cane (Jürgen Prochnow). The suggestion that Cane is an author who is read more widely than anyone else is evident from the comment, 'you can forget about Stephen King'. Reading Cane is reputed to make people paranoid and violent and even though Trent dismisses this claim as a marketing ploy, it does point to one of the dangers of reading Gothic literature. During the 1790s at the heyday of the Gothic novel, it was believed that its terrors could drive a reader to insanity. The most famous author of Gothic romance, Ann Radcliffe, was rumoured to have been driven mad by her own terrors (see Todd 1989: 254). Cane is a writer crazed by his belief that his writing is real and, in his self-imposed isolation, he conducts a reign of terror. The Biblical resonance of his own name with that of the first murderer recorded in the Bible is apocalyptic since his new book 'In the Mouth of Madness' is concerned with the end of the human race. Cane also anticipates that his novel will drive him to absolute madness.

Paranoia starts for Trent when someone tells him in a bookshop: 'He sees you'. This statement is suggestive of the film actor under the gaze of the director and eventually of the viewer in the cinema. In view of this, it is significant that, without escaping the diegetic, Trent will end up watching himself on the screen.

After he has started reading the book, Trent's imagination is so tormented by nightmarish images that he tears it up. Out of a number of covers ripped from Cane's books, Trent constructs a map, which he believes will lead him to the novelist. All the information he needs for facing his fears generated by the texts is contained within the books themselves. Accompanied by Cane's editor, the significantly named Miss Linda Styles (Julie Carmen), Trent, who will discover that he has a life as a fictional character, goes in search of the author. When they arrive at a hotel en route, Miss Styles sees a photographic image of herself and Trent hanging on a wall. It confirms her belief that they are occupying the pages of one of Cane's Gothic horror novels. Her hunch – 'what if Cane's work isn't fiction?' – leads her to treat the novel as a guidebook.

The point at which the main characters begin to literally lose the plot is when Miss Styles realises that they are part of a new novel, which only she and Cane's literary agent have read. True to life imitating art and vice versa, the narrative tells of evil returning to the small town of Hobb's End, the name of which is indicative of the teleological emphasis of the film. Miss Styles confides to Trent that he can escape from the film by skipping to the end of the new book. Earlier, while in the mental hospital, Trent confronts death saying, 'this is not the ending, you haven't read it yet'. He and Miss Styles trace the source of the terror to a church in Hobb's End where they find Cane typing a novel. Cane tells his newly-arrived editor, 'you can edit this one from the inside looking out ... for years I thought I was making all this up – but they were telling me what to write. Giving me the power to make it all real'.

Carpenter, the filmmaker, is also the magician who is capable of making it all seem 'real'. More than that, he can conjure people into existence just like the novelist or the Creator. As in Muriel Spark's metafictional novel *The Comforters* (1957), where the heroine Caroline Rose realises that she is a character in a novel, some of Carpenter's characters know that they are in a text. In *In the Mouth of Madness* one bemused man says, 'I cannot remember what came first, us or the book'. Cane's creativity is a parodic distortion of the opening of St John's Gospel: 'In the beginning was the Word and the Word was made flesh.' Significantly, Cane thrusts Miss Styles's face literally into 'The New Bible' and later tells Trent that 'more people believe in my work than believe in the Bible'. Cane arrogantly declares, 'you are what I write' and 'like this town – it wasn't here before I wrote it ... and neither were you'. Trent's refusal to accept such manipulation is evident from his insistence that 'I am not a piece of fiction' and 'nobody pulls my strings'. Cane's version of Cartesian ontology – 'I think therefore I am' is – 'I think there[fore] you are'. As Linda states, 'Cane's writing me', which she asserts 'is good for the book'. The predestination inherent within this Canian universe implies that for characters in the book and the film of *In the Mouth of Madness*, there is no free will.

Trent's resistance to this lack of freedom may be seen in his frustration at being forced to enact the same sequence of events over and over again as he tries to escape

An epidemic of paranoia sweeps through a community transformed in *In the Mouth of Madness*

from Hobb's End. He now realises that he is a character stuck in an author's narrative. When he eventually breaks out of the text, he finds himself standing literally at the edge of a ripped page. Linda cannot accompany him because she has been imprisoned within the novel as a result of having already read through to the end. Even though she has been taken over by the book, Trent's explanation for her subsequent absence is that she has been written out of the action. Reading, like sleeping in *Prince of Darkness*, is an initiation into another world. After crashing his car, Trent is trapped by Cane in a confined space resembling a confessional box. Through the other side of the grille, Cane makes his own confession to Trent, regarding his belief that religion has failed to convey horror. For this reason, Gothic literature and film have become in Cane's world a new religion. In a bizarre variation of the Catholic doctrine of transubstantiation, Cane's books may be seen as vampire-like since they suck the life-blood from the reader for their own replenishment. Trent's attempt to stop people reading 'In the Mouth of Madness' is futile since the impact of the film version of the book promises to reach an even wider audience (ironically Trent is colluding in this process which is in itself another source of metafictional madness). In the end, even Cane loses control over his own fictional world. He can no longer hold back the evil he has created, for the book in literal terms takes on a life of its own. Unlike Cane, Mary Shelley in her introduction to *Frankenstein* had given her authorial permission for her 'hideous progeny' to 'go forth and prosper' which is now most evident in the proliferation of publications and films spawned from her creation myth (Shelley 1992: 23).

*In the Mouth of Madness* depicts an epidemic of paranoid schizophrenics rather like Mary Shelley's 'race of devils' (1992: 40). As bodies mutate into monstrosity, a voice on the radio warns against trusting family and friends. The film is suggestive of the dilemma of the Gothic reader who has been taken over by fear, paranoia and imagination. Demonic possession by textual and cinematic means underpins that which is sensed by the man in a bar who informs us that 'reality is not what it used to be'. At the end of the film, in a scene which Trent is actually watching, he begins to laugh dementedly. He has discovered finally the Bakhtinian antidote to his fear that 'terror is conquered by laughter' (Morris 1994: 238).

The relationships between author, text and reader, filmmaker, the viewer and the viewed are variations on the paradigm of host and parasite. David Punter applies the logic of parasitism, described by Jacques Derrida, to the Gothic as being an 'essential co-necessity of parasite and host, and therefore … the moment at which we can no longer clearly see what is the bearer and what is being borne' (Byron & Punter 1999: 37). In *The Fog, Prince of Darkness, Christine, Vampires, The Thing* and *In the Mouth of Madness*, the identity of those who are hosts for that which represents the return of the repressed are inextricably bound up with the evil force preying upon them. Punter suggests that we might see stability from the vantage point of the parasite rather than of the host. The 'para-site' is a constituent of the stability of the host and is apparent in the way in which cinema audiences leech on the images in front of them for their own mass consumption. At the same time, they are being drained by the film whose *raison d'être* rests on a vampiric co-dependency with its spectators. *In the Mouth of Madness* and *Vampires*, where the vampire masterminding the various parasitic relationships is a metaphor for the film director, demonstrate this celluloid symbiosis. The Gothic is both predatory and incestuous, for it parasitically preys on the past and on its own conventions. The injunction made in *Vampires*, to 'forget what you've seen in the movies', is a reminder that the film itself is a cinematic pastiche. The final frame of *In the Mouth of Madness* is set in the cinema in order to foreground both the parasitic/host relationship between the viewer and the viewed and the ambiguous boundaries between where the film ends and real life begins.[6]

Gothic terror and horror are achieved by exploding the polar opposites of fiction and reality, sleep and wakefulness and the human and the monstrous that corral our experience of being human. Even Gothic literature itself has its own duality in the traditional division between terror and horror. For example, Ann Radcliffe regarded terror as a source for the sublime. In such a context, *The Fog* could be seen to exhibit a Radcliffean dreadful sublimity. As Radcliffe explains, 'terror and horror are so far opposite that the first expands the soul, and awakens the faculties to a high degree of life; the other contracts, freezes, and nearly annihilates them' (1826: 151). Her contemporary, Matthew Lewis, explored Gothic horror and the supernatural in his novel *The Monk* (1796). The Antarctic setting of *The Thing* is particularly appropriate for the atrophying of the emotions stunned by the spectacle of horror. Unlike Lewis, Radcliffe rationalises the supernatural. To a certain extent, so does Carpenter, through the use of the uncanny in his most well-known Gothic film *Halloween* in which the bogeyman, who is first seen as a child, becomes a serial killer.

The endings of several of Carpenter's films are suggestive of the dissolution of the self about to disappear into the fog, or into the oblivion of the mirror in *Prince of Darkness*, with its final cut to a blank screen. In *The Thing*, the two survivors await to see who will be or has already been assimilated into the formless entity, which is itself a simulacrum of a human being. In *In the Mouth of Madness*, the self becomes illusory through its projection upon a cinema screen, in an expression of Carpenter's admission that 'this idea of the audience projecting their fantasy, is to me the secret of movies'.[7] Directing the Gothic has similarities to creating out of the void: a conduit for the oppositions between matter and anti-matter, darkness and light, being and non-being. It is both a denial and a reminder of the convergence between the other and ourselves. Like the novelist Cane who brings people into existence, the director of the Gothic is a Prince of Darkness rising up from the dark side. Not unlike the master vampire of the night in *Vampires* about to conduct the forbidden ceremony of the sun, Carpenter summons forth, from the darkness of the auditorium, the light of Gothic cinema.

*Notes*

1   In the audio commentary to the laserdisc of *The Fog* (Image).
2   In the audio commentary to the laserdisc of *The Fog*, Carpenter refers to a source of inspiration for the film in an English horror film called *The Crawling Eye* (1958) in the US (original title, *The Trollenberg Terror*), directed by Quentin Lawrence, which he had seen as a boy. It is about a strange cloud hovering around a Swiss village where mountain climbers have been found dead, their heads severed.
3   In an interview that appeared in the programme *The Directors: John Carpenter* (Media Entertainment in association with the American Film Institute, 1997), Carpenter admitted that to make *The Fog* convincing for the audience was more challenging than those films where there is 'a guy chasing you with a knife'.
4   In contrast to the female monster who is dismembered by Victor Frankenstein, this alien being flourishes on fragmentation.
5   Here she draws on the work of the social anthropologist Mary Douglas who is alert to the dangers of that which violates systems of classification. See Douglas (1966).
6   For a Lacanian approach to the film see Mendik (1999).
7   *The Directors: John Carpenter.*

*References*

Byron, G. and D. Punter (1999) *Spectral Readings: Towards a Gothic Geography.* Houndmills: Macmillan.

Douglas, M. (1966) *Purity and Danger: An Analysis of the Concepts of Pollution and Taboo.* London: Routledge.

Freud, S. (1985) 'The Uncanny', in *Art and Literature, Vol. 14.* Trans. James Strachey. Harmondsworth: Penguin, 336–76.

Hurley, K. (1996) *The Gothic Body: Sexuality, Materialism and Degeneration at the Fin de Siècle.* Cambridge: Cambridge University Press.

Kristeva, J. (1982) *Powers of Horror: An Essay on Abjection.* Trans. Leon S. Roudiez. New York: Columbia University Press.

Mendik, X. (1999) '"I Think, Therefore You Are", Or How I Lost Myself in the Mouth of Madness', in A. Black (ed.) *Necronomicon: Book Three.* Hereford: Noir Publishing, 172–86.

Morris, P. (ed.) (1994) *The Bakhtin Reader: Selected Writings of Bakhtin, Medvedev, Voloshinov*. London: Arnold.

Radcliffe, A. (1826) 'On the Supernatural in Poetry', *New Monthly Magazine*, 16, 151.

Scanlon, P. (1979) '*The Fog*: A Spook Ride on Film', *Rolling Stone*, 28 June.

Shelley, M. (1992) *Frankenstein or The Modern Prometheus*. Ed. J. Smith. New York: St Martin's Press.

Todd, J. (1989) *The Sign of Angellica: Women, Writing and Fiction, 1660–1800*. London: Virago.

Wood, R. (1984) 'An Introduction to the American Horror Film', in B. K. Grant (ed.) *Planks of Reason: Essays on the Horror Film*. Metuchen, NJ: Scarecrow Press, 164–200.

CHAPTER SEVEN

# Killing Time … and Time Again: The Popular Appeal of Carpenter's Horrors and the Impact of The Thing and Halloween

Ian Conrich

An article by Kent Jones on John Carpenter, in the film journal *Film Comment*, presented in bold and an enlarged font a quote from the filmmaker: 'In France, I'm an auteur. In Germany, I'm a filmmaker. In the UK, I'm a horror director. In the US, I'm a bum' (1999: 27). Yet, looking back, as a director of horror films there were few who could rival Carpenter's popularity in America especially during and immediately after what I will view as his principal period of production – 1978–82. This was a period in which he directed for theatrical release, *Halloween* (1978), *The Fog* (1979), *Escape From New York* (1981) and *The Thing* (1982).

Why Carpenter's subsequent films have had less of an impact, or why Carpenter perceives that he is regarded in America as 'a bum' will not be the preoccupation of this chapter. The 'classic' status of *Halloween* and *The Thing* in particular, the two films that bookend Carpenter's principal period of production, offer an understanding of the development of the horror genre, moreover the nature of fan appreciation. Understanding Carpenter's popularity in relation to these films and the cultural recognition for his most enduring fictional creation – Michael Myers of the *Halloween* films – will offer a chance to reassess the horror new wave that began in the late 1970s. The American horror fanzine *Fangoria*, as a key example of related print media, offers a revealing series of reactions to Carpenter's films of this period and a fascinating spread of popular support for the genre amongst a distinct group of fans. Drawing on readers' letters, personal messages and poll results, this chapter will argue that Carpenter's impact on the genre was immense. The appeal of Carpenter's films of this period will be explored further through their continuing popularity amongst users of the Internet.

*Veneration*

*Fangoria* was not the sole horror fanzine associated with a new wave of horror film production to have high street and mainstream availability. It was, however, as Mark Kermode writes, the 'new bible of hard-core horror fandom', a publication that was the central voice and visual expression of a genre that had taken a turn towards gore, graphic violence and body horror (1997: 59). The co-publisher, Kerry O'Quinn, authored the readers' welcome in the first issue of *Fangoria*, and wrote that the American horror film fanzine aimed 'to be the first classy, professional, pictorial news magazine covering the world of fantasy'. It also claimed that *Fangoria* was 'much more than just another cheap monster magazine; each issue will include full-colour art, media news, techniques of special effects and makeup' (1979: 4). I have written on *Fangoria* elsewhere, in a discussion on the films of David Cronenberg (see Conrich 2000), where I stated that Cronenberg and Carpenter belonged 'to a group of neo-horror directors who had emerged before the first *Fangoria* [in August 1979]' (2000: 35). These filmmakers – such as George A. Romero, Tobe Hooper, Brian De Palma, Wes Craven and Dario Argento – were, as Philip Brophy writes, producing horror which was distinctly different from its historical definition, and which was 'involved in a violent awareness of itself as a saturated genre' (1986: 5). In my essay on Cronenberg I wrote that he had become one of the leading filmmakers of this new wave, with Carpenter declaring that Cronenberg was 'better than the rest of us combined' (2000: 35). But, I also concluded that essay with the observation that amongst readers of *Fangoria*, Cronenberg was revered, though of the neo-horror 'stars' he was 'surprisingly, not amongst the most honoured' (2000: 46).

The annual *Fangoria* 'Movie Poll Results' provide a regular gauge to popular opinion. From the first readers' poll, Stephen King and special makeup effects artist, Rick Baker, were installed in 'The Hallowed Halls of the *Fangoria* Hall of Fame' – 'parties inducted into this Hallowed Hall will be those people whose life-time achievements in the field of Horror have earned them a permanent place in the Pantheon of Great Ones' (February 1983, number 25: 59). The second movie poll, announced in the July 1983 issue (number 28: 61), extended the honour to Carpenter, Romero and special makeup effects artist Tom Savini. In the same poll, Carpenter was voted the second best director of the year, curiously behind Steven Spielberg, but ahead of Romero, George Miller, Tobe Hooper, Steve Miner and Ridley Scott; *The Thing* was the third best film of the year (placed behind *Creepshow* and *Road Warrior*, first and second respectively) whilst *Halloween III: Season of the Witch* was sixth. For the 'Third Annual Movie Poll Results' (August 1984, number 37: 36–7) an 'All Time Best' list was inaugurated with *Halloween* placed second (behind Romero's *Dawn of the Dead* (aka *Zombies*, 1979)) and *The Thing* placed tenth. Romero was the only other director to have two films so highly nominated and, as *Fangoria* noted, it was interesting that *The Thing*, 'despite its non-performance at the box office, is regarded by our readership as one of the 10 best films ever made' (August 1984: 36).

The commercial reception of *The Thing* will be addressed later. However, it is clear from *Fangoria*'s 'Free Subscriber Ads' that the Polls were no miscalculation, but were faithful reflections of the readership's popular opinion. The ads, which commenced with issue 12 (April 1981), offer a wealth of subjective responses and fan expression. As the magazine's subscription notice proclaimed in its reasons to join, 'in whatever weird way you like (as long as you're not selling anything) in your own little piece of FANGORIA – a three-line [initially 35 characters, later 45 characters per line] non-commercial ad – ABSOLUTELY FREE' (March 1983, number 26: 6). A degree of regulation over the content of the ads would be expected, though what was published leaves an impression that *Fangoria* had quite a tolerant editorial policy. Amongst the first small group of free subscriber ads printed in issue 12, one reader used the space to ask 'Can I really say whatever I want to in this ad? Really?' (April 1981: 63).

It took some time for readers to realise that *Fangoria* was genuinely offering a forum for free expression. The style of these ads developed gradually as a result, and it was not perhaps until issue 23 (November 1982: 64–5) that the standard fan club, 'wanted', and pen-pal messages of the early issues began to be swamped by a wave of 'long live' and 'greatest' lists, and unique public declarations (later subdivided by the magazine under the heading 'Arcane Messages'). In issue 23, readers used the free space to write messages such as 'John Carpenter is great, his movies are true art', 'Fangoria, Kurt Russel [sic] and John Carpenter Forever!', 'Carpenter and Savini are the greatest!!!', and 'I saw *The Thing* and I speak for a lot of people when I say that John Carpenter should make more movies' (November 1982: 65).

By issue 26 (March 1983), adoration for Carpenter was peaking with a noticeable batch of subscribers declaring respect for his film creations. The effect of *The Thing* (released in the US in June 1982) on the *Fangoria* readership was beginning to seep through to the ads. Meanwhile, *Halloween II* (1981) and *Halloween III: Season of the Witch* (1982), had received mixed reviews from *Fangoria* fans (see the readers' letters page 'The Postal Zone' in, respectively, February 1982, number 17: 5; and December 1982, number 24: 7). Combined with the emerging iconic status of Jason Voorhees in *Friday the 13th Part 2* (1981) and *Friday the 13th Part 3 (3D)* (1982), readers were drawn to compare the films with the emergence of Michael Myers in the original modern slasher, *Halloween*. Ads in issue 26 included 'John Carpenter is A#1 with me', 'The Thing and Rob Bottin are the greatest', 'I Love *Halloween II*, Jamie Lee Curtis and *Friday the 13th II*', 'Long live Jason Voorhees, his mother & Michael Myers!' and 'PERSONAL TO STEVE H: There is no "J. Carpenter School of Filmmaking". The phrase refers only to his style, his *oeuvre*, his *mise-en-scène*. Got it?' The pattern continues in issue 28 (July 1983: 65), where the ads include 'Kurt Russell and The Thing are the best!', 'John Carpenter, Tom Savini, Rob Bottin, Rick Baker and FANGORIA #1!', 'Ozzy Osbourne, Michael Myers and Teri make the World go round' and 'My praises to Spielberg, but I much prefer Bottin. "The Thing" should have instead, all the praise that *E.T.* has gotten!' Others scattered throughout later issues include 'Michael Myers Lives! Halloween #1' and 'Death to D. Cronenberg. Long Live John Carpenter. *Halloween* #1; *Videodrome* sux' (October 1983, number 30: 65); 'John Carpenter is king of the horror movie' (December 1983, number 31: 67); and 'Keep the gore coming, Mr. Carpenter!' (January 1984, number 32: 67). It should, however, be noted that not all messages were in praise, with the first ad (though only one of a small number) from a disillusioned fan appearing in issue 27, 'John Carpenter – Please put out a movie worth seeing!' (May 1983: 65).

Determining the demographics of *Fangoria*'s readership, moreover the declared fans of Carpenter, from the magazine's ads and the readers' letters is difficult. It should first be noted that even though there are in excess of two thousand ads in the first fifty issues of *Fangoria*, this can only represent a particular view of the readership; *Fangoria* has enjoyed wide circulation and certainly is read well beyond a subscription base. From just the ads, subscribers would appear firmly centred in North America, and more specifically in the USA. There is, however, a regular smattering of ads from readers in Australia and Europe (particularly Germany, Sweden and the UK). There is the occasional declaration of ethnic identity – 'I'm glad I am Puerto Rican! Puerto Rico #1' (September 1983, number 29: 65) – and religious belief – 'Jesus is the answer! Read the Bible' (number 29: 64). And from the declarations of love, and requests for penpals, it would appear that *Fangoria* was predominantly subscribed to by men. Some of these conclusions are supported by the 'Reader Poll Results', published in May 1983 (number 27: 61), and administered to gain an idea of the magazine's broader readership. Here, it was recorded that 68% of the readers were then students, average age was '19.254555', '95% of Fangorians Responding Liked Girls!' and 'Only 47% … currently has a job – yet 84% are decent Americans!' As expected, the most favoured article content, with 31%, addressed makeup effects.

Fans of Carpenter and Carpenter films continually placed him in ads that also praised the writer Stephen King, directors Hooper, Romero and the makeup effects artists Savini and Bottin. By 1984, Carpenter was also being named in the growing number of ads celebrating old-school heavy metal and new-school glam metal bands: 'Twisted Sister, Bottin, The Thing, Joe and CIRJ are #1' (June 1985, number 45: 67); 'IRON MAIDEN RULES. Fango, Savini, Carpenter #1'; and 'Caprenter [sic], King, Curtis, Jason, Cronenberg, Hooper, Sabbath, Priest, Crue, Motorhead and Fango: Sont les meilleurs, longue vie' (October 1984, number 38: 66). Furthermore, many readers' subscriptions were bought or renewed by parents and Carpenter features within these readers' free ads – 'Thanks for the sub, Mom & Dad. King, Carpenter Rule!' (January 1985, number 41: 67). At the same time, though, Carpenter was also seemingly being appreciated by an older readership – 'In life I have three loves: my wife Valerie, my daughter Regina, and gory movies by Carpenter, Romero and Cronenberg' (January 1984, number 32: 67).

These messages offer themselves to a degree of interpretation, and it can be argued that they establish a skeleton profile of the *Fangoria* reader and Carpenter fan. *The Thing* and *Halloween* are landmark productions within the history of contemporary horror, with Anne Billson describing *The Thing* as 'something of a *Gesamt Kunstwerk* of the genre' (1997: 13). As can be ascertained by the repeated references made to these films within the free subscriber ads, they made a palpable impact on the fan culture of the early to mid-1980s. Placing the popular reception of these films in context with other celebrated and much-discussed fantasy fiction of the period, and next to contemporary films with which Carpenter was associated, will create an understanding of his reception and the reverence he inspired as a skilled genre director.

## Preference

Carpenter fans are best considered as a diverse rather than homogenous group. Despite readers of *Fangoria* sharing similar demographics and declaring their adoration of a congruous and recurring list of filmmakers, there were frequent conflicts of taste and preference amongst the fans (see Conrich 2000: 44–6; 2003: 116–18). Furthermore, in the case of a fan of Carpenter's work, their free ad would be used to promote their appreciation of the filmmaker, but would this necessarily mean high regard for the entirety or bulk of his *oeuvre*? It could, but then in the genre's new wave, a fan's pantheon of glorious horror films was most likely constructed from a range of recent 'classics' and a group of filmmakers. In the free ads, Carpenter is in fact referenced more by films with which he is associated than mentioned directly by name. Commonly, one or two of Carpenter's films are mentioned amongst other titles of films with which he was not involved. Therefore, quite possibly, Carpenter was revered by many of his fans mainly for certain productions and, here, whilst there is pre-1985 the very occasional mention of *Assault on Precinct 13* (1976), *Escape From New York* or *Christine* (1983) in the free subscriber ads (*The Fog* is never mentioned), it is *The Thing* and the *Halloween* series that receive constant citation.

Yet, *The Thing* was a commercial and critical failure. As Billson writes:

> [it] received an almost unanimous critical drubbing on both sides of the Atlantic. 'This movie is more disgusting than frightening, and most of it is just boring', wrote David Denby of *New York* magazine. His words were echoed by Freda Bruce Lockhart of the *Catholic Herald*, who wrote that '*The Thing* achieves the particularly horrid combination of being both dull and absolutely disgusting'. Vincent Canby in the *New York Times* disagreed only in so far as he thought the film 'too phony looking to be disgusting. It qualifies only as instant junk'. (1997: 8)

There are several factors relevant to locating the reasons for *The Thing*'s lack of success. Billson registers the cultural snobbery of the critics of the time (1997: 9), which I have observed too in the critical reaction to Cronenberg's horror films in the adjacent period 1976–81 (Conrich 2000: 37–9). There, I argued that 'there appeared, amongst critics, an unwillingness and an inability to understand a film that … was disturbingly original' (2000: 39). Cronenberg's declared mission at that time was to celebrate and glorify the exquisiteness of the visceral and opened body. He imagined 'a beauty contest for the inside of the human body where people would unzip themselves and show the best spleen, [and] the best heart'. Cronenberg was also quoted as saying 'we've not devised an aesthetic for the inside of the body … Most people are disgusted … but if you develop an aesthetic for it, it ceases to be ugly. I'm trying to force the audience to change its aesthetic sense' (2000: 37).

Cronenberg was frequently regarded as the most artistic and 'intelligent' of the new wave of horror directors, but this still could not prevent his formative horrors – *Shivers* (1976), *Rabid* (1977), *The Brood* (1979) and *Scanners* (1981) – from being savaged by the mainstream press and critics who saw these films as deplorable exploitation. Such films were distinctly part of the new wave's association with body horror in which filmmakers 'demonstrated a desire for producing spectacular set-pieces designed to parade the fantastic anatomical creations of special effects technicians … [and manufactured] the most convincing, visually explicit and fascinatingly original grotesques' (2000: 36). With perhaps the later exception of the heights of splatstick attained by Peter Jackson's *Braindead* (1992), *The Thing*, for many of its fans and those with a developed aesthetic sense, displayed an advanced creative ability and represented the reaching of a peak in body horror.

The explicit fantasies of *The Thing* can be viewed as part of a tradition of surrealism in art, which can be traced back at least to the culturally celebrated visions of the horrific in the imaginary works of the symbolist Odilon Redon. I have discussed elsewhere the possible influence of Redon's drawings of detached, distorted and exaggerated anatomical parts for Brian Desmond Hurst's *The Tell-Tale Heart* (1934) (see Conrich 2002: 64). The associations between Redon and horror cinema are even more striking when considering, for instance, a moment in *The Thing* when the infamous upturned and detached head sprouts spider's legs and scuttles away. This is a memorable image in classic horror cinema which shares fascinating similarities with Redon's vision 'The Crying Spider' (1882), a charcoal drawing of an arachnidan human head supported by spidery legs, which are bristly and multi-jointed. Redon's work hangs in renowned galleries; Carpenter's *The Thing*, in comparison, has been condemned for its outrageous series of visual outbursts. There was even the controversial Academy Award snub of 1983 when *The Thing* was not even nominated as its special makeup effects were defined as being outside the selection rules of the Academy (see Martin 1984: 47–8). Steve Jenkins, in a contemporary review of the film, accuses the effects of functioning in a 'modernist fashion', existing 'in and for themselves' (1982: 159). Jenkins attacks the film essentially for its surrealist nature: he shows his misjudgement when he writes that, 'with regard to the effects, they completely fail to "clarify the weirdness" of the Thing', and that 'because one is never sure exactly how it [the alien] functions, its eruptions from the shells of its victims seem as arbitrary as they are spectacular' (ibid.). Fans had a different understanding and wrote to *Fangoria* to express both their frustration and support: (from Gerry Kimber, in Toronto) 'I'm a little surprised that *The Thing* didn't do as well as I'd hoped it would at the box office; it really knocked me for a loop. I guess the public didn't care for Carpenter's adult approach to the genre' (November 1982, number 23: 5) and (from Mitchell B. Craig, in Lancaster, South Carolina) 'The Thing has a wonderful example of something missing in many fantasy films: a mature perspective' (December 1982, number 24: 7).

The maturity of Carpenter's vision was an issue. Universal, the studio behind *The Thing*, released a second 'outer space visitor' movie the same summer, and this creature was in contrast distinctly wholesome. Spielberg's *E.T.: The Extra Terrestrial* (1982), a family-friendly sci-fi movie, dominated the summer box office and became the yardstick against which to measure future blockbusters. The monstrous force and the apocalyptic all-consuming threat posed by Carpenter's indiscernible Thing, could not compete with a mass market that had been seduced by the appealing wide-eyed features of a compassionate alien drawn to friendship with a young boy. *Fangoria* readers definitely rallied around *The Thing*, but when it came to the annual 'Movie Poll Results', Spielberg was voted the year's best director ahead of Carpenter. True, Spielberg had made *Poltergeist* (1982), though the authorship of that film has been greatly contested with director Tobe Hooper. *Fangoria*'s identity had been forged from a struggle in its early issues over whether it should halt accommodation of a sci-fi content, and as to whether family ties with sister magazines *Starlog* and *Future Life* should be severed (see Conrich 2000: 44–5). *Fangoria*'s readership had evidently not extricated itself entirely from the world beyond body horror. It is also possible that readers, like many critics, may have felt *The Thing* was less a result of Carpenter's directorial mark and more the craft of the lead special makeup effects technician Rob Bottin. Certainly, in the free subscriber ads, Bottin's name appears frequently, and commonly alongside *The Thing*.

*Fangoria*'s features are driven by a cinema of special makeup effects, and it is not surprising if readers promote the importance of an effects technician such as Bottin. But to look elsewhere would suggest that amongst *Fangoria*'s readership Carpenter's

Blair is repulsed by what he sees. The grotesque effects and body horror in *The Thing* divided its audience

authorial weight and responsibility extended to productions where he is not the director. Carpenter was composer, co-producer and co-scriptwriter for *Halloween II*; Rick Rosenthal was the film's director. Similarly, Carpenter was composer and co-producer for *Halloween III: Season of the Witch*; Tommy Lee Wallace the director. Yet, blame or praise for these films was aimed equally at almost Carpenter alone. Mitchell B. Craig began his letter to *Fangoria* thus:

> Steven Spielberg, the modern Disney-cum-Pavlov, fooled millions into believing that *E. T.* and *Poltergeist* were films of great worth. And while many believe this, a devout few held in reverence John Carpenter's similar coup this year. I speak of course about *The Thing* and *Halloween III: Season of the Witch*, two of this year's best SF/horror movies ... Gripping and chilling, *Season of the Witch* is a real 'treat' for horror movie fans. (December 1982, number 24: 7)

A letter on the same page from Dave Berry (Tallahassee, Florida), addressed to 'Mr. Carpenter', disagrees:

> Deplorable! I have just returned from seeing *Halloween III: Season of the Witch*, and I must say that I was embarrassed being seen coming out of the theatre. And from all the moans and groans from the other moviegoers, it was clear that I was not the only one. You have been my idol for many years, but after the piece of sheer trash I was forced to sit through last night, I am truly shocked. Surely, two great minds like yours and [co-producer] Debra Hill's could come up with something more entertaining than that. I truly think an apology is in order. The Shape must be rolling in his grave, if he has one, that is...

Michael Myers (aka The Shape) was by 1983 an established and iconic figure of the horror new wave, who was seen to be synonymous with the *Halloween* films. The Shape was the bogeyman exemplar, indestructible, focused, devoid of a conscience, omnipresent yet also quick to vanish, and operating on the edges of society. To switch the locus of horror to an evil toymaker, who in the manner of a modern fairytale aims to destroy children via a microchip-controlled Halloween mask, challenged a core of purist fans who could not accept a Halloween franchise (with all its original associations with Carpenter) post-Meyers. As one *Fangoria* subscriber ad read, 'Carpenter – You choked on *Halloween III* – Robots?? Try staying in Haddonfield next time, and have Jamie Lee turn psycho, huh? – *Halloween I* and *II* fans' (February 1983, number 25: 64).

Carpenter had acquired a reputation as a skilled director, with an acute awareness of the technique of terror, the ability to build a scene through suspense, tension and suggestion. *The Thing*, with its spectacle of horror, had opened Carpenter to a further level of admiration amongst fans, who now also firmly associated him with a cinema of gore and prosthetic effects. Many of the contemporary reviews of *The Thing* had felt, however, that the effects had been gained at a price and that Carpenter had shown an inability to develop either the characters at the research station, or the fearful confines of the snowbound team. The *Halloween* legend had, by the early 1980s, quickly developed to the point that not only was it influencing an entire sub-genre of slasher movies (see Conrich 1995: 47–8), but it was being established as the refined and artistic original (see Neale 1981: 25–9) of a wave of copy-cats, the 'classic' to what many saw as the exploitation that followed. The effect of *Halloween* was to also elevate Carpenter to a seemingly omnipotent presence in a horror film's production, regardless of the level of his involvement.

*Halloween* gave the slasher film sub-genre, to a degree, its style of prowling camera, the voyeuristic camera positions, the fluid camera movement, the relentless stalker and the threatened teenagers. It was the commercial success of *Friday the 13th* (1980) – part influenced by *Halloween*, more so by Mario Bava and films such as *Sei Donne per l'Assassino* (1964) – that ignited the slasher film, and gave it the explicit violence, and inventive executions. Crucially, *Halloween* was largely bloodless, and compared to *Friday the 13th* presented murders that were less stylised and centre-screen. But by the time of *Halloween II*, in 1981, the slasher had been transformed. More than any other slasher film of the period, *Halloween II* clearly showed the marks of its ancestry, whilst simultaneously embracing an evolving and rampant sub-genre. Films began to compete in producing ever-greater spectacles of death and this meant an increase in murders and the dramatic style of execution. For some fans, the second part of what was to become the *Halloween* saga was too detached from the sophisticated style of the original. Frank Ward (Palatine, Illinois) wrote to *Fangoria* to complain that in *Halloween II*,

> Michael killed too many people. The girl in the house at the beginning was not called for. I don't think that all the hospital deaths were needed … He didn't need to kill twice as many people in the second film … The director made the killings much, much too gory. The first one was great for its lack of blood. He also showed Michael too much. In the first one, he appears and disappears without warning. In the new one, there is shot after shot of him wandering around, especially in the hospital. He took away greatly from his mystique. In short, the whole thing was a major disappointment. (February 1982, number 17: 5)

Just who exactly is the 'he' being blamed for the mistakes in *Halloween II*, is not clear. But printed on the same page was a letter from David Reynolds who, for some reason, felt Carpenter's creative involvement alone was the problem: 'Just saw *Halloween II* and it's not very good. Carpenter went for graphic violence in this one and spoiled it. Nice directorial debut by Rick Rosenthal though.'

*Conflict*

Michael Myers vanished from the screen between *Halloween II*, in 1981, and 1988, when he was revived for *Halloween 4: The Return of Michael Myers*, and a recycling of the series that has to date totalled eight films.[1] As with *Friday the 13th Part VII – The*

*Halloween*'s Michael Myers (aka The Shape), the relentless stalker and bogeyman exemplar

*New Blood* (1988), the success of *A Nightmare on Elm Street Part 3: Dream Warriors* (1987), had brought new life to modern horror's supreme monsters. During Myers' seven-year absence from the screen, the mythical nature of Carpenter's creation was too strong to allow his disappearance from popular culture. Within *Fangoria* there began popular imaginings of Myers' invincibility if faced with Jason Voorhees, who back in 1982 was the ascendant slasher star of the *Friday the 13th* films. An early provocation appeared in the February 1983 (number 25: 65) subscriber ads: 'Michael Myers could whip Jason Voorhees any days [sic]'. Nine issues later (March 1984, number 34: 8) William Boblett (Kingman, Arizona) wrote to *Fangoria* with a suggestion:

> How about something on Jason Voorhees battling Michael Myers? I mean, give it some thought. Wouldn't it be a sight to behold? A real battle of the

heavyweights ... They both seem so indestructible. I mean just think of it ... You could even do a story on it with an artist's rendering of the fight. How about a poll on who would win? Please give it some thought. I'm sure a lot of readers and fans would appreciate it ... Who knows? You could even have the winner go against Leatherface.

*Fangoria* listened to Boblett's plea and two issues later (August 1984, number 36: 7) initiated a comic strip drawing competition for readers, a 'no-holds-barred battle of the terror titans!', with entries judged on 'both artistic and dramatic imagination'. The results of this 'Maniac Match-Up', published in issue 39 (November 1984: 26–30, 38) as 'Battle of the Maniacs!', showed the extent of the reader's commitment to the subject with extracts from a selection of entries: 'the number of responses to our Maniac Match-Up contest was enormous', wrote *Fangoria*, 'and the imagination and enthusiasm that went into the entries surpassed our wildest splatterfilled dreams' (August 1984: 26). The winning entry, a stunning comic strip drawn by readers John Arnold and Linwood Sasser, was printed in full colour over five pages of *Fangoria*. Titled 'The 1st Fangoria Splatterbowl', it established a battle in which Jason plunges his axe into Myers' shoulder, pours boiling fat over him, cuts his body open with a tree saw and removes his internal organs. Myers had taken early and brief control of the fight with 'his patented larynx-crush-neck-hold' and a deep slicing open of Jason's chest, but Jason is soon dictating the violence. That is, until Jason is distracted by a passing, popcorn-munching *Star Trek* fan, which gives Myers enough time to rise up and decapitate Jason. Myers moves to the showdown with Leatherface, who is split in two when he is unable to start his chainsaw. The declared winner is Myers, only for the compere – who bears a close resemblance to *Fangoria* editor Bob Martin – to dramatically erupt into the Thing. Significantly, these fans imagined an ultimate movie death match being won by a Carpenter creation, and then being won again by yet another Carpenter movie monster. Carpenter versus Carpenter appeared the only respectable way to conclude.

This imagined death match shared many similarities with American wrestling, the popular arenas of excess and the carnivalesque, in which fearsome, humongous or hyper-masculine forms have been pitted against each other. Earlier issues of *Fangoria* had contained, for instance, features on Mexican wrestling horror films, and as Bob Martin wrote in his pro-wrestling-laden *Fangoria* editorial for issue 20 (July 1982: 4), 'on the wrestling front, we seem to have struck a raw nerve in the collective consciousness (if you can call it that) of our readers. This issue's letters page says more on that subject than I would dare say'. As with *Fangoria*'s other digressions from the concentration on body horror, readers were split over the value of wrestling-horror. Martin Weiss (Encino, California) wrote to *Fangoria* declaring,

I decided to speak out about my second 'fave', wrestling ... I think of how much wrestling and horror movies have in common. Adding wrestling to *Fangoria* is a great idea. If you have any doubt about combining wrestling and horror, watch Andre the Giant play Bigfoot on the *Six Million Dollar*

*Man* ... [and] 'Killer' Ox Baker as the monstrous opponent of Kurt Russell in *Escape From New York*. (July 1982, number 20: 5)

Others on the same letters page were abhorred at the idea of wrestling-horror, which had first surfaced in the letters page in issue 18: 'Why in the world would you even consider putting articles on wrestling in your magazine. What does wrestling have to do with horror films!? (from Ross Kemp, Milton, Wisconsin) and 'Please don't. I can't think of anything more moronic ... If you started covering wrestling I would immediately cancel my subscription' (from Jeff Carroll, Fairfax, Virginia). In a response to another reader's letter in *Fangoria* issue 23 (November 1982: 7) the editor announced a permanent cessation to the magazine's brief obsession with wrestling-horror with an apology to readers: 'we hate to shatter the hopes of the zillions of wrestling-horror fans who've been ecstatic over our first explorations into that marvellous *oeuvre*.' The comic strip Maniac Match-Up showed that *Fangoria*'s interest in wrestling-horror could never really be repressed and any thought of pitting Jason against Michael against Leatherface, even if only in a series of drawings, was too exciting to ignore.

*Idolatry*

The 'Michael versus Jason' debate would never be resolved and readers continued to assert the superiority of each, though especially Jason, as the *Friday the 13th* films continued with more sequels supported by a hard-core of fans (see Conrich 2003). With the supposed ultimate destruction of Jason in *Friday the 13th: The Final Chapter* (1984), *Fangoria* appeared to go into mourning. *Halloween* fans retaliated: 'You never did any of this for the Shape. I don't have anything against the *Friday the 13th* movies, but the *Halloween* movies were much better (and a lot more believable than the *Friday the 13th*'s). "Shape" up, guys', wrote James Stephens (Waldorf, Maryland). Mike (Miggy) de Necochea (from Menlo Park, California), signing himself off as 'Michael Myer's [sic] friend', wrote in the same issue:

> ARRRGH!!! What is this? Jasonmania? *Halloween* lives!! John Carpenter's all-time classic blows away all *F13*'s, parts 1, 2, 3 and 4! The suspense in *Halloween* is awesome. In the first hour of *Halloween*, you're already jumping out of your seat and wetting your pants! None of the *F13th*'s have any of this!!! *Halloween*'s Michael Myers is better than Jason Voorhees!!! Michael Myers is more psychotic and psychologically confused than Jason. Jason is just some creep running through the woods and killing bad actors in ghastly ways. Michael's murders were *planned* out ... Michael's mask and costume is better!! The director is better! Everything's better'. (December 1984, number 40: 7)

One attempt to resolve the question of monster greatness, has been constructed by a fan on the Internet, to which many of the public debates, previously confined to spaces such as *Fangoria*'s readers' letters page, migrated. Here, following categories such as number of 'Kills', number of movies and 'Average Kills Per Film', a stats table is presented that compares the screen exploits of Jason, Michael and Freddy Krueger.[2] Going by these criteria, Jason is the runaway victor.

The Internet presents a profusion of sites at which fans celebrate, and maintain the memory of an affectionate and exceptional movie experience. The films of Carpenter, especially, have been extended over an astonishing number of fan sites, which simply demonstrate the high regard in which Carpenter as a filmmaker is held. The impact of productions such as *Halloween*, *The Thing* and Snake Plissken and the *Escape* films, is most noticeable. *The Thing*, in particular, appears precious to many fans, where, as Henry Jenkins (1992) writes on fandom and participatory culture, fans united in alternative communities are active as consumers and textual poachers, borrowing from the mass media and constructing new meaning from favoured sources of fiction. *Cinefantastique* has already noted the number of Carpenter-devoted pages and describes the 'Tribute to The Thing' as 'The Mother of All Carpenter film-specific sites' (Thonen 1998: 60).[3] In an interview, the then 27-year-old webmaster, Australian Jamie Horne, said 'the only reason I even got an Internet account was to design a web page on THE THING – to create a place that all fans of the movie could visit to find out all there was to know on it' (ibid.). *Cinefantastique* proposes that 'Carpenter's appeal to film-oriented webmasters is easy to understand. The director's protagonists are outsiders, rebels, distrustful of society and its systems. It's a description of Plissken, MacReady and Nada, and a pretty fair description of the average web fanatic. In Carpenter's creations, Internet fans find a kindred spirit. It's no surprise that some chose to honour him' (ibid.).

Unfortunately, this paints a troubling image of the average Internet user, which, whilst it is perhaps true for some, ignores other factors of fandom. Many mythical figures of popular culture circulate within contemporary society and as fan communities increase the speed and directness of their communication with like-minded individuals – most significantly via the Internet – evolving exchanges of opinion, debates and imaginings can flourish. Such debates appeared in the *Fangoria* free-subscriber ads – 'Michael Myers, Jason Voorhees, Snake Plissken and Raul Fernandez Jr. will rule the world. But is it us, or the Thing? Think about it' (June 1985, number 45: 67) – but they were rhetorical, deprived of a response. In contrast, the Internet fan sites cater for and encourage participation. The death match, such as the one drawn in the pages of *Fangoria*, now thrives on the Internet, where the probable outcome of the battle is continually debated by fans. One such site asks fans to consider Mad Max versus Snake Plissken (62.1 per cent believed Max would be victorious); another, the Thing versus the Blob (the Thing declared the winner); another, Ash, from *The Evil Dead* films, versus Plissken (Ash seems to have the edge), and the Thing versus the Body Snatchers ('the Thing supreme winner').[4]

The indomitability, invincibility and perceived all-conquering nature of certain Carpenter creations – Myers, the Thing and Plissken – combined with their distinct popular appeal amongst a sizeable fan-base, makes them highly attractive competitors in the Internet's virtual arenas of one-on-one battle. The fantasised struggles are continued in associated comic books, such as those for *The Thing* and Plissken, and fan fiction, most noticeably for *The Thing*, where it battles variously and in different

The indomitable and all-conquering Snake Plissken (Kurt Russell) defeats Slag (Ox Baker) in *Escape from New York*'s arena of death

stories, Godzilla, Batman, Aliens and Predator.[5] The manufacturing of computer games for *The Thing* and (proposed) for Plissken, allows the fan to become further involved and actively manipulate the imagined space of action.[6]

Participating in the mythology of these fictional creations is paramount for the fans, and if they are not playing the computer game, writing fan fiction or inventing titanic battles, they may be purchasing the merchandise or crafting scaled models (often unique and private creations).[7] Fan devotion can be seen most explicitly at the Outpost31 website devoted to *The Thing*, which promotes the annual 'Thing-Fest', held in Ontario, Canada, a gathering built mainly around a large-screen showing of *The Thing* and, so it would appear, ample opportunities for socialising.[8] There is on this website, too, examples of fan artwork, which includes one fan's tattoo on his leg of a poster image for *The Thing*, and another's tattoo on their upper arm of a head and shoulders shot of MacReady.[9] There is, here, a recycling of images and popular myths, a return to an original creation, and a desire to repeat yet simultaneously invent a new dimension for interaction. Fan culture is the truest indicator of a film's impact, which survives beyond any contemporary reviews or notions of commercial success. Carpenter, himself, was an avid fan of horror and fantasy films, who produced for sale, at the age of sixteen, his own mimeographed fanzine, *Fantastic Films Illustrated*, which lasted for three issues (see Clarke 1980: 11). As Carpenter would surely realise, the respect and admiration shown by fans to a given film is the real sign of its cultural value.

## Notes

1   The other films in the series are *Halloween 5: The Revenge of Michael Myers* (1989), *Halloween: The Curse of Michael Myers* (1995), *Halloween H20: 20 Years Later* (1998) and *Halloween: Resurrection* (2002).

2   Available online. See <http://www.geocities.com/madnessmike/Michael_vs.htm>.

3   Available online. See <http:homepage.powerup.com.au/~vampire/thing/thing.htm>.

4   Available online. See <http://www.grudge-match.com/History/maxsnake.shtml>, <http:electricfenet.com/fights/blob.htm>, <http://www.crossoveruniverse.com/vs 31.htm>, <http://www.crossoveruniverse.com/vs30.htm>, <http://www.crossover universe.com/vsrules.htm>.

5   Available online. See <http:homepage.powerup.com.au/~vampire/thing/t-comics. htm>, <http://www.comics2film.com/StoryFrame.php?f_id=1422>, <http:/www. outpost31.com/vistar/fanstory.html>.

6   Available online. See <http:homepage.powerup.com.au/~vampire/thing/t-game. htm>, <http://softwaremart.biz/software/prods/-n=9030.htm>, <http://www.mega games.com/news/html/pc/escapetopcforsnakeplissken.shtml>.

7   Available online. See <homepage.powerup.com.au/~vampire/thing/t-misc.htm>, <http://perso.club-Internet.fr/resinkit/version%20anglaise/galleries/Thing_ carpenter/thing_carpenter.htm>,<http://www.outpost31.com/vistar/fanimage. html>, <http://www.sphosting.com/theefnypage/snaketoys800600.htm>.

8   Available online. See <http://www.outpost31.com/todd/thingfest.htm>.

9   Available online. See <http://www.outpost31.com/vistar/tattoos.html>.

## References

Billson, A. (1997) *The Thing*. London: British Film Institute.

Brophy, P. (1986) 'Horrality – the Textuality of Contemporary Horror Films', *Screen*, 27, 1, 2–13.

Clarke, F. S. (1980) 'Roots of Imagination', *Cinefantastique*, 10, 1, 11.

Conrich, I. (1995) 'How to Make a "Slasher" Film', *Invasion*, 11, 48–9.

_____ (2000) 'An Aesthetic Sense: Cronenberg and Neo-Horror Film Culture', in M. Grant (ed.) *The Modern Fantastic: The Films of David Cronenberg*. Trowbridge: Flicks Books, 35–49.

_____ (2002) 'Horrific films and 1930s British cinema', in S. Chibnall and J. Petley (eds) *British Horror Cinema*. London and New York: Routledge, 58–70.

_____ (2003) 'La série des *Vendredi 13* et la fonction culturelle d'un Grand-Guignol moderne', in F. Lafond (ed.) *Cauchemars américains: Fantastique et horreur dans le cinema moderne*. Liège: Éditions du Céfal, 103–18.

Jenkins, H. (1992) *Textual Poachers: Television Fans and Participatory Culture*. London and New York: Routledge.

Jenkins, S. (1982) '*The Thing*', *Monthly Film Bulletin*, 49, 583, 158–60.

Jones, K. (1999) 'John Carpenter: american movie classic', *Film Comment*, 35, 1, 26–31.

Kermode, M. (1997) 'I was a teenage horror fan, Or, "How I learned to stop worrying and love Linda Blair"', in M. Barker and J. Petley (eds) *Ill Effects: The Media/ Violence Debate*. London and New York: Routledge, 57–66.

Martin, R. H. (1984) 'The Makeup Oscar 1983', *Fangoria*, 36, 47–8.

Neale, S. (1981) 'Halloween: Suspense, Aggression and the Look', *Framework*, 14, 25–9. [Reprinted in B. K. Grant (1984) (ed.) *Planks of Reason: Essays on the Horror Film*. Metuchen, NJ: Scarecrow Press, 331–45.]

O'Quinn, K. (1979) 'Welcome to the World of Fangoria!', *Fangoria*, 1, 4.

Thonen, J. (1998) '*Vampires*: Carpenter's Web', *Cinefantastique*, 30, 7/8, 60.

# CHAPTER EIGHT

# Masculinity, Kurt Russell and the Escape Films

## Robert Shail

Kurt Russell occupies a position in relation to John Carpenter's films which could be seen as being a mirror to that of John Wayne in Howard Hawks's work or of Clint Eastwood in Don Siegel's. The Russell-Carpenter association has stretched across five films in 17 years, from the made-for-television *Elvis* (1979) to *Escape From L.A.* (1996), by way of *Escape From New York* (1981), *The Thing* (1982) and *Big Trouble in Little China* (1986). Russell seems to represent for Carpenter the closest thing he has found to a cinematic alter ego, a term which Carpenter himself has used to describe their working relationship. However, whereas in the case of the Eastwood/Siegel and Wayne/Hawks partnerships the stars seem to bear a fairly unproblematic and direct relation to the director's personal thematic and narrative concerns, the affinity between Russell and Carpenter is far more equivocal and ambiguous. Their own comments on their working relationship do not shed much constructive light on this, with Carpenter characteristically describing Russell as 'a total professional' and as being able to 'do what I'm thinking without me saying a word' (Udo 1996). Russell similarly refers to working with Carpenter as 'the most ideal actor-director relationship one could possibly hope for'.[1] This guardedness on both their parts cannot disguise the sense of distance between director and star which tends to mark their work together and which goes towards making Russell's personification of male heroism in Carpenter's work particularly distinctive. It is this disjunction in thematic and ideological positions which is especially apparent in the *Escape* films.

Russell's reputation in contemporary American cinema is built largely around his appearance in films which have cast him in fairly typical action-hero roles. This persona has been constructed both in Carpenter's films and with other, often more overtly macho, appearances in the likes of *Backdraft* (1991), *Tombstone* (1993) and *Tango and Cash* (1989), a film in which he was cast as half of a double act with Sylvester Stallone. In line with other contemporary action genre stars, like Arnold Schwarzenegger, his deviations from this persona have tended to be in light comedies intended to play against roles of violence and aggression; such films include *Overboard* (1987). Russell's particular variation on the well-established all-purpose tough guy persona has been to heighten the level of stylisation audiences have come to expect from such genre roles, with their characteristic minimalistic acting, cartoon violence and deadpan sarcasm. His use of this stylisation places him in a referential context which takes in Eastwood and Mel Gibson, as well as referring back to John Wayne, Robert Mitchum and even Charles Bronson. There is an affinity between Russell's Snake Plissken, decorated war hero turned renegade outlaw, and Stallone's role as the equally intense John Rambo in Ted Kotcheff's *First Blood* (1982), although Russell has attempted to drain his character of any clarifying sense of psychological sympathy:

> I think he's unique. Most of these characters who are 'on the edge' as it were, doing all these disputable things, explain why their characters got this way. In other words they have a socially redeemable manner. What I like about Snake is that he doesn't. He's a sociopath. And it is a challenge to make people understand that, but at the same time to root for the guy to pull through. (Udo 1996)

If Carpenter's films have always been marked by his own referential use and acknowledgement of other favoured filmic sources, then the same is true of Russell's performances for Carpenter. There is an overt combined visual mirroring of Eastwood and Gibson in his slick muscularity (usually carefully displayed through slightly ragged clothing), his inevitable dark sunglasses, stubbled chin and rock-star hair styling. In addition, specific connections are established by Russell through his adopting the physical and vocal mannerisms of other male stars, so that Snake Plissken speaks with the same whispered, tight-lipped delivery characteristic of Eastwood's Dirty Harry Callahan. In *Big Trouble in Little China* the reference point is John Wayne, right down to the drawling delivery and slouching, lumbering gait.

A useful framework through which to examine the specifics of Russell's variation of this film persona can be found by applying some of the typologies defined by Richard Dyer. The characterisation of Snake Plissken combines elements from at least three of Dyer's 'star types' (1998: 47–54). The first – the 'tough guy' – is a character who exhibits modes of behaviour, particularly with regard to violence, which would normally be seen as morally negative, but which, within genre conventions, can be used in a morally positive way. The second type – the 'good guy' – is

On the edge: the anti-heroic individualism of Snake Plissken (Kurt Russell)

a less problematic and more conventional embodiment of dominant cultural and social values. The third type – the 'rebel' – is an 'alternative and subversive' character who is allowed to carry the audience's feelings of disquiet or ambivalence towards the dominant value system within which these texts operate. The conventions of the male hero of the contemporary action film genre, into which Russell's Plissken fits, is an amalgamation of these qualities.

Snake Plissken is a 'tough guy' who demonstrates in both the *Escape* films cynicism and lack of respect for authority, along with a typical concern for physical prowess and controlled violence. He also has something of the tough guy's characteristic moral ambiguities, with the audience frequently left to ponder whether his violence is a means to an end or something he enjoys, and his lack of human warmth often taken to extremes (both films are almost completely devoid of any humanising love interest). At the same time Plissken's actions are always rationalised within an individualistic creed which has its own moral structure. Plissken may be morally deviant in a conventional sense, but his position remains relatively humane in comparison with surrounding characters. As such he conforms to more of the traditional values of the 'good guy' than might be expected. Whereas tough guys are frequently punished for transgressions outside of the dominant value system, or learn to return to more conventional behaviour, Plissken remains essentially represented as an unproblematic moral centre of the films. Within a context of moral confusion depicted in both films, he remains true to an ethical code which still allows him to be the focus for the audience's affiliations. The fact that his heroism has to be framed in oppositional terms, rather than celebrated as a given certainty, as might be the case in Hawks's use of John Wayne, tends to move his persona into the territory of the rebel, or more accurately the anti-hero. It would seem that for a contemporary audience qualities of moral integrity can be more convincingly represented by the outsider rather than by the traditionally approved hero figure. The targets for Plissken's derision are both corrupt, hypocritical politicians and idealistic revolutionaries. The rebel here is an outlet for the audience's ambivalence and anxiety towards both the dominant ideology and its alternatives. What becomes characteristic of Plissken, and many another star personae of this ilk, is a kind of nihilism in which only an almost existential sense of individual morality remains.

This combining of different male star types is characteristic of the direction taken by action hero roles since the 1970s and can be linked within American culture to the need to reassign moral value in ways which could side-step the public's increasing sense of disillusionment with more conventional representations of masculine moral worth. If both politicians and revolutionaries had been discredited in post-Watergate, post-Vietnam America, then a new form of cinematic hero was about to emerge, and if John Wayne's masculine persona was now too good to be true, then a different kind of hero could exhibit all the outward indications of that current cynicism and disillusionment, but still provide some indication of the possible continuation of masculine moral value. It is this generic type, the violent, individualistic and cynical anti-hero, into which Russell's performances fall. In *Escape From New York* Russell's central character is at first established as an outsider and individualist (as with his role in *The Thing*) who, despite the war record and previous acts of state-sanctioned bravery, is now more at home with the misfits and social deviants of the New York prison state. Plissken is constantly recognised, if only by reputation, amongst the punks, oddballs and criminals with whom he finds himself and he is for them an almost mythic figure. One of the film's running jokes has those who meet him surprised to discover he is still alive (a parodic reference to Lee Marvin's character, Walker, in John Boorman's *Point Blank* (1960), whom everyone believes is dead). His positioning with social outcasts is emphasised by his adoption of a similar style of dress and even by the pirate eyepatch. He is clearly only a servant of order to the extent that he is being forced to take on that role by the tricky and deceitful President (Donald Pleasence) and his manipulative henchman, Hauk (Lee Van Cleef). Despite this, he has no particular corresponding personal affinity with the position of the rebel criminal army and its chief, the Duke of New York (Isaac Hayes). This narrative structure is repeated in *Escape From L.A.* where an even more morally dubious President (Cliff Robertson) and a vainglorious rebel leader, the Che Guevara-like Cuervo Jones (George Corraface), represent the two negatives between which Plissken operates. Nonetheless, Plissken remains as morally certain as almost any John Wayne hero of the 1950s and exhibits an equivalent sense of physical invincibility. His moral creed leads him to unmask and destroy all the false prophets who surround him. Even if this code offers little that is intrinsically positive in itself, it still retains its audience appeal in the conviction that Plissken remains an uncompromised figure, rather like Eastwood's 'Man With No Name'. For a post-Vietnam American audience such a figure could be seen to offer the best available version of masculine honour and courage.

What remains intriguing here is the way in which this generic type, and Russell's own version of it, offers the opportunity for a problematisation of its more reactionary ideological aspects to take place alongside the construction of that reactionary mythology. The most troubling element in the ideological content of the contemporary male action hero, particularly for many liberal commentators, and for some audiences, has been the association of individualistic moral certainties with the use of lethal violence, so that characterisations like Snake Plissken seem to take on the methodology of the vigilante. Here, the self-righteous rugged individualist of American mythology becomes the self-appointed urban commando, handing out rough justice on the streets where conventional authority has failed. Certainly, the image of Plissken striding down half-lit, post-apocalyptic streets, fending off the threat of 'semi-human' undesirables who rise out of the sewers, is a potent representation of modern America's social anxieties over urban decay and youth gang culture. The streets in both *Escape* films do seem to be populated largely by gangs of degenerate young punks whose identity is dependent upon gang affiliations.

In her essay examining the *Terminator* films, Susan Jeffords points to the development of the reactionary, ultra-masculine hero of the 1980s action genre as a response to other attempts to reawaken America's sense of its own political and military virility during the early years of the Reagan Presidency. Referring specifically to Sylvester Stallone's role in *Rambo: First Blood II* (1985), she suggests that these films pushed 'outward into increasingly extravagant spectacles of violence and power', but also that they ultimately failed: 'as Rambo and Ronald Reagan showed, these displays had become their own form of parody'(1993: 259). This can be attributed

The urban commando: Plissken as a post-Vietnam figure of uncompromised masculinity in *Escape From L.A.*

partly to the context of a changing political climate, which Jeffords acknowledges when she argues that in order to deal with the shifting parameters of male identity in the late 1980s and 1990s the action genre had to offer a version of masculinity that was more in keeping with an audience which increasingly expected men to be able to show tenderness and vulnerability, as well as be strong. Such representations needed to demonstrate the ability of the male to make sound moral judgements in the form of an open commitment to the family, to women and to children. Hence the shift in Schwarzenegger's Terminator character from killing machine to defender of the mother-of-future-civilisations, Sarah Connor (Linda Hamilton). A similar characterisation was apparent in Bruce Willis's persona as policeman John McClane, whose underlying motivation in *Die Hard* (1988) is to be reconciled with his wife and two children, as soon as he has dispatched the foreign bad guys. The value system being defended may have largely remained unchanged, but the means available to the male hero to defend that system had to be reshaped to accommodate the sense of disquiet apparent amongst late 1980s and 1990s audiences towards overstated demonstrations of reactionary male violence.

The *Escape* films largely disassociate themselves from these ideological connotations by deploying a conscious level of parody in the depiction of Russell's Snake Plissken and in the use of pastiche in the staging of the action scenes. The high level of stylisation used throughout both films invites a sense of distance on the part of the spectator and suggests an attitude of irony on the part of star and director. Plissken appears at the beginning of *Escape From New York* as a silhouetted figure being escorted under heavy guard. This exaggeration is taken a stage further in *Escape From L.A.* when Plissken is introduced by a reporter as someone who has been convicted of 27 'moral crimes'. The self-conscious recognition of Russell's established generic status is consistently signalled in a knowing manner, so that another observer on seeing him for the first time comments: 'He looks so retro, kind of twentieth century.' The clichés of the 1980s macho action hero are consistently made absurd by the exaggeration of emblematic scenes and key motifs. The phallic weaponry in *Escape From L.A.* reaches bizarre proportions and Plissken is frequently depicted as a futuristic western gunslinger, with holsters on both hips. This attains its appropriate apogee in a gunfight sequence, modelled on Spaghetti westerns, which Plissken subverts by drawing his gun and killing all his opponents before the agreed moment to draw. A car and motorcycle chase similarly becomes a genre parody, turning into a western stagecoach pursuit complete with a horserider galloping down the city streets.

A shift is also apparent between the two films, which tends to indicate further the changing attitude towards the macho archetypes of the 1980s action genre. The pleasure for the audience in *Escape From New York* resides first in their shared recognition of the genre conventions on display and then from the overtly playful stylisation which pushes those conventions to the edge of absurdity. In *Escape From L.A.* we have moved into more open parody, where Plissken himself becomes the object of a good deal of the humour. Through these means Carpenter and Russell turn Plissken into a postmodern creature, a kind of identikit of genre references and motifs who operates on the furthest edges of fantasy. If in *Escape From New York* he resembles a parody videogame character, by *Escape From L.A.* he has become a pastiche of himself.

Of course it is possible to argue that such strategies do not significantly alter the ideological content of the characterisation. This kind of argument has been applied to the 1980s action hero, including Russell's appearance in *Tango and Cash*, by Yvonne Tasker. She rightly identifies Russell's variation on the usual conventions of the genre hero, calling it the 'macho slob' style, and she supports this by specifically referring to his persona in Carpenter's *Big Trouble in Little China* (1993: 235). Here, Russell played heavily on his characterisation as a dishevelled and rather disorganised truck driver, whose final amble off onto the road at the end of the film is a parodic homage to John Wayne's final scene in Ford's *The Searchers* (1956). Tasker identifies similar myth-deflating strategies in *Tango and Cash*, such as Russell appearing in drag, but suggests their purpose is largely to find another means to recycle the essentially conservative and reactionary ethics of the genre and its male stars. She expresses doubt at 'the possibility of making a distinction between a parodic performance of masculinity and the oppressive enactment of that performance' (1993: 243).

It is certainly the case that the self-consciousness of Russell's performances for Carpenter does not completely alter the essential content of his narrative function, which is often centred on the use of violence to dispose of anything problematic, as well as the fetishisation of male aggression and the marginalising of female characters. At the same time, as Tasker herself suggests, the performative stylisation and distancing humour used in these roles tend to signal a sense of disquiet with the ideological connotations normally associated with such representations. She argues that 'the enactment of a drama of power and powerlessness is intrinsic to the anxieties about masculine identity and authority that are embodied in the figure of the struggling hero' (ibid.). If such strategies do not entirely subvert the ideological conservatism of the traditional action hero, then they do give expression to substantive doubts as to the continued potency and relevance of such representations of masculinity. It is symptomatic of the changing context within which these films function that Russell's Plissken has to shift ground from self-conscious artifice to outright self-parody.

A further level of complexity is added to the *Escape* films by the tensions and ambiguities apparent in the relationship between Carpenter and Russell. These tensions are verifiable both through the strikingly different attitudes publicly expressed by director and star in relation to the material they have worked on and in the political values played out on-screen through the character of Snake Plissken. Russell's own political position has always been clear and he has shown little reticence in making his own views public. In an interview for *Village Voice* he revealingly positioned himself as being in opposition to the dominant ethical trends of his own generation: 'I basically hate my generation. I never got along with them. They were all bullshit' (Trebay 1981: 51). He proceeds to give an account of running into an old high-school friend who had become part of his generation's common rebellion against the government over civil rights and the Vietnam war. He takes open pleasure in parading his own financial success and fame in contrast to his friend's life of comparative obscurity. He says: 'My generation couldn't stand me and I couldn't stand them. In high school I was to the right of being straight. I believed in the work ethic, making money and they all had this beef with the nation. Vietnam disappointed me because we didn't win' (ibid.). His continuing public identification with a very traditionally macho, Hemingwayesque lifestyle has brought him attention from the liberal American media, who took particular exception to his charity hunting parties at his Colorado home (oddly, the good cause chosen to benefit from one of these was the World Wildlife Fund). It is also clear from his interview with *Village Voice* that his characterisation of Snake Plissken is for him an extension of some of his own values. For Russell, Plissken's invulnerability is a way of externalising his own anger and frustration with post-1960s America: 'There are things about Plissken that all of us have felt. His anguishes, desires, fears. But when he walks down the street, he's in control, an island, totally alone. I like that' (ibid.).

Elements of Russell's attitudes are evident in the ideological iconography of his presentation of Plissken. Particularly in *Escape From New York*, Plissken is presented as the embodiment of a righteous sense of justice that is beyond the law. He is positioned within a schematic narrative structure that balances punkish ghetto villains on one side, against a weak, vacillating president on the other. Plissken metes out justice to both in appropriate ways. The punks are violently dispatched, whilst the President receives an execution of a different kind, when exposed as an incompetent and self-seeking politician during a live television broadcast. Plissken's macho sexual virility is even given symbolic representation by the tattoo of a snake which winds its way out of his trousers and up over his midriff.

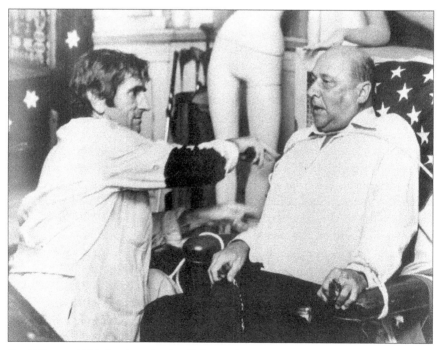

Donald Pleasence (right) plays the weak and vacillating president in *Escape From New York*

It is easy to see how Plissken could be interpreted as a fetishised hero of the political right. In a review in *Rolling Stone*, Michael Sragow (1981) argued that 'what *Escape From New York* tries to tell us is that the US is out of control – its citizens crazy and its cities virtual insane asylums: the only objective standard and reforming force is the power of a gun'. In Britain, a fairly typical review in the *Daily Telegraph* expressed similar misgivings about Plissken, describing him as 'one of those appalling anti-heroes of our times, a master criminal complete with a pirate's eye-patch, paramilitary gear from the he-man waist down and armed with a snarling mouthful of cynical quips' (Nurse 1981).

In *Escape From L.A.* Russell's views are given expression in the choice of some of the targets set up for ridicule. It is also perhaps easier to link Russell directly to these views as for the sequel he acted as co-producer, along with Carpenter's long-term collaborator Debra Hill, and as co-scriptwriter with both Hill and Carpenter. Russell has acknowledged in an interview that 'I am politically incorrect, I realise that. I say what I think and that at times can be a problem' (Elmer 1996: 28). The targets for parody in *Escape From L.A.* centre around the depiction of a future utopian/dystopian America presided over by a politically-correct administration. Here swearing is prohibited, no one is allowed to own a gun and the eating of red meat has been banned. Plissken's final victory over the forces of liberal autocracy is celebrated by another illegal activity, the smoking of a cigar, which forms the film's closing image. The inmates of L.A.'s prison enclave become the inverted, politically incorrect heroes of the film. In one scene Plissken's futuristic L.A., which he sees as a 'dark paradise', is described as the only place where an individual can be free, and where 'a girl can buy a fur coat'.

A second target for the film's critique is contemporary L.A. and, in particular, Hollywood. It is wholly predictable that Russell should feel himself to be somewhat at odds with the frequently liberal values of much of Hollywood's contemporary elite and this is reflected in the film's persistent jokes at the expense of Hollywood and L.A. society. Steve Buscemi's character is a crude parody of a Hollywood agent, who tries to ingratiate himself with Plissken by offering him access to his 'map to the stars'. Referring to Beverly Hills, another character laments 'no one gets out of there alive'. In another wonderfully grotesque sequence Plissken finds himself cornered by a gang of mutants who are the product of excessive plastic surgery and whose leader, the 'surgeon general' (Bruce Campbell), wants Plissken for his fresh body parts.

At the same time, many of the targets of the film's humour are markedly different in their ideological base, something which can be traced to the quite different position taken by Carpenter. In an interview with the Director's Guild of America, Carpenter suggested a very different agenda, although it is apparent that he shares something of Russell's sense of being an outsider in the Hollywood community. Talking about *Escape From L.A.*, Carpenter says:

> It's got a little subversive message to it. The United States is a theocracy and it deports the morally guilty to L.A. So they send atheists, teenage runaways and abortion doctors over to L.A.; they get them out of the new Moral America. Cliff Robertson is the president, so there's a little juice to it. (Elrick 1996: 3)

The figure of the President here is a fairly blatant caricature of America's moral majority politicians, such as Pat Buchanan and Newt Gingrich. Robertson's President is a singularly self-righteous individual who is quite willing to send his own daughter to the electric chair to punish her for having taken sides against him. He has declared himself President for life and subsequently withdrawn to his hometown of Lynchburg, Virginia (now the nation's capital) from where he runs the country. Quoting repeatedly from the Bible, he has designated L.A. a kind of Sodom and Gomorrah, or 'island of the damned'. The sense of America being ruled by an ultra- right-wing Christian orthodoxy is accentuated by the fact that one character has been sentenced to the prison for 'being a Muslim in South Dakota'. Plissken's only real ally for most of the film is an anachronistic counter-cultural figure, played appropriately by Peter Fonda, who helps Plissken to escape from pursuit in a manner worthy of the most spaced-out of psychedelic visions from the 1960s: they surf to freedom on a tidal wave that sweeps them down Wiltshire Boulevard. The sense of Carpenter's sympathies lying rather to the left of Russell's is also confirmed by the similarly hippie sensibility which informed his feature debut, *Dark Star* (1974), and which is apparent at intervals in his other films.

Where these apparent contradictions between Carpenter and Russell become fused is in the creation of the appropriate ethic for the figure of the rebel. This is apparent as early as their first teaming on the television movie *Elvis*, where the focus is almost always on emphasising the singer as an outsider and an opponent of authority: Presley is shown as a self-conscious dandy at school, using his clothing and hairstyle to separate himself from the other students, and his period in the army is shown largely as one of confusion and misdirection. Plissken is a similar rebel against authority, but that authority can take different forms. It can be the dictates of liberal political correctness or the threat of urban disintegration and anarchy. Alternatively it can take the form of corrupt politicians, America's moral majority or even the machinations of the Hollywood system. Whatever its contemporary manifestation, Plissken's refuge is always in individualism. Russell has stated:

> The constitution said, 'there's a place on Earth where you can go do what you want to do, think what you want to think, as long as you don't step on other people's toes'. I like that, being a libertarian. I'm Jeffersonian in my thoughts, so is John. We feel that Snake is the ultimate in his total disdain for authority, because he was under the control of authority in this country and proved that to be totally futile and useless. (Elmer 1996: 28)

It is this sense of the individual at odds with a malevolent social and cultural environment which links Carpenter's counter-cultural sensibility with Russell's macho backwoodsman, and which brings out the surprising affinities between the two. Plissken is both an anti-authoritarian figure and a vigilante moral crusader. In the context of a dystopian future America, where the ruling elite are duplicitous beyond belief and the masses anarchic and beyond restraint, the embodiment of moral value becomes the isolated individual. Such an amalgamation of disparate masculine archetypes as that represented by Snake Plissken may not always convince as a fully developed hero, something to which Carpenter alludes with his knowing sense of ironic detachment from the character, but, in its own self-conscious way, it manages to give a reinvented voice to a form of American rugged individualism which has been at the centre of discourses of American male identity since the establishment of the frontier.

*Notes*

1   Kurt Russell quoted in a press release for *The Thing*, issued by Universal Studios (11 February 1982).

*References*

Dyer, R. (1998) *Stars*. London: British Film Institute.

Elmer, D. (1996) 'Boom towns', *Time Out*, 11 September, 28.

Elrick, T. (1996) 'Fires ... floods ... riots ... earthquakes ... John Carpenter!', *Director's Guild of America Magazine*, 21, 3.

Jeffords, S. (1993) 'Can Masculinity Be Terminated?', in S. Cohan and I. R. Hark (eds) *Screening the Male: Exploring Masculinities in Hollywood Cinema*. London: Routledge, 245–62.

Nurse, K. (1981) 'Snake in the Criminal Jungle', *Daily Telegraph*, 21 August.

Sragow, M. (1981) 'John Carpenter's Escape to Nowhere', *Rolling Stone*, 20 August.

Tasker, Y. (1993) 'Dumb Movies for Dumb People: Masculinity, the Body, and the Voice in Contemporary Action Cinema', in S. Cohan and I. R. Hark (eds) *Screening the Male: Exploring Masculinities in Hollywood Cinema*. London: Routledge, 230–44.

Trebay, G. (1981) 'Talking Heads: Kurt Russell's Escape From Nowhere', *Village Voice*, 8 July, 51.

Udo, T. (1996) 'Getaway out west', *New Musical Express*, September.

# CHAPTER NINE

# From Elvis to L.A.: Reflections on the Carpenter-Russell Films

## Tony Williams

A consistent feature of John Carpenter's filmmaking is his collaborations with actor Kurt Russell. Excluding the television movie *Elvis* (1979), Carpenter and Russell have to date collaborated on four films. Although this number appears small in comparison to the extent to which many directors, stars and character actors worked together in the heyday of the old studio system, it is a respectable figure for a post-classical Hollywood era characterised by increasing production costs and the independence of the star.

Russell has received less critical attention than Carpenter. However, he is not only that rare phenomenon of the child actor who graduated into adult stardom but he has been active in film and television since the age of four.[1] Although less definable as a star in comparison to high-profile contemporaries such as Clint Eastwood, Arnold Schwarzenegger and Bruce Willis, Russell does, however, have a fair track record. His early years as a child actor in television and film and his move towards adolescent and mature roles enabled him to deliver competent, journeyman performances. Like Eastwood, Russell performed acting apprentice work in television series, and although his usual type of performance is less charismatic and flamboyant than most of his star contemporaries, it reflects hard work and knowledge of the tools of the trade. Russell has spoken highly of Walt Disney and the training he received working as a child actor in 'Uncle Walt's' studio during the 1960s (Ward

1980; Chase 1981; Trebay 1981). In many ways, these films were the equivalent of the old 'B' westerns in which John Wayne polished his acting abilities in the 1930s.

Like Wayne, Russell is an actor who understands performance technique by learning on the job rather than at acting school. Russell made his starring debut in the short-lived television series *The Travels of Jaimie McPheeters* (1963–64), which he followed with appearances in more Disney features. Many of his television performances appear in works unquestioningly accepting the benefits of the American way of life. However, his role as Charles Whitman in the television documentary-drama *The Deadly Tower* (1975) revealed that Russell could also play deranged (as well as socially well-balanced) characters. His low-key, but menacing, Whitman role revealed depths in his performance skills very few directors (with the exception of Carpenter) recognised. Russell later decided to follow his father's earlier vocation by leaving acting to train for a career in professional baseball.[2] However, an injury led to his return to acting and an Emmy-nominated award for his role in *Elvis*.

The significance of Russell's collaboration with Carpenter lies in the fusion of two personalities whose work reinforces, rather than drastically contradicts, negative features within classical Hollywood ideology. Superficially, *Escape From New York* (1981), *Escape From L.A.* (1996) and *Big Trouble in Little China* (1986) aim at satirising now defunct images of screen masculinity. Also, Carpenter appears to use Russell to send up the masculine roles he frequently plays in his other films. Rather than subversively rejecting masculine archetypes Carpenter and Russell merely use them for superficial humour and leave intact the ideological system from which they were created. The *Escape* films may express discontent with the status quo, but they also operate in a nihilistic manner, taking pleasure in chaos for its own sake rather than suggesting alternative directions for the survivors of a debased political system to follow. This course is impossible anyway, since the films demonise any representations of the 'other' which might undermine Carpenter's ideological assumptions and his star's construction of masculinity.[3]

Russell is used by Carpenter to parody one of two key Hollywood masculine performances. In *Big Trouble in Little China*, Russell sends up the John Wayne persona. In *Escape From New York*, *The Thing* (1982) and *Escape From L.A.* Russell also borrows recognisable Eastwood performance traits in a deliberate and self-aware manner. Russell's roles in his other non-Carpenter films are revealing. These vary from playing the 'slob' he satirises in *Big Trouble in Little China* in *The Best of Times* (1986), *Overboard* (1987) and *Captain Ron* (1992), to the sensitive males of *Silkwood* (1983), *Swing Shift* (1984) and *Winter People* (1989). Russell plays a regular guy facing dangerous circumstances in *Tequila Sunrise* (1988) and *Executive Decision* (1996), but his most interesting non-Carpenter performances are in films such as *The Mean Season* (1985), *Unlawful Entry* (1992) and *Breakdown* (1998), which represent distinctive class variants of this role.

Carpenter usually casts Russell in films containing chaotic situations threatening both social stability and the affluent, conservative attitudes of Beverly Hills. *The Mean Season*, *Unlawful Entry* and *Breakdown* parallel the roles Russell plays in the Carpenter films, as a character less in control of a situation and actually a victim of circumstances. Although the Russell persona in all these films generally believes in the status quo and the secure nature of his masculine identity, he more often than not finds it threatened by demonised representatives of dark forces within a hostile universe.

The television movie *Elvis* was the first time Carpenter and Russell collaborated. Despite its broadcast origins as a Dick Clark production, it was released as a theatrical feature in Britain. Carpenter filmed it very much like a theatrical feature with elements of a cinematic style such as the predominant use of the mobile camera. Despite appearing two years after Elvis's death and preceding the many revelatory biographies and television movies, *Elvis* is not as reverential as reviewers such as Richard Combs (1979) suppose.[4] Carpenter knowingly employs the *Citizen Kane* (1941) formula to depict a rise and fall trajectory for his chosen hero. The film begins with Elvis arriving in Las Vegas, hiding himself in a hotel room, facing a death threat. One brief shot reveals Elvis and his associates walking along a shadowy hotel corridor whose dark-red walls resemble a womb-like interior. Carpenter introduces Russell's Elvis by dollying left into his hotel room to reveal a huge shadow of the King's head on the wall before tracking in to show the actual figure. This shadow motif occurs frequently throughout the film and parallels the expressionistic and film noir techniques Welles uses in *Citizen Kane*. It represents Elvis's traumatic survivor guilt feelings over the death, at birth, of his twin brother Jesse, and as a death wish he himself cherishes throughout his life. During the prologue, Elvis doubts his own abilities, ignores the support of his ex-wife Priscilla (Season Hubley), compares his unseen assassin to Lee Harvey Oswald, and fires at a television screen when the announcer speculates that the Vegas debut could be the beginning or end of Elvis's career.

Like Charles Foster Kane, Elvis suffers from a problematic family upbringing. His devoted mother Gladys (Shelley Winters) is by far the stronger parent, rather than the weak Vernon Presley (Bing Russell). She encourages her son in his ambition to become an entertainer and confuses him with Jesse before she dies. Earlier, she states, 'you've just got so much energy in your young body ... I think sometimes maybe you got the energy of two'. Elvis's Graceland soon resembles Kane's Xanadu, and Priscilla is the King's version of Susan Alexander Kane. Like Susan, Priscilla becomes fascinated by encountering a living legend but soon finds him lacking, and desires her own independence. Anthony Lawrence's screenplay explicitly states Priscilla's attraction to Elvis originates from his seeing her as a younger version of Gladys. Elvis not only notes parallels between Priscilla's hair and Gladys's but also dyes his own hair which emphasises his closeness to his devoted mother. Although Carpenter never includes a breakfast table montage sequence depicting the deterioration of a marital relationship, he does include a scene with both partners separated on different sides of a long dining table. Towards the end of the film, Elvis is shown comparing himself to John F. Kennedy and Martin Luther King – who were both cut short at the height of their fame – and desiring a final reunion with Gladys and Jesse. After Elvis phones Lisa Marie (Felicia Fenske) before his first Vegas cabaret performance, in a manner resembling archetypal cinematic farewells between loved ones, the camera pans left to reveal the shadow of his head. Elvis then turns his head towards the wall and he finally merges with his own shadow. The twins now become one and Elvis achieves his dream.

Although *Elvis* shows the King performing before a shadowy audience of younger and older spectators, it concludes on a much more ominous note. The final image shows Elvis finally immobile, like a statue, as the camera tracks in for a close-up of his head, while mixed dissolves at the right show extracts from his past life, before ending with a black screen against an extreme close-up of the King's face. This sequence parallels archetypal imagery of a dying person seeing the past rapidly flow before their eyes prior to death. It also resembles the concluding images in *Citizen Kane* which end with the letter 'K', an abstract memorial still affirming the identity of a once living person whose life has been a waste. Similarly, *Elvis* concludes with an extreme close-up of its title character's head, lit up like a Greek god, before a fade to black. Elvis achieves his goal of immortality, but his pursuit of success has cost him dearly by draining him of life. He disavows his masculine crisis by engaging in an exaggerated performance which deprives him of any possibility of personal growth or change.

By inflecting a straightforward television biography with subversive elements, *Elvis* reveals its male hero facing powerful institutional and social forces which render his attempts at controlling situations either difficult or futile. Family trauma and pursuit of the American Dream destroy Elvis. He also chooses contemporary heroic role models which are actually irrelevant to his own personal dilemmas. The hair-dyeing scenes show his desire to emulate Tony Curtis, but the King cannot admit unconscious forces in his personality which make him want to be closer to his mother. Despite two scenes showing Elvis practising martial arts, the film makes clear that his expertise is only a desperate veneer to cover boredom and insecurity. It is as meaningless as the ballet exercises performed by Priscilla in an empty Graceland to compensate for her loneliness. Another scene reveals Elvis watching, on 16mm, James Dean's confession scene to Officer Ray (Edward Platt) in *Rebel Without a Cause* (1955). Like Howard Hughes, who would later constantly replay *Ice Station Zebra* (1968), the King is clearly familiar with the film and even repeats the dialogue, identifying himself with the screen character as a 'crazy mixed-up kid'. But *Elvis* makes clear that the King can find no adequate role models. Instead, he manufactures his gaudy jump-suited 'late Elvis' Vegas personality and finally becomes frozen in time. Although the final scenes of *Elvis* are played reverentially, more than a touch of irony remains in the concluding images. Elvis finally becomes an image of spectacular excess, his Vegas jump-suit contrasting with the more sober costumes worn during his earlier career reprised during the final scenes. Denial and excess compensate for male inadequacy. Unfortunately, these significant implications never develop to their logical conclusions in the Carpenter-Russell films that followed.

In *Escape From New York*, *The Thing*, *Big Trouble in Little China* and *Escape From L.A.*, the characters Russell plays are merely variants of the male masquerade which conclude the scenes of his first collaboration with Carpenter. In *Escape From L.A.*, Russell appears costumed like a bondage fantasy version of Eastwood's 'Man With No Name', complete with leather duster. In both *Escape* films, Snake's costumes represent different versions of the absurd jump-suit worn by Elvis in the concluding scenes of the television movie. The eye-patch worn by Snake resembles that worn by John Wayne in *True Grit* (1969). This is more than accidental since Russell mimics both Wayne and Eastwood in *Escape From New York*: as Snake he begins threatening Brain (Harry Dean Stanton) in Wayne-like intonations before relapsing back into his Eastwood whisper. Furthermore, throughout *Escape From New York*, characters often confront Plissken with the line, 'I heard you were dead', a line Carpenter borrows from the John Wayne film *Big Jake* (1971), in which there is the repetitive utterance 'I thought you'd be taller' (a line which is then borrowed for *Escape From L.A.*). *Big Trouble in Little China* sees a rough-looking Russell wearing a tasteless white vest, while his MacReady character from *The Thing* is really Snake without the eye-patch.

In *The Thing* Russell plays gruff loner J. R. MacReady, a character invested with subdued Eastwood overtones and various western generic attributes. Whereas Captain Hendry (Kenneth Tobey) in the Hawks version, *The Thing From Another World* (1951), functioned as part of a team and depended on the contributions of others, MacReady is always alone as a prospective leader during the ensuing chaos.[5] After the opening scenes, the film shows a group of frustrated males already at odds with each other and scarcely needing the presence of a Thing to introduce chaos into their universe. Like the crew members in *Dark Star* (1974), they exhibit no Hawksian sense of professionalism. Near the film's beginning MacReady plays chess with a female computer, but loses. Sneering at this challenge to his masculinity (the first of several throughout the film), he mutters 'Cheating bitch!' and blows her circuits by pouring his glass of whisky into the machine. MacReady's passage of fluids during his particular 'blow job' finds an ironic counterpart in the various ways the Thing processes both animal and human bodies on the base. Although able to act intuitively, and realise the imminent danger, MacReady also has to fight his suspicious colleagues, and combat a less identifiable entity than the figure originally played by James Arness in the Hawks version. During the Cold War era, the enemy was at least identifiable. But, in a film shot during Reagan's attempt to return to the future, the threat is less clear. Indeed, it threatens masculinity itself by taking over the male body, penetrating its very being. Although MacReady's masculinity suspends the threat, the victory is a Pyrrhic one. The saviour can be viewed as perishing in a nihilistic conclusion in which each of the survivors, without being aware of it, may, or may not, be another embodiment of the Thing. Nothing is certain any longer. Even if victorious, MacReady's masculinity is now both absurd and anachronistic.

*Big Trouble in Little China* is a difficult film. Shot a decade before widespread knowledge of Hong Kong New Wave productions such as *A Chinese Ghost Story* (1987) became common in the West, the film confounds the viewer by its eccentric handling of martial arts sequences and yellow journalistic perceptions of the Chinese community. Like the *Escape* films, *Big Trouble* regards the non-Westernised ethnic entity as a demonic threat. And women fare little better. Although the refusal of Jack Burton (Kurt Russell) to kiss the leading lady at the climax may be read as satirical, it also indicates a fear of the feminine, which functions as both an internal and external

Masculinity imperilled: MacReady (Kurt Russell) encounters the unknown in *The Thing*

threat to the hero in many of the Carpenter-Russell collaborations.[6] This feature is seen, for instance, in the *Escape* films, which also contain reactionary features first seen in *Assault on Precinct 13*.

Both *Escape* films begin with an opening apocalyptic scenario. In the 1997 world of *Escape From New York*, Manhattan is now a top security prison, while Los Angeles serves the same function in the right-wing Christian fundamentalist world of 2013 depicted in *Escape From L.A.* Both films contain an introductory voiceover by a female commentator describing reasons for the chaos. In *Escape From New York* a Marxist female kamikaze stewardess crashes Air Force One into Manhattan, while the President's daughter steals a secret doomsday weapon and flees to Los Angeles in the later film. The remaining fragments of the President's daughter's virtual reality tape ascribe her decision to the malign influence of Che Guevara figurehead, Cuervo Jones (George Corraface). Jones not only resembles the Marxist alternative embodied in Carpenter's demonically depicted Street Thunder gang of *Assault on Precinct 13* but also parallels the equally ethnic and one-dimensional threat presented by the Duke of New York (Isaac Hayes) in the earlier film. Although Snake's Establishment adversaries are equally unpleasant in both films, alternative potentials for a better society represented by women and other ethnic groups are represented negatively. *Escape From New York* presents its threats in the form of bi-sexual punks, Native Americans and gypsies while *Escape From L.A.* sees the return of the city to its original inhabitants as nightmarish.

Romero (Frank Doubleday) is one of the bi-sexual punks in *Escape From New York* and, before he emerges, a shrill form of hysterical laughter occurs off-screen in the darkness. Romero then appears warning Hauk (Lee Van Cleef) and his men away from Manhattan and showing them one of the President's fingers, a symbol of castration. Later in the film, Romero is seen threatening the President (Donald Pleasence) who wears a blonde female wig which Romero has made him wear. When Brain (Harry Dean Stanton) arrives to rescue the President, it is just in time to save the Chief from a 'fate worse than death'. In *Escape From L.A.*, Brain's character becomes the trans-sexual figure of Hershe (Pam Grier), formerly Snake's male associate Carjack. Naturally, she does not escape from L.A. at the climax. Hershe also echoes the degenerate figures of the male transvestite chorus enjoyed by Cabbie (Ernest Borgnine) during a theatrical performance in *Escape From New York*. As with Grier, Carpenter depicts Borgnine like a grotesque gargoyle, and he too, must not escape from New York. Cabbie's decision to remain in the Big Apple

Romero, the figure of an alternative culture in the nightmarish metropolis, in *Escape From New York*

and enjoy some dubious entertainment casts doubt on his suitability for living in a 'cleaner' society. In *Escape From L.A.* Cabbie's replacement is sleazy 'Map to the Stars Eddie' played by Steve Buscemi, who attempts to out-mug Borgnine's earlier performance.

In *Escape From New York*, Snake encounters a mysterious woman (Season Hubley) hiding from a group of nocturnal cannibalistic scavengers, the crazies. Before she has the chance to make Snake 'whistle' as 'Slim' does to 'Steve' in *To Have and Have Not* (1944), she is pulled down into the depths by the crazies so the hero can continue on his mission without further delays. Later, Brain's 'squeeze' Maggie (Adrienne Barbeau) makes the heroic sacrifice for Snake by attempting to stop the Duke's car, if not stopping a bullet meant for the hero like the western's traditional dance-hall girl. In *Escape From L.A.* Valeria Golino's character Taslima also offers a Hawksian female alternative to Snake's dominant masculinity, with her role more developed than Season Hubley's in *Escape From New York* both in terms of screen time and significance. When following Snake to a used-car lot, they view a group of Christians praying. She tells him, 'They're new. They don't belong to any gang. They're just scared.' Taslima also tells Snake that she is a Muslim from South Dakota who was deported to Los Angeles when her religion became a crime. But she also emphasises that the dark paradise of Los Angeles is better 'than the other side of the world' and offers to take care of Snake. Taslima soon dies from a bullet fired by a group of child assassins, but she does attempt to awaken Snake to the idea that Los Angeles may contain alternative possibilities. Despite her affront to the male-narrative trajectory by attempting to hinder Snake's mission, she does take the initiative in reaching out to him. Taslima also suggests that the dark world of Los Angeles is more real than the one outside, a world which encompasses both right-wing fundamentalism and Snake's macho activities. Even though Carpenter represents Los Angeles as a demonic realm encompassing independent women, racially mixed groups and outcasts from society, the screenplay recognises that it contains some potential for alternative existence; an idea which does not occur in the earlier film. A child's bullet, however, terminates both Taslima's life and the offer she makes to Snake.

It is not accidental that the bullet comes from a male child gang member. As a girl, Taslima comes dangerously close to disrupting the boy's game. She must be eliminated from the text so that it may return to the structure of its predecessor. Eventually, Snake undergoes the same type of leg wound, gladiatorial combat and escape as in the earlier film.

As Peter Lehman coherently argues in his study of screen masculinity, Hollywood productions, classical and post-classical, often contain revealing insights into both the nature of the male body and its relationship to the female counterpart. Referring to *Rio Bravo* (1959), *Rio Lobo* (1970) and *The Searchers* (1956), Lehman notes that loss of power affects males and females in different ways. Whereas the female loss usually involves scarring, male vulnerability 'is marked not by a disfigurement but by a crippling, that is, a limitation of the power to act. For this reason, leg injuries are probably the most common male equivalent of the female scarred face' (1993: 61). However, Lehman also notes that 'in the cinema, a scar on a man's face frequently enhances rather than detracts from his power, providing a sign that he has been tested in the violent and dangerous world of male action and has survived' (1993: 63). Snake's eyepatch fulfills this function in the *Escape* films while female deaths represent the ultimate 'scarring' process in this conservative male scenario. Snake's leg wounds in the two films represent homages to the John Wayne character's disabilities in both *El Dorado* (1967) and *Rio Lobo*, but they also function as empty plot devices; neither *Escape* film contains the significant implications contained in Carpenter's favoured mentor. As Lehman again notes, 'the powerful men in Hawks's action films are never quite so powerful and secure as they may seem; Chance and McNally are not that far away from Tony Camonte' (1993: 66). Vulnerability is never far away from the supposedly strong hero. To their credit, Hawks's films recognise this. But, apart from *Elvis*, Carpenter's Russell films do not.

*Notes*

1   The *Internet Movie Database* lists Russell's first appearance in a 1955 episode of the television western *Gunsmoke*.
2   Kurt's father was actor Bing Russell, well-known for his role as the deputy sheriff in the long-running *Bonanza* television series. He also appeared as Elvis's father in *Elvis* as well as other films such as *Overboard* (1987).
3   I have elsewhere expressed reservations concerning Carpenter's refusal to examine the implications of his material in demonising the 'other'. These appear in Williams (1979). Wood also persuasively includes *Halloween* (1978) among the reactionary wing of horror films. See Wood (1979: 24–7); and Williams (1996: 216). *Halloween* also spawned the 1980s cycle of reactionary horror films represented by the *Friday the 13th* and *A Nightmare on Elm Street* series.
4   Ironically, both Elvis and Russell appeared together in *It Happened at the World's Fair* (1963), the latter playing the role of the boy who kicks Elvis.
5   As Russell points out, his character is 'in the outpost group but not of it … He's just a helicopter pilot out to make a lot of money in a very short amount of time. He's a Vietnam vet, and he's isolated from the rest of the group … He's as scared as the others, but the war has taught him how to act instinctively. The script pits an outsider against another outsider, the pilot against the alien.' Quoted in Billson (1997: 29).
6   For an alternative perspective see Cumbow (1990: 110). Cumbow comments that it is 'interesting to note that all of the women in *Assault on Precinct 13*, *Halloween* and *Escape From New York* are either wounded or killed – a phenomenon that suggests not a sadistic attitude toward women but a willingness to place them – as Hawks did – alongside men in the centre of the arena of physical action'.

*References*

Billson, A. (1997) *The Thing*. London: British Film Institute.
Chase, C. (1981) 'Kurt Russell: From Baseball to the Screen', *New York Times*, 10

July, C6.

Combs, R. (1979) '*Elvis*', *Monthly Film Bulletin*, 46, 547, 170–1.

Cumbow, R. C. (1990) *Order in the Universe: The Films of John Carpenter*. Metuchen, NJ: Scarecrow Press.

Lehman, P. (1993) *Running Scared: Masculinity and the Representation of the Male Body*. Philadelphia: Temple University Press.

Trebay, G. (1981) 'Talking Heads: Kurt Russell's Escape From Nowhere', *Village Voice*, 8 July, 51.

Ward, A. (1980) 'Ex-Infielder Now Stars in "Used Cars Lot"', *New York Times*, 12 September, C11.

Williams, T. (1979) '*Assault on Precinct 13*: The Mechanics of Repression', in R. Wood and R. Lippe (eds) *The American Nightmare: Essays on the Horror Film*. Toronto: Festival of Festivals, 67–73.

_____ (1996) *Hearths of Darkness: The Family in the American Horror Film*. Cranbury, NJ: Associated University Presses.

Wood, R. (1979) 'An Introduction to the American Horror Film', in R. Wood and R. Lippe (eds) *The American Nightmare: Essays on the Horror Film*. Toronto: Festival of Festivals, 7–28.

CHAPTER TEN

# Restorative and Destructive: Carpenter and Maternal Authority

Suzie Young

*The Subversion of Paternal Law*

John Carpenter's cinema fusses and frets over the masculine world with spectacular enthusiasm, offering beachball aliens in outer space (*Dark Star* (1974)), glowing fog and black cloud in idyllic smalltown-USA (*The Fog* (1979) and *Village of the Damned* (1995)), a candy-apple red Plymouth Fury in a greasy garage (*Christine* (1983)), and pure eruptive joys in prison-cities (*Escape From New York* (1981) and *Escape From L.A.* (1996)). These are anxious spectacles in narratives that suggest civilisation is deeply flawed. Neither the formless seepage that escorts the righteous, vengeful, ghoulish figures in *The Fog* nor the chrome-overdosed vintage car that gives the power of vindictive violence to he who loves her best in *Christine* has a human face. In contrast, the prison-cities in the two *Escape* films shelter those who are most clearly *alive*, society's criminals and outcasts expelled there (for life, we might pun) to play the deadliest games for survival; however much the *mise-en-scène* suggests a dreadful decadence, in these dystopias we also see human faces and passions, exacting and paying their prices, quite unlike the 'civilised' authorities who stew in rituals of power in the outside world.

Like Heracles who descended into the underworld, often for the sake of weak or evil kings,[1] Snake Plissken (Kurt Russell) in the *Escape* films harrows hell to retrieve a lost treasure because he alone can. If the sun shines somewhere, it decidedly does not in Carpenter's great prison metropolis in *Escape From New York*. The film's immense penal colony is so unmitigatedly dark that, despite the evil system which thrusts Plissken into this place of chaos and disintegration, it is impossible not to share his goal and hope for triumph and escape. His return with the President (Donald Pleasence) may be applauded, though the audience is more likely to approve when he brings the latter to ridicule and undercuts his authority. The second *Escape* film is less successful because L.A. is never as dark: it is simply too much fun, and it moves close to camp with hang-glider rescues, guided tours to the homes of the stars and big-wave seekers who hang ten even as the world ends. But if *Escape From L.A.* is more playful and even, at times, silly, it also has a darker vision. The President in the New York film is evil but there is at least the suggestion at the end that if he was removed, then the system might be fixed. There is no such possibility at the end of *Escape From L.A.*: it must all come crashing down.

That Carpenter means to suggest this is our world, or at least a logical extension of it, seems certain. The name of Russell's character – 'Snake' – of course makes immediate reference to his dangerous and quick nature but it also recalls the serpent in the Garden, who heralded the beginning of a new era for humanity. Snake Plissken, too, ushers in a new age, albeit in reverse to the traditional story: out of the Garden we have grown distant from nature, and so it is with Plissken's destruction of all electronic technology (in *Escape From L.A.*) that we may have a chance at return. In fact it was wrong to blame the serpent in the first place, since it only gave us *knowledge* of good and evil; in the end, it was the *choice* for evil that led to humanity's expulsion from the Garden. Accordingly, Carpenter's protagonists do not combat for omnipotence in the world but for freedom from it. In Carpenter's films, society's institutions are shown to be corrupt and villainous or confused and ineffectual. The clergy, for example, are secretive and hypocritical. They murder, sell their souls, or give in to doubts in *The Fog*, *Vampires* (1998) and *Village of the Damned*; they are invariably 'unmanned' when 'manliness' is what typically matters in their desperate situations. In *Prince of Darkness* (1987), the church is the very portal through which Hell erupts. While religion's Fathers fail as men, the military, the police, and the government fall so short as to become the monsters themselves. In *They Live* (1988), the authorities are power-driven evil aliens who enslave a good humanity, or they are human Judases who sell out their own kind for any share of power; in *Village of the Damned*, they are helpless bystanders susceptible to the aliens' mind-control, or they are deceptive, callous murderers intent upon military and political advantage even at the expense of human lives; and in the two *Escape* films, the police lie, cheat and bully others into perilous reconnaissance and rescues that they themselves dare not undertake.

Scientists, too, most often fail to rise above a self-serving interest, be it intellectual, financial or existential: in *Starman* (1984), NASA researchers are sweet and childlike in their wonder for other planets but they are also irresponsibly docile in this world, submissive to their Department of National Defense bosses who lack compassion and even curiosity and who are fuelled only by murderous greed for geopolitical dominance. In *Village of the Damned*, doctors from the National Science

Foundation and the National Institute of Health favour research grants over the welfare of the mysterious children and their earthling families; in *The Thing* (1982), researchers in the Antarctic are so anti-social that they cannot distinguish friend from foe when their station is invaded by an alien force that hides inside human bodies. Even language-centred institutions such as the school, the university and the publishing house are the site of monstrosity rather than the order that eliminates chaos. The high school in *Christine* breeds cliques and bullies, bigotry and harm; the university's research conducted in the church in *Prince of Darkness* overlays the subterranean evil that breeds in the basement below; and the publishing house – a mainstay of popular enlightenment – is the very means and mechanism by which a particularly hideous Armegeddon is let loose upon the earth in *In the Mouth of Madness* (1995).

In fact, the subversion of paternal Law is a central pleasure in Carpenter's films as they reveal the faults in the pillars of society; time and again, the films expose the hypocrisy of civil society, often displaying the violated male body for spectatorial pleasure and as evidence of the fragility of the Law. But what obtains from such unease with the masculine world? I suggest that against the horrors of civilisation is an ambivalent nostalgia for kinder/gentler times, before the trappings of normative society or after technocracy has maximised its destructive potential. A pattern emerges: deliverance from failed homosociality is achieved by mother-goddesses who, as sole parent and originating womb, are both redemptive and appalling, restorative and destructive, enticing and vile.

### Flirtation with Maternal Authority

In Carpenter's cinema, it may be men who fight the battles but frequently it is women – mother-figures – who guide them. Indeed, the future is gendered feminine narratively and ideologically in several films, most pointedly in *Escape From L.A.* in which the fascist president's daughter – named Utopia – rejects the patriarch(s) and thereby collapses the repressive status quo. The goal of this chapter is to draw attention to Carpenter's reverie: so enchanted is he by the maternal that the mother-son dyad or its poetical equivalent appears repeatedly in his films. In some, the maternal is configured as the source of conflict resolution and site of hope and salvation (*The Fog, Starman, Village of the Damned*) while in others, it is the devil's portal through which evil is given new life and unleashed on the world (*Prince of Darkness, In the Mouth of Madness, Christine*).

### The womb-tomb

Two things unspoken in Western culture are: death, or the silence beyond the grave, and birth, or the pain of tearing open one for another. That irreversible expulsion from our first place of plentitude is the model of all loss that we find in our second, longer life. In that first home we grew many times bigger, so great was the womb; in the final enclosure we will dwindle to nothing, enveloped in cold. Haunted by this rhyme between the womb-tomb, our first and last homes, Carpenter's cinema obsesses with loss – constant and endless – and fantasises a comfort that can reach us, engulf us, from and to the beyond.

Noting the etymological relation between 'vulva' and 'valve', Carol J. Clover observes that female characters are typically figured in occult films as 'more open to the supernatural' (1992: 74). In *Prince of Darkness*, it is in and through a woman – as maternal womb, to be precise – that ultimate evil will be unleashed on the world. Of course, this finds more poetic expression through the myths of Eve and of Pandora. Eve opens her ears and then her mouth to the fruit of the Tree of Knowledge and, through her, Adam and all (hu)mankind must know evil and suffering; Pandora opens that infamous box and thereby allows all the evils to escape and to henceforth plague humanity, ending the golden age and bringing decay and disintegration. In other words, woman's perversion is her double openness – her curiosity and attraction to evil, and her ever-ready status as its conduit. Evil enters her and, through her, enters the world; easily seduced, she is the guilty womb that readily infects, for she is not only vulnerable to seduction but also proficient at it.

In *In the Mouth of Madness*, book editor Linda Styles (Julie Carmen) hires and then guides an insurance investigator, John Trent (Sam Neill), to search for a missing horror writer. Trent does not fare well for, finding the mouth to madness, he *enters* rather than seals it; from then on, he truly knows madness because he lacks the necessary distance between subject (investigator) and object (enigma), between detection and infection. Trapped in Hobb's End, a small town that is not even on the map, his (con)fusion in this un-represented – pre-symbolic – space binds him to the imaginary in both the ordinary sense of illusion and fantasy and the Lacanian use of the term to designate that kaleidoscope of images that precedes the subject's entry into language. Certainly, once in Hobb's End, the film abandons narrative logic in favour of fantastic spectacles that a tracking camera reveals (such as a naked man in chains behind the hotel reception counter) or ghouls and nightmarish apparitions that leap suddenly into view.

This descent into pre-symbolic or pre-Oedipal pandemonium is most anxiously articulated by Carpenter in *Christine*, his adaptation of Stephen King's novel of the same title. Arnie Cunningham (Keith Gordon), a teenage nerd, buys an old beat-up car and restores it with his college-fund savings; he names it 'Christine'. Protective and indignant, Christine takes the place of Arnie's uncaring mother, defending him from the school's bullies who make his life a constant misery. In this tale of love and metamorphosis, Christine erects Arnie's manhood as her transformation makes him feel masterful. He achieves a conventional masculinity he could only dream of before – his girlfriend is 'the most beautiful girl in the school', and he stands up to his father whilst putting his mother in her place. But even as he ascends to high-school cool, it is always Christine who provides Arnie with his deepest and most satisfying 'social' relationship. Soon he is investing all his erotic desire in the car. Arnie's devotion to Christine can be seen partially to conceal and partially to heal a past disappointment: in the place of his real-life phallic mother who is indifferent to his needs, he produces a surrogate – Christine – who is pro-active and self-sacrificing in his defence.[2] This pattern of masculine 'redress' takes us reasonably to Julia Kristeva's theory of abjection – the 'mourning for an "object" that has always already been lost' (1982: 15) – and to Freud's equally tragic view of an original bliss (during the infant's initial 'oneness' with the mother) and the subsequent loss and

The surrogate mother: chrome-bodied Christine as object of teenage devotion

forfeiture of that bliss (a necessary separation from her and a later psychic renunciation of her).

Kristeva characterises abjection as doubly constructed by desire for and fear of the maternal body, a '*land of oblivion* that is constantly remembered' and abjected in the subject (1982: 8, emphasis in original). Freud's (dangerously prescriptive) theory of normative development for the boy also posits repression of erotic desire for the mother as the resolution of his Oedipus Complex (jealousy and fear of his father); that is, the boy 'gives up' his mother as erotic love object in the hope that he will, in future, find someone similar to her with whom he will have the sexual and social privileges now enjoyed exclusively by his father (Freud 1983: 318–20; see also 1960: 22–36 ). Successful maturation from pre- to post-Oedipal conflict requires that the initial psychic fusion with (and subsequent desire for) the mother be replaced by a psychic separation from (and rejection of) her. In other words, effective masculine sovereignty is predicated on psychological matricide.

The horror in *Christine* is produced precisely in Arnie's less-than-successful masculine matricide for, although he achieves independence from his real-life mother and ascends to become a sexual subject with a girlfriend, Leigh (Alexandra Paul), he finds himself increasingly tied to Christine; in fact, as Christine is turned from wreck to vintage-collectible, Arnie's personality disappears, absorbed into the diffuse and unabated destructiveness of the monstrous-feminine.[3] The vengeance against the bullies is his violent fantasy, but horror is signified in the film when sovereignty is abandoned – his will is her will is his will.

If Satanic possession is once again gendered feminine, as Clover observes it typically is in the American horror genre (1992: 72), we also have, in *Christine*, the 'all-incorporating mother' (1992: 23) whose malevolence is represented less in her murderous revenges – there is, after all, pleasure in seeing the bullies receive their comeuppance – than in her double obliteration of boundary between mother and son: incest and feminisation, or the monstrous-feminine as vagina dentata and as (s)mother. With a history of devouring men who dare enter her (the auto-workers, her previous owners, the proprietor of the garage where she is parked, the school bullies), Christine transfigures Arnie from nervous underdog to foul-mouthed tough guy; but in his compulsion for her he finally descends into hysteria (from the Greek word *husterikos* which means 'a suffering in the womb') (Fischer 1993: 83 n.1).

In the end, Arnie dies while his buddy (Dennis (John Stockwell)) ascends to proper heterosexual coupledom with the right feminine target (Leigh). If horror theorist James Twitchell is correct, and horror films teach adolescents how they should behave,[4] then Carpenter's Christine leaves no room for doubt. The object (abject) lesson here – in a collapse and collaboration of metaphor and literalness – is that excessive mimesis or fusion with the mother will lead inevitably to the death of the subject. Outside morality and paternal law, the womb-tomb engulfs the lapsing subject until all boundaries are dissolved and he is no more.

*Rebirth*

Carpenter approaches death through bliss once again in *Vampires* but this time he is unequivocal that one is impossible without the other. Jack Crow (James Woods) leads a team of vampire slayers, men who are most alive when they are in confrontation with their adversaries – their only other 'activity' is post-work drunken dissipation with whores. Near the beginning of the film, after a successful daytime hunt, the men nuzzle into the sumptuous bosoms of a group of prostitutes in a motel party in a dusty nowhere, but their indulgence is cut short in a bloody revenge led by vampire master, Valek (Thomas Ian Griffith). The sight of sexualised femininity doubles as the site of spectacular monstrosity, and may be read in terms of Linda Williams' observations on the horror genre. In an essay on the female gaze in and at the horror film (by the film's female characters and its female audiences, respectively), Williams directs our attention to the affinity between the woman and the monster: she suggests that the woman 'recognises the sense in which [the monster's] freakishness is similar to her own difference' in patriarchal culture (1996: 21). In *Vampires* this identity of woman-and-monster is given full expression when, in the aftermath of the bloodthirsty massacre that left only two survivors – Crow and Tony Montoya (Daniel Baldwin) – it is vampire-bitten prostitute, Katrina (Sheryl Lee), who precipitates male victory because her mental synchronicity with the vampire master can reveal his location and lead them to his nest.

Significantly, before the dénouement about evil Fathers and their centuries of diabolical deceit in the Roman Catholic Church, something else happens: in his carelessness, Montoya allows Katrina to bite (infect) him, and he begins to fall in love with her. He eventually rejects all that he had been with his vampire-slayer brothers, opting instead to follow Katrina into the grave … and out of it again. Every night, theirs is love without end, because what he had sought lifelong to destroy and what he loves more than life itself are, it turns out, *one and the same*. Katrina is the redemptive, restorative (m)other who, as Kristeva writes, 'shores up,

The protecting mother: Stevie Wayne, a local radio DJ, alerts the townspeople to impending danger in *The Fog*

in the individual, the fantasy of the loss in which he is engulfed or becomes inebriated' (1982: 20).

More endangered sons and evil fathers from the past emerge in *The Fog* but, here, a mother fights alone, and alone fights effectively to protect her son and her town. In the film's story about a sinister ghost-fog that invades a fishing town, Stevie Wayne (a woman bearing men's names) is a single mother who is mostly a 'disembodied voice' (typically a male privilege) from the radio station situated in the (phallic) lighthouse. Alongside these masculine signifiers, the film clearly provides us with a female body in casting Adrienne Barbeau as Stevie.[5] What obtains from this apparent antithesis of masculine and feminine?

During the evening festivities to celebrate Antonio Bay's 100th birthday, only Stevie, who is alone at the lighthouse radio-station, can see the totality of the glowing fog creeping in from the sea. She reports its movement along the coast, but when it heads inland she cries out to her young son over the radio: 'Andy, get out of the house! Run!' In what seems like a re-enactment of the protective mother whose voice is the first 'voice-off' (from beyond the infant's range of vision) that inserts 'otherness' into – and thereby ruptures – the child's blissful non-differentiation (Silverman 1988: 83), the film simultaneously offers a fantastic recovery, or a retroactive fantasy, of oneness-with-mother whose voice is also the 'sonorous envelope' of plenitude and bliss.[6] Indeed, Andy (Ty Mitchell) is retrieved from the claws of death because of his mother's broadcast appeal, 'my son is trapped by the fog!' However, in a disappointingly familiar move, Carpenter's flirtation with maternal authority is undermined when Andy's sanctuary is provided by none other than the film's representative heterosexual couple – the coast guard, Nick (Tom Atkins) and his girlfriend, Elizabeth (Jamie Lee Curtis) – while his mother publicly voices her regret: 'Andy ... I'm sorry that I didn't come for you, that I wasn't there. Andy, please understand, I have to stay here...'. Thus, the fog and its ghostly fathers succeed in separating mother from son. Nevertheless, kept on the edge of town, at the borders of consciousness, the mother remains the 'lookout' who provides, however marginally, the voice of interdiction: 'Something came out of the fog and tried to destroy us. In one moment it vanished, but ... it could come again. To the ships at sea who can hear my voice, look across the water, into the darkness; look for the fog.'

In fact, Carpenter frequently puts mothers in a wild zone between civilisation and the unknown. In addition to *Vampires* and *The Fog* discussed above, *Starman* and *Village of the Damned* also locate women – protective and procreative – on the cusp of chaos, or let them stand alone heroically between the men they love and the forces of evil that will destroy them. In *Starman*, near the film's beginning, the recently widowed Jenny Hayden (Karen Allen) is shown alone in her grief and despair in a house she had shared too briefly with her husband, Scott. In the night, an alien (Jeff Bridges) crashes his spacecraft and finds shelter in Jenny's house, taking the shape of the man – Scott – that is found preserved in her photo albums. As the film's story unfolds, it is Jenny's love for her dead husband, for ordinary life itself and, eventually, for the alien who comes to inhabit partial aspects of both, that ensures homosociality, for she protects not only the alien (from capture and murder by the FBI in the name of science) but also humankind (from intergalactic isolation). In a final scene that typically invites spectacular attention to 'the lift off' (the alien is reunited with his colleagues in their spaceship), Carpenter's camera focuses, instead, on Jenny: a close-up of her face fills the screen. However important the alien contact, however important her compassion for the alien (representative of

Mother-to-be Jenny is entrusted with the Starman's knowledge which will enable the salvation of humankind

humanity's triumph over the military and the entire superstructure of irresponsible government), what matters in the end is Jenny, and the half-alien child she carries inside her. The boy, we understand from his father, will grow up to be a teacher: thus, the *right* kind of compassionate male will return justice to an unbalanced world. The film's final long take on Jenny's upturned face suggests it is at least a bitter-sweet if not happy ending, one in which the womb matters most, even if the mother will be a 'single parent' like no other on earth.

This concern with the generative mother resurfaces most clearly in Carpenter's remake of *Village of the Damned*. Based on John Wyndham's novel, *The Midwich Cuckoos* (1957), Carpenter's film tells the story of a town in which the women are impregnated without consort during a mass blackout. Later, they give birth to identical, emotionless children who share one mind and one will; an alien race who will kill any human who hinders their taking over the Earth. Significantly, under Carpenter's direction, it is the fainting of the female protagonist, Jill (played by Linda Koslowski), that first causes our anxiety, whereas in Wolf Rilla's 1960 film version, it is the fainting of a man, Gordon (George Sanders), that initially signifies a supernatural disturbance. The leader of the alien children in Rilla's film is David (Martin Stephens), son of Gordon and Anthea (Barbara Shelley), and he is closer to his father than to his mother, who is afraid of the children. This film meticulously depicts the love between Gordon and his wife, and the developing bond between Gordon and his son, before the climax in which David and all his alien siblings are killed, together with Gordon who explodes a bomb in self-sacrifice. Though alone, Anthea survives – it was her husband's plan because he loved her so. In Carpenter's film, however, David (Thomas Dekker) is saved. It is a *mother*'s love – her hope, her belief in the uniqueness of her son – that delivers him from the bomb that kills his siblings.

Jill is the town's school principal who is widowed early in the narrative when her husband Frank (Michael Paré) is killed in a car crash at the initial moment of the blackout; afterwards, she is pregnant and gives birth to a son, David. The town doctor ('Doc', played by Christopher Reeve) and his wife Barbara (Karen Kahn) have a daughter, Mara (Lyndsey Haun), who turns out to be the leader of the alien children; Mara kills her mother by inciting her to suicide. One by one, the other parents are also murdered. Each child is partnered with another of the opposite sex who will be its reproductive mate. Doc tries, with encouragement from Jill, to teach the children 'humanity' (an ideal that the film naturalises), but Mara dismisses her father: 'You are a prisoner of your values.' The only child who seems different from the group – because he feels and desires – is Jill's son, David, who is single because his mate was stillborn. Because he is alone and lonely, David shows signs of sociability: at the cemetery where he searches unsuccessfully for the grave of his mate ('she was to be with me; we were to be together'), he recognises and responds to Doc's pain: 'You've lost someone too.'

In the film's climax, Jill saves David seconds before the bomb explodes. As they speed into the night, she hugs him and tells him, 'don't worry, David, we'll go some place where nobody knows who we are'. The camera pans to a sombre David, resting on his dark-eyed face, and the screen goes to black. Though the film's narrative open ending does not secure the future for David or Jill, Carpenter's *Village of the Damned* fantasises a reparation of masculine crisis through maternal authority: in this (re)imagined community, the mother is the boy's best support and his only chance.

Released sixteen years after David Cronenberg's *The Brood* (1979), Carpenter's *Village of the Damned* has an almost identical final scene, but the two films make contrasting arguments. In *The Brood*, a film in which a monstrous mother reproduces murderous children without male impregnation, the family – the idea and the ideal – is strongly indicted as a fantasy, a deception we play upon ourselves, and a site that breeds and conceals horrific relations. Tania Modleski cites *The Brood* as a contemporary horror film which is 'engaged in an unprecedented assault on all that bourgeois culture is supposed to cherish – like the ideological apparatuses of the family and the school' (1986: 158). In the final scene, Frank (Art Hindle) rescues his daughter Candy (Cindy Hinds), snatching her away from her mother and the murderous brood. Together they drive away to escape the horror, but we see in the passenger seat, in close-up, a tear-stained, almost comatose Candy who begins to have the same physical eruptions on her skin as her mother. Though Frank does not know it yet (does not know it *still*), rebuilding the family is not the end but the beginning of the nightmare. Carpenter's *Village of the Damned*, in contrast, fantasises a maternal authority that both protects and emancipates, just as a mother's faith and compassion defeats the military and government (*Starman*), and the avenging dead (*The Fog*). Insofar as 'femininity' and 'masculinity' are naturalised in the narratives and the spectacles rather than problematised as constructed, Carpenter's discontent with civilisation remains a masculinist dream for nurturing mothers and gentle-hearted muses, rather than a feminist scrutiny of patriarchy.

The credo that the feminine ideal is fully realised in she who propels men towards their manifest destiny – in *Village of the Damned*, *The Fog* and *Starman* – is restated in *Escape From L.A.* with an almost mathematical elegance in the character of Utopia, whose name signifies an age of heaven on Earth. Of course there is no heaven without excess (moderation being the ultimate antithesis of bliss), and since excess is prohibited in the repressive future, Utopia escapes – first into a virtual simulator after the suicide of her mother (who escaped, obviously, too) and then, with a top-secret defence weapon prototype, to the prison island of Los Angeles. This supplies the premise and necessity for Plissken's rescue attempt, but when Utopia sees his courage and capability displayed in the impossible-to-win basketball game (he wins), she changes her mind about the gang leader whom she had once loved. Back in civilisation, she is strapped to the electric chair. Utopia will survive only if the world turns away from its utter dependency on technology, yields to the primordial cycles of the sky, and allows night to return. Enter again, as if from the beginning of time, the Snake.

Masculinity is not 'always "about men"', as Eve Kosofsky Sedgwick has reminded us (1995: 12), but Carpenter's films invariably confess an anxiety that men are in constant danger – of being cut off/set adrift, of being tied/bound, of their inviolability threatened. Nostalgic for a humanity that precedes the social contract and exceeds its repressive discipline, Carpenter's cinema celebrates the subversion of patriarchy but, in the end, does not resist the age-old, misogynist question of how to build a man, rationally and efficiently, on a feminine foundation.

*Notes*

1  Interestingly, Heracles is known for having strangled two snakes while in his cradle. But Robert Graves suggests that this is based on a misreading of an icon which showed Heracles having his ears licked by serpents while he caressed them, which is what gave him his oracular powers (1990: 94).

2  E. Ann Kaplan identifies the dominant paradigms in fictional representation of the mother; she suggests that the 'evil "phallic" or witch mother [is] the underside of the self-sacrificing ideal mother' (1992: 13).

3  Barbara Creed (1993) has famously introduced this term to refer to more than simply a monster that is female rather than male. She illustrates that the woman-as-monster may take many forms, such as vampire, monstrous womb, *femme castratrice* or aged psychopath, but she is always defined in terms of sexuality, and she horrifies the audience in very different ways than does the conventional male monster because gender is crucial to the construction of her monstrosity.

4  James Twitchell concludes that horror films are 'dreadful pleasures' which respond mythically to pubescent angst – for example, by distinguishing socially correct from socially incorrect sexual behaviours: 'we need myths when we need information, and because we need information when we are confused, fantasy structures are given by a society as maps ... by which a lost audience can find its way' (1985: 87). See also his discussion of horror films as 'memory banks' of wisdom (1985: 88–104).

5  Barbeau was already known for her 'feminine curves' (cleavage and tight tops) in the American television sitcom, *Maude* (1972–78).

6  In *La voix, entre corps et langue*, Guy Rosolato theorises the mother's voice as our first model of auditory pleasure (music). See Silverman (1988: 84–6).

*References*

Clover, C. J. (1992) *Men, Women, and Chain Saws: Gender in the Modern Horror Film*. Princeton, NJ: Princeton University Press.

Creed, B. (1993) *The Monstrous-Feminine: Film, Feminism, Psychoanalysis*. London: Routledge.

Fischer, L. (1993) 'Mama's Boy: Filial Hysteria in *White Heat*', in S. Cohan and I. R. Hark (eds) *Screening the Male: Exploring Masculinities in Hollywood Cinema*. London: Routledge, 70–84.

Freud, S. (1960) 'The Ego and the Super-Ego (Ego Ideal)', in *The Ego and the Id*. Trans. Joan Riviere. London: W. W. Norton, 18–29.

_____ (1983) 'Dissolution of the Oedipus Complex', in *On Sexuality: Three Essays on the Theory of Sexuality, and Other Works, Vol. 7*. Trans. James Strachey. London: Penguin, 313–22.

Graves, R. (1990) *Greek Myths, 2*. London: Penguin.

Kaplan, E. A. (1992) *Motherhood and Representation: The Mother in Popular Culture and Melodrama*. London: Routledge.

Kristeva, J. (1982) *Powers of Horror: An Essay on Abjection*. Trans. Leon S. Roudiez. New York: Columbia University Press.

Modleski, T. (1986) 'Terror of Pleasure: The Contemporary Horror Film and Post-modern Theory', in T. Modleski (ed.) *Studies in Entertainment: Critical Approaches to Mass Culture*. Bloomington: Indiana University Press.

Sedgwick, E. K. (1995) 'Gosh, Boy George, You Must Be Awfully Secure in Your Masculinity!', in M. Berger, B. Wallis, S. Watson and C. M. Weems (eds) *Constructing Masculinity*. New York: Routledge, 11–20.

Silverman, K. (1988) *The Acoustic Mirror: The Female Voice in Psychoanalysis and Cinema*. Bloomington: Indiana University Press.

Twitchell, J. (1985) *Dreadful Pleasures: An Anatomy of Modern Horror*. New York: Oxford University Press.

Williams, L. (1996) 'When the Woman Looks', in B. K. Grant (ed.) *Dread of Difference: Gender and the Horror Film*. Austin: University of Texas Press, 15–34.

# CHAPTER ELEVEN

# 'Something Came Leaking Out': Carpenter's Unholy Abominations

## Anna Powell

This chapter explores three of John Carpenter's occult-themed films – *Christine* (1983), *Prince of Darkness* (1987) and *In the Mouth of Madness* (1995). It focuses on his presentation of the demonic in a contemporary secular context, and argues the irredeemable evil of his entities. This reading will be informed by Western occult traditions and their usage in the fantasy fiction of Stephen King and also H. P. Lovecraft who, it will be argued, is a seminal influence on Carpenter's metaphysics. The discussion will be situated within psychoanalytical, theological and social parameters.

The motiveless anti-human malice of Carpenter's demonic forces thrives within secular society. The films reveal the impotence of Enlightenment paradigms such as science, in *Prince of Darkness*, and clinical psychology, in *In the Mouth of Madness*. When confronted by primal evil, they are rendered unable either to explain or protect. By encouraging scepticism towards the supernatural, reason enables the irrational to flourish and psychoanalysis offers only the inadequate method of treating possession as psychosis. The Church's role is rendered anomalous in this secular milieu as its traditional ability to contain the diabolical was dependent on faith. In the age of reason, churches are depicted as separated from the everyday world. Their powerlessness is such that they actually form spawning grounds for malign entities.

Carpenter's supernatural beings are both alien and demon. Most predate Christianity and originate beyond this world, either in deep space or another dimension outside our perception. Nevertheless, they are driven to manifest themselves in everyday reality by their need to infect and subsume the human species, plunging society into violence and chaos. Carpenter's supernaturalism is marked by an insistence that mundane materiality is being undermined. Everyday objects such as cars and paperback books are imbued with a sinister intelligence mobilised through their use by susceptible humans. The more attention is focused on them, via the temptations of epistemophilia or materialistic consumption, the quicker they breed as their virus parasitises human psyches and bodies.[1]

The films generate tension and suspense as the nature of evil is concealed from us. Personal appearances by demons are kept to a minimum, apart from the entity which is the car Christine. They are glimpsed as tentacles, viscous slime, swirls of ectoplasm, reptiles and insects, and they manifest their power in multifarious ways: by generating darkness or light, invading the bodies or the minds of their hosts and shape-shifting. Their deceptions are aided by the creation of plausible simulacra (Baudrillard 1993: 50–3). No-one is immune from their influence. Female characters are more easily susceptible, but men are frequently chosen as their chief targets, seduced by knowledge, success and power. In the film *In the Mouth of Madness*, Sutter Cane (Jürgen Prochnow) owes his best-seller fame to them, and Christine turns a shy geek into a charismatic bad boy who scores with the high-school beauty. Their contemporary Faustian trajectory is fulfilled within the gratifications of consumer culture.

In his study of the historical origins of the 'weird tale', 'Supernatural Horror in Literature', H. P. Lovecraft contends that conventional religion focuses on the benevolent aspects of the unknown, so it has fallen to 'the darker and more malefi-

Despite appearing to be contained, primal evil is able to exert control over the investigating scientists in *Prince of Darkness*

cent side of cosmic mystery to figure chiefly in our popular supernatural folklore' (1985b: 425). Carpenter and Lovecraft have produced modern popular cultural versions of supernatural folklore, which seek to address the epistemology and metaphysics of evil.

*Lovecraft in Carpenter's Films*

Lovecraft's influence on Carpenter is profound, ranging from metaphysical perspective to character names. *The Thing* (1982), for example, references Lovecraft's 'At the Mountains of Madness', in which a team of Antarctic explorers encounter an unknown life-form, then mysteriously vanish; the title is echoed again in *In the Mouth of Madness*. Although Carpenter lacks Lovecraft's scorn for the evolutionary weakness of the human race, both share an apocalyptic vision and depict relentless persecution of humans by cosmic demons who plan to invade Earth. Lovecraft's short stories, published in the pulp fantasy magazine *Weird Tales* in the 1920s and 1930s, combine non-Euclidean physics, science fiction and the European occult tradition as adapted by the witchcraft of New England. Interestingly, Carpenter's film style also fulfils Lovecraft's criteria for successful horror fantasy, in which 'plot is everywhere negligible, and atmosphere reigns untrammelled' (1985b: 503). Narrative structure is secondary to the films' evocation of psychological states and atmosphere. Carpenter's cinematography notably uses the expressionistic devices of dynamic framing, darkness imbued by an unseen presence, monster's point-of-view shots and the fluid camera swoop of victim pursuit. His horror films, especially *Prince of Darkness*, also have the 'seriousness and portentousness' (1985b: 426) required by Lovecraft, depicting characters under metaphysical siege, or in a potential Armageddon.

Both Carpenter and Lovecraft situate the demonic within the mundane. Lovecraft advocated cutting out Gothic paraphernalia to locate the uncanny within contemporary American life. He compares himself to Nathaniel Hawthorne, in that both see 'a dismal throng of vague spectres behind the common phenomena of life' (1985b: 469) and he seeks verisimilitude by grounding his monsters in actuality, with recognisable geographical locations, historical characters and allusions to familiar events. Carpenter also situates primal evil within contemporary artefacts, such as computers and cars, whilst retaining traditional diabolism in the wake of *The Exorcist* (1973). As Robert C. Cumbow comments on Tom and Jerry's cartoon devil used in *Prince of Darkness*, the film 'mingles the ancient and the modern, the primordial with the futuristic, interlacing traditional mythic images with its contemporary story' (1990: 161). Behind such mixes of the numinous and the mundane lies a Platonic world of transcendent essences parallel to everyday appearance and, in 'The Unnameable', Lovecraft expresses a 'faith in the existence of spectral substances on the Earth apart from and subsequent to their material counterparts' (1970: 83).

Lovecraft incorporated the science of his day to enlarge the parameters of fantasy fiction. This led to a particular blend of science fiction and horror fantasy, also retained in Carpenter's films. Lovecraft aimed at 'the stimulation of wonder and fancy by such enlarged vistas and broken barriers as modern science has given us with its intra-atomic chemistry, advancing astrophysics, doctrines of relativity, and probings into biology and human thought' (1985b: 512). In common with Modernism, he recognised Relativity's radical fracture of anthropocentrism, already weakened by evolutionary theories and the decline of Christianity. He suggested that the magical and religious elements inherent in the human psyche had shifted focus, 'for though the area of the unknown has been steadily contracting for thousands of years, an infinite reservoir of mystery still engulfs most of the outer cosmos' (1985b: 425). He thus regarded science fiction as a fertile new field.

Sensory abjection is central to Lovecraft's monsters, such as 'The Unnameable', of which he writes 'it was everywhere – a gelatin – a slime ... it was the pit – the maelstrom – the ultimate abomination'. Sliminess is conveyed chiefly by visuals in Carpenter's work. He usually insists on the repellent abjection of demonic entities, which generates his most repulsive imagery, particularly in *Prince of Darkness*, with its ants, maggots, roaches and degenerate street-people. Maggots crawl in the beggar woman's cup and beetles first devour then reanimate their victim, Wyndham (Robert Grasmere). The schizos' possessed state is signified by a zombiedom not unlike the film's presentation of their customary condition.

In *Powers of Horror*, the French psychoanalytic and linguistic theorist Julia Kristeva investigates the nature of abjection. She suggests that Biblical identification of impurity attempts to fix it within the subjective and symbolic order, to prevent its actualisation as demonic evil. According to her, 'Biblical impurity is thus always already a *logicising* of what departs from the symbolic' (1982: 91). She also suggests that Christianity displaced evil to within the subject as sin. Christ, as both God and man, is heterogeneous, thus he is able to deal more effectively with human evil, and 'resorbs and cleanses the demoniacal' (1982: 122).

In the films considered here, Carpenter also depicts the resurgence of an age-old evil, biding its time until circumstances convene to awaken its slumbering power. Although the influence of Lovecraft can be mapped onto *Prince of Darkness* with its apocalyptic science fiction combined with traditional demonism, it is in *In the Mouth of Madness* that Lovecraft's occult mythos is overtly referenced.

### In the Mouth of Madness: Words of Power

*In the Mouth of Madness* follows John Trent (Sam Neill), an insurance investigator on the case of Sutter Cane, an absconded novelist who has left his last novel unfinished. Trent becomes increasingly absorbed in Cane's pulp horror stories, which give him nightmares. He cuts and pastes their covers to discover a coded map of Hobb's End, the fictional setting of Cane's last novel. As he seeks Cane, Trent's sense of reality is dissolved and his sanity undermined by malevolent projections. In his review of the film Philip Kemp states that 'the ingenious twist in Carpenter's film is ... [a result of] the writings of someone like Lovecraft himself, whose imagination has created the requisite alternative reality, centring on the archetypal spooky New England village of Hobb's End' (1995: 53). Lovecraft's notion of the book that comes to life is literalised by Carpenter when the contents of the horror tales of the villainous writer manifest themselves both as simulacra and as empirical reality. In this case, pulp fiction functions as a grimoire to awaken and invoke demonic forces. Central to systems of ceremonial occultism, a grimoire was a handbook for sorcerers, and included details about infernal spirits and rituals for summoning and banishing. Lovecraft's work evinces a degree of familiarity with Western occult history, and he references Renaissance 'magicians' and seers John Dee, Robert Fludd and Nostradamus. In his story 'The Book', he recollects reading something 'in furtive paragraphs of mixed abhorrence and fascination penned by those strange ancient delvers into the universe's guarded secrets whose decaying texts I loved to absorb' (1985a: 414).

Among Lovecraft's fictional grimoires is, most famously, the *Necronomicon* by the 'mad Arab, Abdul Alhazrad' for which he provides a history and chronology.[2] Unlike modern magic, which aims to effect change in accordance with the magician's will, this book's rituals are solely designed to summon the demonic Old Ones. The *Necronomicon* is referred to as an 'accursed' book because its use causes insanity and could destroy humanity. To Lovecraft, a grimoire is 'a key – a guide – to certain gateways and transitions' (ibid.), and Cane's novels also act as a literal gate via which abominations are manifest as he gradually replaces normality with a diabolical version of reality, playing mind games and driving the population insane to facilitate the victory of the Old Ones. In a climactic scene in Carpenter's film which foregrounds the novels' role as grimoires, Cane mockingly pronounces that his books are more popular than the Bible. Handing Trent the completed manuscript which finalises the end of humanity, the novelist as First Cause undermines Trent's claims of autonomy by announcing, 'you are what I write', whilst Trent persists in affirming, 'I know what I am ... I am not a piece of fiction.' Cane stands before a wooden door that glistens and drips with bloody slime, and bends in a way reminiscent of the door in *The Haunting* (1963), an earlier filmic depiction of a demonic presence barely restrained.

Cane's face becomes paper, which he proceeds to tear apart, leaving the torn pages of a book to form a hole in space, which is also a doorway. As Trent peers into this abyss, Linda (Julie Carmen), apparently Cane's editor but actually another puppet from his fiction, opens the manuscript and summons the demons from deep space by the words of power. The book from which Linda reads describes Trent's actions as he performs them and the monsters are invoked: 'Trent's eyes refused to close ... as in the same second he saw them, spill and tumble upward out of an enormous carrion-black pit, choked with the gleaming white bones of countless unhallowed centuries.' The style here is deliberately Lovecraftian, and the scene acknowledges an indebtedness to his vision of ultimate horror.

Cane's book is typically Gothic in its euphemistic elision of monstrous details. It describes 'hideous, unholy abominations' and 'the army of unspeakable figures twilit by the glow from the bottomless pit'. Precision would be superfluous here and might detract from Carpenter's own visualisation of the entities. We have already been prepared for them by Cane's book covers, the painting in the Pickman Hotel and Mrs Pickman's (Frances Bay) briefly-glimpsed companion. Elsewhere, we see their shadows and writhing tentacles. Even when these demons are manifest, Carpenter avoids overstatement. Amid disorientating flashes, we glimpse amorphous, repellently fleshy, slimy creatures; tentacled, heavy and with crushing feet. Back in a motel room, in a 'reality' which is becoming increasingly tenuous, Trent grimaces as he watches a clip on television from the low-budget science fiction movie *Robot Monster* (1953), in which a space-creature carries off a woman. We suspect that the monstrous entities we have seen were subject to the limitations of yet another fiction. Their true likeness may be beyond the powers of both representation and perception.

Existing in a dimension beyond human sensory grasp, Lovecraft's entities, the Great Old Ones, are more fearsome and dangerous than the Earth-bound vampire or ghost. His mythos recounts that prior to human evolution, the Great Old Ones came here from deep space to rule. They were essentially demonic beings, and when humankind developed, it was forced to worship them. Subsequently, the Old Ones lapsed in their rule and either slumbered in the Earth's remote places or vanished into other dimensions of space and time. Small enclaves of regressive human beings remained dedicated to them, practising abominable rites as found in books like the *Necronomicon*, in order to facilitate their reinheritance of Earth. Lovecraft's tales modify historical accounts of occult practices by suggesting that the Black Arts are also focused to this end.[3]

In Lovecraft's story 'The Haunter of the Dark', in Cane's novel and in Carpenter's film, the locale for rites to conjure up the Old Ones is a desecrated church.[4] At the centre of Hobb's End, the focal point of Cane's evil projections is an abandoned church, traditionally a favourite site for Satanic inversions of sanctity. The first shot in which the church is seen is from the Pickman Hotel and it has the appearance of a matte; in the next scene architectural details such as Byzantian domes and Eastern Orthodox iconic mosaics are highlighted by Trent as he reads from the novel. Viewer control is undermined by temporal and spatial disorientation, with a shot of Trent and Linda standing before a mosaic of Satan's fall being immediately followed by a long shot of the townsfolks' cars driving towards the building. Such jump cuts serve to emphasise the church as an image projected by Cane. Later, while Trent sleeps, Linda enters the dimly-lit church alone, where she sees an inverted crucifix, and upon touching the walls feels a sticky substance evocative of the 'black ichor' trail of Lovecraft's monster. Throughout, the characteristic Carpenter prowling camera suggests that Linda is being followed and watched. The inversion of Christian symbolism continues with Cane housed in the vestry, clad in a black, cowl-neck sweater and using the diabolical typewriter to produce the 'New Bible'. In this space, the gelatinous, pulsating door holds back the demons until he has written their advent. As Linda embraces him, Cane's monstrous identity as 'One of Them' is revealed, suggesting that he may also be a simulacrum or a human body impregnated and possessed by an entity.

Again, Carpenter's antecedents are overt. In 'The Haunter of the Dark', the writer of horror stories Robert Blake discovers a horror beyond any priestly powers of exorcism lurking in the abandoned Gothic church on Federal Hill. He learns that the church has been the headquarters of a bizarre ritual cult, and that its steeple is the lair of an amorphous monster confined only by daylight. In this story, the entity from space had formerly been summoned by an apostate minister and reawakened when a naïve protagonist stumbled upon the design of powers that exist beyond time and space. *In the Mouth of Madness* stresses the extra-terrestrial origins of the horror. In contrast, *Prince of Darkness*, an earlier film by Carpenter, depicts the occult but also suggests how far from traditional occultism such entities are. This disparity is highlighted by a dialogue between the Catholic Church and the New Physics, neither of which is able to contain a power which is beyond their scope.

*Prince of Darkness: Antichrist and Anti-Matter*

In *Prince of Darkness*, Carpenter investigates the interrelated contemporary paradigms of science and religion as they attempt to analyse and control diabolical powers. Cumbow has noted the film's plethora of references from the horror and science fiction genres, in particular the British film *Quatermass and the Pit* (1967), directed by Roy Ward Baker,[5] and Carpenter's own earlier usage of 'the extraterrestrial as a metaphor for the demonic' in *The Thing* (1990: 153). The film combines scientific technology with Biblical abominations and Gothic demons, and ultimately implies the unregenerate nature of occult forces, which elude and exceed human attempts at control.

In his essay on the film, Bryan Dietrich asserts that *Prince of Darkness* exceeds its slasher trappings and presents 'a direct metaphor for the paradigm shift' (1991: 92) affected by quantum theory's engagement with metaphysics as it investigates, like religion, the nature of the First Cause.[6] Further concepts advocated by the New Science are chaos theory, Heisenberg's uncertainty principle and the inseparability of observer and observed. Within this context, Dietrich argues that Carpenter breaks the mad scientist mould and casts Faust in the role of redeemer. Professor Birack (Victor Wong) engages in metaphysics, teaching his graduate students to question traditional concepts of time, matter and perception and to 'say goodbye to classical reality, because our logic collapses on the subatomic level into ghosts and shadows … [and] while order does exist in the universe, it is not at all what we had in mind'.[7] Intrigued by the unknown phenomena in the crypt of a decaying Catholic mission, he assembles a research team of physicists, biochemists, engineers and cryptanalysts in order to examine an occult entity traditionally falling under the Church's jurisdiction. The failure of a secret Catholic sect, the Brotherhood of Sleep, to restrain this being leads to the priest's appeal to the Doppler Institute to save humankind from a Satanic Armageddon.[8] This indicates that science has entered and colonised areas of knowledge previously the realm of theologians. The priest is forced to acknowledge the superior knowledge afforded by the scientific model. 'He lives', says the priest, 'in the atom. He lives in all things … no prison can hold him now.' From the appearance of a new supernova to the unnatural swarming of insects, the entity's power operates on particles, changing their laws on a macrocosmic as well as a microcosmic level, thus usurping and perverting the traditional prerogative of God the creator.

Ultimately, however, science also proves unable to contain this excessive force, and Christian teachings apparently resurface in the self-sacrifice of Catherine (Lisa

Blount), who, while the priest suffers a breakdown, goes through the mirror to prevent the entity from bringing about the Apocalypse. However, the efforts of both the Church and science, seduced by their own epistemological hunger, the Original Sin,[9] have been directed towards investigating an entity which has already incorporated this very process within its purposes.

The process of detection gradually uncovers details of the entity's history and identity. Inferential sources are the diary of the last Brother of Sleep; the ancient text in the shrine; the messages sent out by the demon itself; and the communal dreams/visions from the future. The Vatican kept the existence of the Brotherhood of Sleep secret. It was their duty to guard a container buried aeons ago in the Middle East by Satan's father, 'a god who once walked the Earth before man, but was somehow banished to "the dark side"'. Carpenter's screenplay contends that Jesus was an alien sent to warn humankind, but that the canister was kept hidden until the advent of a science 'sophisticated enough to prove what Christ was saying'.

Indeed, Birack supplements the Church's interpretation by suggesting the possible equation of evil with anti-matter:

Suppose there is a universal mind controlling everything, a god willing the behaviour of every subatomic particle. Now every particle has an anti-particle, its mirror image, its negative side. Maybe this universal mind resides in the mirror image instead of in our universe as we have wanted to believe. Maybe he's Anti-God, bringing darkness instead of light.

To the sometimes-elided Biblical concepts of Antichrist and Satan, Birack adds an originary antithesis to God the Father, mistakenly presented by theology as omnipotent and autonomous. This Anti-God is not reliant on the canister to gain a foothold in the human world, and has greater powers than the Christian Devil, being ultimately part of the Divine plan. The canister contains a manifestation of his emissary, a demonic antichrist who heralds the advent of the Prince of Darkness.

Given that the entity is limited in scope, it begins its work on the world of humans by influencing and physically possessing those who venture near it, initially entering the street schizos who are already susceptible due to their social and mental marginality. They are visually elided in a common abjection with cockroaches, beetles and maggots. The next victims in order of susceptibility are women scientists. Kelly (Susan Blanchard), the demon's chosen bride, develops a bruise on her arm which spreads and darkens into the occult symbol of a squared circle. This visible sign of abjection spreads to sores and pustules over her whole body as possession progresses, in a manner reminiscent of Regan's (Linda Blair) disfigurement in *The Exorcist*. Susan (Anne Marie Howard) is drawn to the vessel and is possessed by a squirt of its life-fluid which turns her into an automaton spreading contagion orally. Kristeva has identified Levitical taboos on bodily secretions, noting that 'any secretion or discharge, anything that leaks out of the feminine or masculine body defiles' (1982: 102). Cumbow references a relevant verse from the apocalyptic Book of Revelation: 'And the serpent vomited water from his mouth, like a river, after the woman' (1990: 155). The demon in *Prince of Darkness* secretes a green slime,

Susan is infected by a jet of fluid from the demonic entity in *Prince of Darkness*

which shoots upwards in defiance of the laws of gravity and impregnates Kelly. The abomination here is both biblical and sexual, and, as with *The Thing*, can be read as expressing contemporary AIDS anxieties. Demonic possession is spread like a communicable disease, via a fluid passed between bodies. Shock impact is compounded by a cluster of deviant practices which are suggestive of oral sex, female ejaculation and bisexual penetration.

Again tracing the literary antecedents for Carpenter's vision, we find in Lovecraft's story 'Dreams in the Witch House' (1968) a version of the traditional figure of witchcraft, the Black Man, who was supposedly either the Devil himself or his emissary, and who made pacts and had sexual congress with worshippers. This figure is Nyarlahotep, a messenger from the Other Gods who adopts the guise expected by the witch cult. He appeared as a man with jet black but Caucasian features, and was clad in the black robes of a cleric to disguise his true abhorrent form. Carpenter's usage of such Satanic imagery suggests the survival of traditional occult symbols as resonant signifiers of evil. Ironically, however, when this figure finally reveals itself, it has taken the shadow shape of Catherine, the heroine.

### Christine: The Mean Machine

Four years before making *Prince of Darkness*, Carpenter directed *Christine*, based on the novel of the same name by Stephen King, another writer who has influenced Carpenter's work. The uncharacteristically linear cause and effect structure of the film's plot is a drastic reduction of King's prose. Bill Phillips's screenplay compresses a five hundred-page novel, and thereby cuts several supernatural events, speculation on Christine's nature, the ghosts or zombies of victims, and the car's evil smell. It affords a more conventional perspective for audience empowerment, with dramatic irony paramount as we watch the driverless car perpetrate crimes which baffle other characters. Despite such anomalies, and its predominant tone of black humour, the film still presents a substantive occult diegesis.

King foregrounds the car's ability to move back in time by the mileometer's reverse action, thus providing a technical rationale for its regenerative capacity. This also allows for an elaboration of the theme of the 'eternal' glamour of the 1950s in American culture. In the present, Christine conjures up a vision of 1958 for Dennis, 'as if Libertyville of the late 1970s had been drawn on Saran Wrap and laid over a time that was somehow more real, and I could feel that time reaching its dead hands out toward us, trying to catch us and draw us in for ever' (King 1983: 401). Carpenter's version conveys the era's mystique chiefly by the car's design, the music and Arnie's (Keith Gordon) espousal of sideburns and a black leather waistcoat. These serve to depict the car as 'a vampiric exploiter' (Cumbow 1990: 130) who represents the haunting of one era by another. As well as being an autonomously baleful being, Christine is also a desirable consumer item as an idealised emblem of American masculinity from a time of economic boom.

The design of many 1950s American cars incorporated animal and bird references, for example in the Pontiac Firebird and Ford Mustang. Exaggerated tail fins connote a fish, a bird or a bat.[10] This may be interpreted as a kind of Shamanic fantasy of shape-shifting and metamorphosis which conveys extra-human power to the driver as well as adding the qualities of the animal to the machine. The car afforded a fetish object of particular potency for the teenager in the 1950s, as evinced in the James Dean/*Rebel Without a Cause* (1955) phenomenon and the cult of teenage car and death songs quoted as chapter headings in King's novel. As well as being an enviable fashion item the car was valued as a means of freedom from parental jurisdiction, affording speed and danger, and a private space for intimacy and sex.

Originally fetishised by designer, advertiser and customer, the car became invested with the extraneous power of the owner's object cathexis. Gratifying the driver's desires, it was in turn lavished with worshipful attention. King exaggerates this pre-existing cultural and psychic process of mutual exchange and adds magical dimensions to Roland Le Bay's (Roberts Blossom) agreement with Christine. Le Bay, wishing to pass on his mantle of power to a younger apprentice magician, advises Arnie: 'all you got to do is go on believing in her and she'll take care of you', suggesting the contract of magician and demonic servitor. This pact, like that of Faustus and Mephistopheles, turns out to be deceptive and Arnie's soul is forfeit as payment for services rendered. The fledgling magician is unable to control the forces he is initially glad to invoke.

The influential Magus, Aleister Crowley, defines Magick as 'the science and art of causing change to occur in conformity with Will' (1976: xii). Self-fulfilment is the ultimate goal here, provided that the magician develops the Higher Self and True Will through rigorous spiritual training. Those who interfere with the fulfilment of True Will risk destruction. In occult terms, Arnie uses Christine as his magical weapon.[11] The blood sacrifice used to summon and appease demons is also provided by her. She enacts the vengeance which Arnie desires, but dares not perpetrate, and exonerates him from blame.

King suggests that Christine may be autonomously evil, or that the 'changeling', Le Bay, may have impregnated her material fabric by the force of his sadistic paranoia. As well as possessing the car, the sinister old man gains possession of the body and personality of Arnie, so that the youth's signature changes and he uncharacteristically adopts Le Bay's favourite term of abuse, calling his enemies 'shitters'. He becomes aggressive, lecherous, attacks his parents, and plans to drop out of school to go on the road with Christine, in the teenage rebel tradition. For Carpenter, Le Bay is relatively marginal. The camera shoots Christine as a diabolical presence from the start as we share the wing mirror's point-of-view of a potential victim on the assembly line in Detroit. She motivelessly crashes the bonnet on the mechanic's hand, then kills a supervisor who drops cigarette ash on her blood-red upholstery. As her theme tune tells us, she is inherently 'Bad to the Bone'.

King's novel focuses on character psychology under stress. Dennis and Leigh, our 'normal' perspective on events, struggle to retain their sanity under supernatural onslaught. Dreams of a Jungian rather than Freudian type are featured. Dennis significantly envisions Christine as a demonic archetype:

> she was ancient, a terrible hulk of a car, something you would expect to see in a Tarot deck: instead of the hanged man, the Death Car. Something you could almost believe was as old as the pyramids ... [and] as I raised my hands in a stupid, useless, warding off gesture, I thought *God, its unending fury*! (1983: 81)

Such dreams afford occult insight, as they do in other films by Carpenter, but are omitted here to preserve the predominantly realist tone.

The car becomes a haunted prison, with an intermittent smell which 'came and went like the "mouldering stench" in a Gothic Horror story' (1983: 266). This olfactory quality is difficult to convey on film, as is the tactility described by Dennis: 'the door handle didn't feel like chromed steel; dear Christ, it felt like skin' (1983: 399). Also limited by cinematic representation is King's metamorphosis of car into monster through simile and metaphor. Her uncanny shape-shifting capacity, with dashboard instruments becoming eyes before Leigh is choked, assaults Dennis's reason as he wonders: 'What was it? Some sort of *Afreet*? An ordinary car that had, somehow become the dangerous, stinking dwelling-place of a demon?' (ibid.). Carpenter instead uses reverse time effects to melt, extend and weld the car's body and conveys an impossible fluidity to the fixed properties of metal as the car magically regenerates.

Carpenter foregrounds Christine's gender, although King had also stressed Le Bay's masculine agency. In the novel, even the well-balanced Dennis honours the patriarchal magic of gendering vehicles female, and he asserts that 'its from your father that you get the magic, the talismans, the words of power. If the car won't start, curse it ... and be sure you curse it female' (1983: 35). The eroticism of Arnie's relations with Christine is overt. Arnie's girlfriend, herself a gift from Christine, feels as though he and his car were 'welded together in a disturbing parody of the act of love' (1983: 189).

Carpenter's version continues this theme as Leigh jealously complains that Arnie spends most of his time with Christine. A bizarre affirmation of sexuality occurs in the scene when Arnie wants Christine to fix herself and he invites her to 'show me'. To the accompaniment of the strip-club tune 'Harlem Nocturne', he watches her perform the regeneration as though it were, in both senses, an auto-erotic act. King describes Christine as a 'terrible female force' (1983: 410) and compares her to 'an insanely angry, murderous woman' (1983: 231).

Cumbow also asserts that the film's key image is the Plymouth's grille, 'a cryptic *vagina dentata*' (1990: 131) with its V for victory sign connoting the female genitalia. Significantly, this grille is used to kill her enemies by crushing. Although she finally demands monogamous devotion, initially she gives Arnie the Faustian gift of sexual charisma but, like Mephistopheles, exacts a dreadful price, draining psychic energy and alienating family, friend and lover.

Christine's diabolic power in Carpenter's film is conveyed by both the soundtrack's culturally-charged music of teen rebellion and by visual car-worship through cinematography. As well as using subjective camera-work for Christine's point-of-view, Carpenter fetishises the car's design with slow, lingering shots of her gleaming chrome and flamboyant tail fins. He emphasises the car as an American emblem of Eros but also of Thanatos. The Hellish symbols of fire and smoke are effectively deployed when she catches fire and chases Buddy Repperton (William Ostrander) in the form of an infernal fireball. Her charred and blackened shell, wreathed in smoke, still drives with consummate dignity into her lair at Darnell's (Robert Prosky) garage, and convinces us that she is much more than a car.

Christine, the 'terrible female force', crushes another adversary

The films *In the Mouth of Madness*, *Prince of Darkness* and *Christine* underline Carpenter's pessimism and the inability of the heroes to tackle occult forces. Each initially appears to offer a happy ending in which the demon has been exorcised or the heroes escape. This is immediately undercut by an ironic coda which implies that the evil is still alive, will return or has ultimately triumphed. The conventional relief of closure erodes into unease as viewer satisfaction is withheld. All Carpenter's monstrous entities appear capable of self-regeneration and continued onslaught on humanity, attacking both societal and subjective defences.

*In the Mouth of Madness* shows Trent's escape from the unguarded asylum after a night of chaos. Trent's optimism is deflated by the desolate scene outside, as a radio news broadcast describes an alien attack and the spreading epidemic of insanity. In a self-reflexive final scene, he enters a cinema playing *In the Mouth of Madness*, directed by John Carpenter. We watch both Trent watching a replay of his experiences and a replay of the film we have been watching. Our sense of reality is further dislocated as spectatorial omnipotence dissolves. On realising the totality of Cane's diabolical triumph over his personal subjectivity and over humanity, Trent's manic laughter turns into a yell of horror as the titles come up. Fictionality and reality have been radically undermined for him and, with the Abominations beginning their reinheritance of Earth, the one remaining human with whom we identify is devastated by a bitter mockery of his illusions of reality.

*Prince of Darkness* has a similarly disconcerting ending as a satisfying narrative closure is withheld. After the apparent defeat of the Anti-God by Catherine's sacrifice, the priest is hospitalised due to a nervous breakdown and the street psychos shamble off to resume their disempowered roles. Exhausted by trauma and grief, Brian (Jameson Parker) sleeps. We see again the fuzzy video signals of the earlier dreams, with their tracking shot past the front of St. Godard's to the portals where a shadowy figure awaits. As it moves towards the camera, we recognise the shape, then the features, of Catherine. Brian wakes to see a hideous face on the pillow next to him, but it proves hallucinatory as he wakes for a second time. The inference here seems to be that Catherine has taken up Kelly's former role as Satan's Bride. Stumbling to the bathroom, Brian looks at his own face in the mirror, in a shot reminiscent of Calder's (Jessie Lawrence Ferguson) horrified fascination with the mirror after his impregnation. A shot of Brian from the front cuts to another from the side. Thus, he reaches out to us, as the screen becomes the mirror with the audience on the other side. Cumbow recounts how Brian's hand 'reaches out toward its own reflection … if it *is* a reflection … and just before flesh contacts screen, just before fingertips touch anti-fingertips, Carpenter cuts away … to darkness' (1990: 171). Brian may be impelled to bring back Satan's father himself, in an attempt to rescue his lover. Evil has hence proved indestructible, and this ending mocks the apparent triumph of redemption as Catherine might herself prove to be the avatar of evil.

King's novel of *Christine* ends with Dennis discovering the car's possible regeneration and attendant revenge. The final sequence of the film, however, is a darkly comic vision of the heroes standing by Christine's graveside. On hearing a demolition worker's radio playing the 1950s number 'Come On, Let's Go', Leigh comments that she hates rock 'n' roll. The camera then moves to a close-up of the cube of crushed metal that Christine has become, and we see a couple of rods begin to stir and writhe like organic matter. At that point, the car's theme tune 'Bad to the Bone' swells to accompany the end titles. Carpenter presents the car's defeat as merely a temporary setback for the indwelling force, which is already regenerating.

Clearly, the commercial horror film enables sequels, as with the *Halloween* series. Despite these commercial demands of the industry and the considerable use of ironic self-reflexivity in Carpenter's work, the ambiguous, downbeat endings of the films discussed here indicates a mood of unremitting pessimism when confronted with malign forces which exceed our understanding. The apocalyptic themes of *Prince of Darkness* and *In the Mouth of Madness* suggest that the evolutionary development of humanity has stagnated and that the time is ripe for takeover by entities from the Hell of religion or the deep space of science fiction. Whatever their origin and form, Carpenter's demons afford a potent fantasy of unrecuperable evil and the actuality of the occult.

*Notes*

1   This process recalls the 'replicator power' of the viral meme posited by genetic biologist Richard Dawkins. According to him, memes are self-replicating ideas which 'propagate themselves from brain to brain, from brain to book … as they propagate they can change – mutate' and thus influence cultural evolution (1986: 158).
2   For a collection of essays on this fictional book see Hay (1978).
3   For a history of occult practices see Guiley (1989).
4   Although ancient Indian stones on lonely hilltops are also used for seasonal rituals on May Eve and Halloween in Lovecraft's tales.
5   Roy Ward Baker's Hammer film, *Quatermass and the Pit*, is set in a tube station called Hobbs End. Hobb is a folk-euphemism for the Devil.
6   Popularised by such books as Pirsig (1974), Zukan (1979) and Capra (1984).
7   Birack's name recalls that of Dirac, the physicist who predicted the existence of anti-matter.
8   The name of the Institute underlines the theme of the evil double.
9   Adam was tempted by Eve to eat of the fruit of the tree of knowledge of good and evil, which made them feel as though they were like God.
10  Given supreme fantasy apotheosis in the Batmobile.
11  Cf. Kenneth Anger's use of the Hell's Angels' motorbikes in *Scorpio Rising* (1963) and the 'dream buggy' in *Kustom Kar Kommandos* (1965) as examples of vehicles as magical weapons. Anger is a follower of Crowley's occult system.

*References*

Baudrillard, J. (1993) *Symbolic Exchange and Death*. London: Sage.
Capra, F. (1984) *The Tao of Physics: An Exploration of the Parallels Between Modern*

*Physics and Eastern Mysticism*. New York: Bantam.

Crowley, A. (1976) *Magick in Theory and Practice*. New York: Dover.

Cumbow, R. C. (1990) *Order in the Universe: The Films of John Carpenter*. Metuchen, NJ: Scarecrow Press.

Dawkins, R. (1986) *The Blind Watchmaker*. Harlow: Longman.

Dietrich, B. (1991) '*Prince of Darkness*, Prince of Light: From Faust to Physicist', *Journal of Popular Film and Television*, 19, 2, 91–6.

Guiley, R. E. (1989) *The Encyclopedia of Witches and Witchcraft*. New York and Oxford: Facts on File.

Hay, G. (ed.) (1978) *The Necronomicon*. London: Skoob.

Kemp, P. (1995) '*In the Mouth of Madness*', *Sight and Sound*, 5, 8, 52–3.

King, S. (1983) *Christine*. London: Book Club Associates.

Kristeva, J. (1982) *Powers of Horror: An Essay on Abjection*. Trans. Leon S. Roudiez. New York: Columbia University Press.

Lovecraft, H. P. (1968) 'Dreams in the Witch House', in *At the Mountains of Madness and other Tales of Terror*. St. Albans: Panther, 143–8.

____ (1970) 'The Unnameable', in *The Lurking Fear and Other Stories*. London: Panther, 82–8.

____ (1985a) 'The Book', in *H. P. Lovecraft Omnibus 2: Dagon and other Macabre Tales*. London: Panther.

____ (1985b) 'Supernatural Horror in Literature', in *H. P. Lovecraft Omnibus 2: Dagon and other Macabre Tales*. London: Panther, 423–512.

Pirsig, R. M. (1974) *Zen and the Art of Motorcycle Maintenance: An Enquiry into Values*. New York: Bantam.

Zukan, G. (1979) *An Overview of the New Physics*. New York: Bantam.

# CHAPTER TWELVE

# Revisionings: Repetition as Creative Nostalgia in the Films of John Carpenter

## Raiford Guins and Omayra Zaragoza Cruz

I must stop. I must will myself an end of this joy.
— John Carpenter (1996: 53)

Mass culture. By this term, we loosely designate media forms geared towards mass consumption and the ways in which such commodities impact other spheres of cultural production. One of the most long-standing and powerful critiques of mass culture has been voiced by Max Horkheimer and Theodor Adorno in 'The Culture Industry: Enlightenment as Mass Deception' (1993: 120–67).[1] For Horkeimer and Adorno, mass entertainment, a 'machine [that] rotates on the same spot' (1993: 134), churns out a predictable series of oppressively unoriginal dross, of which 'every detail is so firmly stamped with sameness that nothing can appear that is not marked at birth, or does not meet with approval at first sight' (1993: 128). Cutting to the point, one may safely grant that Horkheimer and Adorno have serious misgivings about mass culture because it is repetitive. American horror films in the 1990s pose no exception.

Yet this is not a chapter dedicated to the ageing debates about mass versus modernist culture. Ours is a piece dedicated to the 1990s horror films of John Carpenter, and Carpenter positively revels in repetition. Remakes, adaptations and sequels, as well as recurring themes, images, sounds and actors firmly imprint his *oeuvre*. His is a repetition which aspires to disrupt the parameters of homogeneity. Specifically, repetition in Carpenter's films responds to emergent social trends, especially the state of the contemporary horror genre.

The film industry readily acknowledges this mass appeal of Carpenter's work. Unlike fellow genre director David Cronenberg whose films often play the independent/art-house circuit, Carpenter's films enjoy a general release. They play mall cinemas and multiplexes, as well as the remaining drive-ins scattered across the United States. This is not to imply that playing mall cinemas is in any way a distinguishing characteristic. After all, so do the other hundreds of films that make their way out of Hollywood. What does merit observation is that Carpenter uses his films to comment on mass culture in a very distinct, even personal manner. One need only think of the way in which popular fiction drives *In the Mouth of Madness* (1995) or a standard rock 'n' roll riff and 1950s automobile culture animates *Christine* (1983).

In this respect, it seems Carpenter would rank among the guiltiest of mass culture purveyors that Horkheimer and Adorno could have imagined. If it is the case that repetition is irremediable, then a discussion of Carpenter's films need go no further. Yet at another, more productive register is the possibility that it is just this repetitive quality of mass entertainment that bears consideration. To determine the function of likeness within the complex networks of repetition that course through Carpenter's films involves attention to the imaginative in homogeneity and the ways in which familiarity, or the recognition of yesterday's detail, becomes significant in its own right. To this end, we will review Carpenter's place within and practices of standard film industry repetition such as genre and the studio system. Such a review paves the way for the main purpose of this chapter: to track the ways in which Carpenter uses some of his later films to comment on his own position as filmmaker and film lover.

*Placing Carpenter/Practising Repetition*

Carpenter's films express close ties to the cycle-based film production of the classical Hollywood studio system. He has explicitly expressed an affiliation to the perceived measure of control which the studio system allowed certain filmmakers. For example, Howard Hawks and Alfred Hitchcock made personal films within a commercial context (McCarthy 1980: 18). As such, Carpenter's ideal self-image conjures a nostalgic view of the director and resembles a Hollywood from the past. In other words, Carpenter identifies with strong genre directors. We would not go so far as to support Kent Jones' bold assertion that 'Carpenter stands completely and utterly alone as the last genre filmmaker in America' (1999: 26). However, we do agree that Carpenter does participate in the conventions of genre, a decision that goes against contemporary Hollywood's tendency to target youth audiences, a tactic meant to maximise profit potential through the meta-generic.

Generic expressions of repetition fuel Carpenter's auteuristic litany, and surround his cinematic universe. Of all forms of repetition present within Carpenter's *oeuvre*, the remake stands out as most conspicuous. For example, Carpenter has

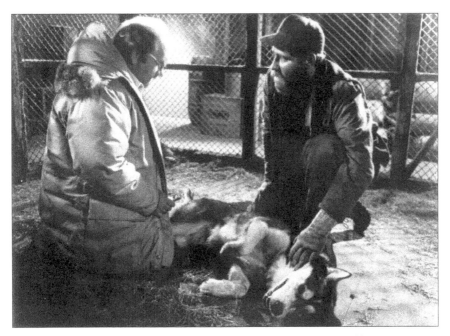

The amorphous Thing lurks unseen in Carpenter's reworking of Hawks's classic 1950s sci-fi horror

drawn inspiration from classic sci-fi horror films: *The Thing* (aka *The Thing From Another World*, 1951), *The Invisible Man* (1933) and *Village of the Damned* (1960). According to Andrew Horton and Stuart Y. McDougal, the remake occupies an anxious space 'between unabashed larceny and subtle originality' (1998: 4). Carpenter's *The Thing* (1982), made thirty years after Hawks's filmic adaptation of John W. Campbell, Jr's short story 'Who Goes There?', operates within these two poles. As a remake, Carpenter's *The Thing* also endeavours to makeover genre expectations, particularly secure conventions of the horror film. Like the amorphous lifeform terrorising the Antarctic research team, the remake can absorb, copy, but also re-work and create. Transformations and re-creations in *The Thing* are so abundant in terms of special effects and generic codes, that one can empathise with the spirited self-realisation: 'You've got to be fucking kidding!'

Sequels are a second form of repetition readily associated with Carpenter. Following the unexpected success of *Halloween* (1978) were, understandably, *Halloween II* (1981), *Halloween III: Season of the Witch* (1982), *Halloween 4: The Return of Michael Myers* (1988), *Halloween 5: The Revenge of Michael Myers* (1989), *Halloween: The Curse of Michael Myers* (1995) and *Halloween H20: 20 Years Later* (1998). The series appears to have culminated with *Halloween: Resurrection* (2002). Although not given directorial responsibilities on any of the sequels, Carpenter was associated with screenplays, musical score and executive production. The 1990s did, however, witness a genuine sequel by Carpenter: *Escape From L.A.* (1996). Much like an old television serial, Snake Plissken (Kurt Russell) finds himself *once again* facing entrapment in a futuristic prison much like the one he escaped from in the earlier film, *Escape From New York* (1981). The coasts may be different, yet Snake remains the same: he and his appearance are described as 'retro', an anachronistic reversion to the days before political correctness.

Finally, Carpenter's films are not merely influential, they are responsible for igniting sub-genres. Within horror, one must take note of Carpenter's impact on the slasher film. Shortly after *Halloween*'s 1978 debut came *Friday the 13th* (1980) (and its hordes of sequels), *Prom Night* (1979), *Terror Train* (1979), *My Bloody Valentine* (1980), *Night School* (1980), *The Burning* (1980), *Graduation Day* (1980), *Happy Birthday to Me* (1980) and *Hell Night* (1980). And in a slightly different register, *Escape From New York* (in particular the film's setting and character Snake Plissken) has served as a significant model for Italian productions such as *1990: The Bronx Warrior* (1982) and *2019: After the Fall of New York* (1983). Where amidst all of this repetition might one locate Carpenter?

The repetition outlined thus far is obvious: a catalogue of brief descriptions based on filmic observations. To approach the aims of this chapter, Carpenter's commentary on mass culture and the state of the horror genre in the 1990s, requires the less obvious. By 'less obvious', we mean attention to a syncopated chronology within Carpenter's 1990s filmic production that bespeaks a creative approach to nostalgia.

Between 1993 and 1999, Carpenter directed five horror and fantasy films: *Body Bags* (1993), *Escape From L.A.*, *Village of the Damned* (1995), *In the Mouth of Madness* and *Vampires* (1998). His films would then seem to fall within the general trajectory of contemporary self-reflexive horror outlined by writers such as Michael A. Arnzen (1994) and Jeffrey Sconce (1993) (for an additional discussion see Brophy 1986). *Body Bags*, an early 1990s cable television production, takes a very playful approach to self-reflexivity. *Escape From L.A.* surrenders to self-reflexivity. *Village of the Damned* evokes a recontextualised nostalgia, with experimental genetics, bio-engineering and government conspiracies routed through updated 1950s imagery. *In the Mouth of Madness* is overpowered by self-reflexivity, to the point of insanity. And *Vampires*, we will argue, aspires to respond to the dominant cycle of 1990s horror and, in the end, a possible renegotiation of the cyclical.

Rather than settle for another catalogue of Carpenter's films, we have opted to thread our discussion through three of these titles: *Body Bags*, *In the Mouth of Madness* and *Vampires*. We distinguish these from *Escape From L.A.* and *Village of the Damned*, a sequel and remake, since our purpose is to trace how Carpenter's relationship to self-reflexivity is revised – or echoing our title, is revisioned.

## Body Bags

In a 1980 interview, Carpenter stated: 'I fight against becoming self-conscious. It's the death of a filmmaker, when he starts parodying himself' (McCarthy 1980: 23). Thirteen years and nine films later, Carpenter released *Body Bags*. Does *Body Bags* represent Carpenter's alignment with the trajectories of parody and self-reflexivity that many have pointed to as a postmodern turn in the horror genre? Does *Body Bags* evoke the same trend towards playful self-reflexivity characteristic of Sam Raimi's *Evil Dead* trilogy (1983, 1987 and 1993) or *Wes Craven's New Nightmare* (1994)?

(After all, both Raimi and Craven make cameo appearances in *Body Bags*.) Well, not exactly.

*Body Bags*, a series of three genre shorts directed by Carpenter and Tobe Hooper, also incidentally features Carpenter himself as horror host. In this sense, *Body Bags* is very much in the vein of other television horror-variety shows such as *Tales From the Crypt*, *The Twilight Zone*, *Alfred Hitchcock Presents* and *The Outer Limits*, and filmic adaptations of this form like *Creepshow* (1982) and *Trilogy of Terror* (1975). And Carpenter's role as host – in this case, a ghoulish coroner – is reminiscent of other traditional post-war television horror hosts such as 'Zacherley', 'Dr. Paul Bearer', 'Vampira' and, of course, 'Elvira – Mistress of the Dark'. Overall, these programmes used their schlock personalities to playfully introduce bad (usually older) films.

Wryly enough, in *Body Bags* Carpenter's host character is ostensibly introducing his own and fellow director Hooper's films as equally bad. Or perhaps more appropriately, Carpenter assumes the persona of horror host to align the skits with a specific history of the movies. But this is nothing new. Carpenter bluntly situates himself within the margins of legitimate film history in 'John Carpenter's Guilty Pleasures':

> In film school, we studied all the classics – silents, German expressionism, Russian montage, Italian neorealism, you know the litany. I realised right away that with a few exceptions I didn't really enjoy or love any of the classic films. I mean, how can you really love *Greed*? … So let's talk about flops and trash. The Poor, The Awful, The Stupid – movies I dearly love and would much rather watch than classics. (1996: 50)

In other words, Carpenter wilfully acknowledges his participation in what he knows to be 'bad', low-budget productions.

Does this make *Body Bags* self-parody? Yes. Is it the death of the filmmaker? Yes, but with a twist. Sure, *Body Bags* takes advantage of the usual props – rubber eyeballs, humorous gross-out puns and creepy setting. And Carpenter as monstrous, yet playful, host does the honours of introducing each short. After the final short, it is revealed to the viewer that the coroner is himself a stiff awaiting autopsy. That is, the narrator, after ridiculing those bodies occupying the morgue due to their natural deaths and the frightening situations befalling the characters in the three short films is, himself, revealed to be part of the same structure. When the real coroners (Tobe Hooper and Tom Arnold) enter, the quirky coroner quickly zips himself up in … you guessed it, a body bag. Carpenter's authoritative voice as horror host and director is playfully undone. 'It's the death of a filmmaker, when he starts parodying himself.' Literally.

With *Body Bags*, Carpenter and his fellow directors abandon themselves to a game of nostalgia: dress-up fun with the horror genre. Directorial enunciation is here conceived as a relationship to the past. Although Carpenter's coroner never attempts to escape from the spatial dimensions of the morgue/genre, his raspy voice expresses the discontent faced in his routine career(s): 'death by natural causes … I hate natural causes. Give me a big ol' stab wound to poke around in, then I'm happy.' After all, as Carpenter's character states: 'Myself, I love stories about our national pastime – violent death.' But who is being murdered? Well, the coroner was already dead. Gimme an old wound to play with – let's say ... the horror film?

*In the Mouth of Madness*

When, however, does self-reflexivity within horror stop being so much fun? What leads it to assume a relentless, overbearing presence? This is the question that animates our discussion of *In the Mouth of Madness*. It is not that Carpenter's movie introduces any radically new ideas into the horror genre – the relationship between reality and fiction, sanity and insanity are addressed at the most banal level. For example, *In the Mouth of Madness* relies on two major tropes of the horror genre: the fantastic, or an invasion of the inexplicable into reality – especially the parallel reality of fiction in *The Dark Half* (1993); and the social and psychological effects of an epidemic, characteristic of such films as *The Crazies* (1973) and the long tradition of contagious aberrance that organises zombie films.

A truly cruel cynic might even dismiss the film's dependence on recursive images as a surreptitious minimisation of production costs. Yet for all its repetition of hackneyed themes and images, *In the Mouth of Madness* touches upon the nucleus of many debates on the character and impact of mass culture. The film portrays a horrific descent into insanity. However, it is not merely an individual who is subjected to such a tortuous journey. The entire world descends into madness. It is a special kind of madness though: a schizophrenia of consumption. Fanatical readers consume the horror fiction of novelist Sutter Cane (Jürgen Prochnow). His fiction in turn consumes the world – after all, Cane's work is translated into eighteen languages. Reality becomes nothing more than a marketing tie-in: the printed text and subsequent film spawn movie posters, coffee mugs and other novelties – the least of which is an entire small town: Hobb's End.

This transformation of reality is tracked through the experiences of John Trent (Sam Neill) and, to a lesser extent, his companion Linda Styles (Julie Carmen). An especially telling scene in the film occurs as Trent and Styles traverse deserted New Hampshire roads in search of the imaginary Hobb's End of horror writer Cane's eerie *Hobb's End Horror*. A young man on a bicycle crosses the path of their speeding automobile. But what initially appeared to be a young man, on closer inspection turns out to be a strangely decrepit version of youth. The words, 'I can't get out. He won't let me out', signal that the young man has been and is trapped in a cycle – on a cycle. He is condemned to incessantly traverse, of all things, his bicycle route. There is more than a hint of dark humour about the scene. Expressed along with this comedic, perhaps cynically playful representation of the cyclical is a formidable terror of repetition.

The boy, trapped by the signifiers of youth – a paper route and the incessant clicking of a playing card wedged into the spokes of his bicycle wheels – continues to appear within the film. We would go so far as to contend that the scene presages the entire theme of the film. It marks Trent's inability to escape the bounds of the mass cultural products in which his existence is implicated, for he too is caught within a cycle, a narrative cycle expressed through two forms of mass media: the horror novel and a movie, duly entitled '*In the Mouth of Madness*'.

Although initially introduced as an insurance fraud investigator, a bastion of sanity rooted so firmly in the operations of the real world that he delights in sniffing out a con, Trent is himself revealed to be a fiction. He is a Sutter Cane creation. Of course, Trent protests that he knows what is real and that no-one 'pulls my strings'. His protests are useless. Though he represents the 'last man', the final link to the previously ordered reality of the film, Trent is also the essential catalyst by which a fiction of mass culture overruns reality. Through him neither time nor reality bear their normal countenance. For example, Styles reads Trent's actions from a mass circulation horror novel as he performs them.

This action ironically cements Horkheimer and Adorno's claim that one can predict an entire film from the first glance. *In the Mouth of Madness* situates Trent within a script that speaks him more directly than any psychoanalytic or Marxist formulation of overdetermination. He operates within this script just as he should, literally existing only by virtue of this mass-produced madness which speaks him into being. His actions are correct, perhaps even too correct. He does not stray from the words which Styles reads. He is the perfect actor in the story of which he is a part since he acts without knowledge of himself acting.

Moreover, this scene portends the very last image we have of John Trent. He is seated in an ransacked empty cinema. As he consumes his popcorn, the blue light of the silver screen illuminates his face. The camera turns to reveal Trent's own performance in the feature: *In the Mouth of Madness*. Trent's response? Psychotic, uncontrollable laughter. Such laughter is a far cry from the prankish chuckles of Carpenter's coroner in *Body Bags*. In *Body Bags*, laughter and the accompanying comedic performance of the horror host are celebratory and participatory, both indicative of the film's self-reflexive form. However, the laughter witnessed at the end of *In the Mouth of Madness* marks a total capitulation. This speaks a different experience of self-reflexivity as oppressive. In other words, there is as yet no clearly enunciated response, no talking out of the cycle.

Laughter. One of the defining characteristics of horror in the 1990s has been the merger between terror and humour or, as Jonathan Lake Crane points out, '[t]he contemporary horror film moves from laughter to terror with unsettling ease' (1994: 37). This may be the case when horror is going for gags – using its own history and conventions to produce hybrids like 'splatstick'. *In the Mouth of Madness*, most notably Trent's last laugh, is anything but easy. We have emphasised this scene and those which lead to it because they appear to comment on Carpenter's attitudes toward the generic tendencies that have become hallmarks for horror in the 1990s.

Whereas in *Body Bags*, his largest acting role, Carpenter appears enthusiastic, pleased with the joke, *In the Mouth of Madness* suggests Carpenter may consider the horror genre's joke on itself to have grown constricting, claustrophobic, and even possibly a step towards generic dementia. The cycle(s) within which John Trent is trapped are not entirely unlike those which constrain the horror genre, that is, where it is forced to see itself perform.

*In the Mouth of Madness* leaves the viewer in the cinema in the company of a laughter it would not want to share. There is no answer, no 'out' to the repetition which mass culture has utilised in the construction of generic self-reflexivity. Conceding to Horkheimer and Adorno's point, mass culture does imprint every aspect of culture. The issue then, is to determine what knowledge may be secured from within. The image of the young man trapped in a redundancy and John Trent's psychotic laughter as he watches himself in the film *In the Mouth of Madness* demonstrate the commentary which Carpenter's work, firmly rooted within the codes of commercial cinema, simultaneously places on the status of the horror genre within contemporary mass culture.

*Vampires*

*In the Mouth of Madness* was released in the US in 1995. Unknowingly, its commentary on horror and genre cycles antedated the arrival of a particularly banal period for the American horror film. Films constitutive of this period, and littered by screaming teenage television personalities, included: *Scream* (1996), *Scream 2* (1997), *Scream 3* (1999), *I Know What You Did Last Summer* (1997), *I Still Know What You Did Last Summer* (1998) and *The Faculty* (1998). The hegemony of Kevin Williamson's scripts came to define the horror film in the US during the mid-late 1990s.[2] Assisted by directors such as Wes Craven and Robert Rodriguez, Williamson's stories are frighteningly transparent and conservative in their marked preference for the safety of horror sub-genre conventions and in-on-the-joke horror giggles. David Sanjek shares this sentiment:

> *Scream* ... in particular depends upon the characters', and the audience's, willingness to abide by the rules of the game. At the same time, neither Williamson nor very many of his contemporaries appear to be interested in critiquing or subverting those parameters. Instead, they merely call attention to them in the most blunt and obvious fashion. (2000: 113–14)

What, given this context, can be said of the relatively late appearance of Carpenter's *Vampires* – a film which is extraordinary for its glaring absence of teenagers?

Whereas *Body Bags* wilfully participated in 1990s horror genre self-reflexivity, and *In the Mouth of Madness* expressed consternation at this same condition, *Vampires* mounts a studied response to the demands of recent, clean-teen horror conventions and overdramatic period pieces. No high schools. No castles. So what does appear in *Vampires*? Creative nostalgia: a brand of repetition which rejects contentment in tongue-in-cheek self-reflexivity. Specifically, Carpenter's reinvestment in and return to horror through genre materialises as the figure of the vampire takes on the western.

Repetition figures in *Vampires* most blatantly through the actual figure of the vampire. Standard vampire practice requires that each feed regularly and avoid sunlight. As such, vampires are bound to two cycles: the passage of day into night, and replenishment through the blood of victims. It would seem, then, that of all classic horror figures, vampires are the most stringently bound by the compulsion to repeat. Carpenter's vampires are even marked by an additional repetitive pattern. Master slayer Jack Crow (James Woods) reveals to Father Adam Guiteau (Tim Guinee) that the film's vampires display a special travel/attack pattern:

> See this map? This map shows all the [vampire] encounters in the United States as far back as the 1800s ... Look at the Southwest. See the spiral pattern? If you time sequence all the encounters, you get a logarithmic pattern ever-widening. It's a search pattern, Padre. They're looking for something...

That which eludes the vampires, and the reason that master vampire Valek (Thomas Ian Griffith) has travelled to the southwestern United States is an ancient relic that has for centuries been hidden in Spanish monasteries, The Berziers Cross. This is a vital element of a special ceremony meant to relieve vampires of the final cumber on immortality that he experiences: vulnerability to daylight. In other words, immortality is construed as an end to the vampire's compulsion to repeat.

As might be expected, the vampires fail to escape the confines of their repetitive existence. This is the West, and the West means heroes, or at the very least, anti-heroic tough guys. Although many of Carpenter's films draw on the codes of the western, it is *Vampires* which most closely approximates the western in terms of setting – the Southwest – and character development, most significantly portrayed by the figure of Jack Crow and sidekick Montoya (Daniel Baldwin). Once again, Carpenter need not be viewed as in some way blazing a trail because he set his vampire narrative in the West. Both Kathryn Bigelow's *Near Dark* (1987) and Robert Rodriguez's *From Dusk till Dawn* (1996) share this quality (for more on this connection, see Cruz and Guins 2000). What does stand out is that Carpenter

Reinvestment in genre in Carpenter's *Vampires*: the undead are reborn in the sun-drenched American Southwest

makes his western in the late 1990s when it is uncouth to occupy the Hawksian and Fordian legacy. We are presented with an extreme model, with characters who are emblematic of a particular type of western, as well as a particular period in horror: the misogyny of 1970s savage cinema. Consequently, *Vampires* recreates horror after the manner of largely buried cinematic practices of the past. It expands the parameters of late 1990s horror to such an extent that, when compared to films like *Scream* and *I Know What You Did Last Summer*, it appears to be a crude joke. Working-class guys in black leather jackets, and with stolen automobiles, whose entertainment consists of cheap booze and loose women. These men do not gather in suburban homes to watch scary movies.

Carpenter's *Vampires* insists that all repetition is not the same. *Vampires* repeats, but it repeats while guarding against the stagnation which limits to repetition impose. Even though Carpenter all but invented the American slasher genre, a sub-genre which films like *Scream* continue to pastiche, it also appears to be the case that through *Vampires*, he calls his progeny to task. The existence of such a film at the tail end of such a homogenous period in the history of the horror film could be understood to advocate a move away from the slasher genre which is, of course, just one aspect of horror. For horror that reflects only earlier horror taps into a now exhausted well. Diverse terrains from which to draw in the production of horror are required, and employed in Carpenter's *Vampires*. In this respect, *Vampires* is in keeping with his earlier films. To illustrate, *The Fog* (1979) takes its cue from the ghost story, while *Christine* tests the parameters of a haunting, and *Prince of Darkness* (1987) addresses the supernatural. *The Thing* and *They Live* (1988) take on the fears associated with alien invasion, while *Assault on Precinct 13* (1976) offers an electric image of urban terror.

The horror genre is complex and demands to be traversed. It may be mass culture, yet to return to our earlier contention, it is not repetition *per se* which must be avoided. Only repetition in its most banal and entrapping state poses a danger of fatuousness. Following on from this, if all mass culture is, as Adorno's *The Culture Industry* (1991) contends, a matter of adaptation, then what Carpenter attempts to demonstrate with *Vampires* is that mass culture is a rich and diverse field. Mass culture may dominate, but there is hardly a shortage of materials from which to choose. If mass culture is being critiqued, then it is for too narrowly limiting itself not because it is limiting.

*Conclusion*

On the one hand *Body Bags*, *In the Mouth of Madness* and *Vampires* manifest the inability to evade cycles; one only need recall John Trent's laughter. On the other, they demonstrate a certain sanguine value, the value of selecting the type of cycle to occupy, even if for only a brief moment. Participation, reaction and response are the actions engendering Carpenter's generic *coup d'état*. These three actions point to the uneasy position that Carpenter occupies within Hollywood: an acknowledgedly commercial context that exhibits an affinity for the mass culture of another era. If Carpenter is to be understood as an invested critic of mass culture, then it may be because of his optimistic willingness to fully embrace the cyclical nature of genre.

As such, Carpenter's generic manoeuvrings are not an escape attempt, in that he does not resort to uncompromising refusal of or flight from genre films altogether. Like the character Jack Crow, the genre may be bruised, betrayed or even crucified; yet it remains ever resilient always with another trick up its sleeve. The trick? Working within repetition, Carpenter thwarts the common expectations and routine acceptance largely associated with the horror film of the 1990s, by returning to less habituated moments, motifs, themes and styles from the past.

Cycles do not end, they repeat. Carpenter's films do not end. They are left unresolved. This too seems to be the expectation for mass culture: a terrifying openness and the failure of a final resolution. The power and terror of repetition that marks commercial filmmaking is destructive – witness John Trent and the trapped young boy from *In the Mouth of Madness*. But if cycles are unable to end, begin again. Repetition simultaneously fosters the emergence of an alternative world, alternative values and another way of doing things. Call it a revision.

*Notes*

1   This chapter of *Dialectic of Enlightenment* discusses the ways in which mass culture conditions people to fascism. The argument is that since mass culture operates in an economic register, it is unable, or perhaps refuses to vary from its own patterns to waylay financial risk. The homogeneity of its products then exercises a levelling effect on all forms of culture. Horkheimer and Adorno's basic programme is to maintain distinctions and diversity in the hope that doing so will annul the threat of sameness associated with fascism (especially in its anti-Semitic implications).

2   New directions for the horror film in the late 1980s and 1990s were found to reside outside of the US in works by Peter Jackson (New Zealand), Guillermo Del Toro (Mexico), Jörg Buttgereit (Germany), Toshiharu Ikeda (Japan) and Michele Soavi (Italy).

*References*

Adorno, T. (1991) *The Culture Industry: Selected Essays on Mass Culture*. Ed. J. M. Bernstein. London: Routledge.

Arnzen, M. (1994) 'Who's Laughing Now?... The Postmodern Splatter Film', *Journal of Popular Film and Television*, 21, 4, 176–84.

Brophy, P. (1986) 'Horrality – The Textuality of Contemporary Horror Films', *Screen*, 27, 1, 2–13.

Carpenter, J. (1996) 'John Carpenter's Guilty Pleasures', *Film Comment*, 32, 5, 50–3.

Crane, J. L. (1994) *Terror and everyday Life: Singular Moments in the History of the Horror Film*. London: Sage.

Cruz, O. and R. Guins (2000) 'Asphalt Veins: On and Off the Road with the Vampire', in J. Sargeant and S. Watson (eds) *Lost Highways: An Illustrated History of*

*Road Movies*. London: Creation, 129–46.

Horheimer, A. and T. Adorno (1993) *Dialectic of Enlightenment*. Trans. John Cumming. New York: Continuum.

Horton, A. and S. Y. McDougal (1998) *Play It Again, Sam: Retakes on Remakes*. Berkeley: University of California Press.

Jones, K. (1999) 'John Carpenter: american movie classic', *Film Comment*, 35, 1, 26–31.

McCarthy, T. (1980) 'Trick and Treat', *Film Comment*, 16, 1, 17–24.

Sanjek, D. (2000) 'Same as It Ever Was: Innovation and Exhaustion in the Horror and Science Fiction Films of the 1990s', in W. W. Dixon (ed.) *Film Genre 2000: New Critical Essays*. Albany: State University of New York Press.

Sconce, J. (1993) 'Spectacles of Death: Identification, Reflexivity and Contemporary Horror', in J. Collins, H. Radner and A. P. Collins (eds) *Film Theory Goes to the Movies*. London: Routledge, 103–19.

# CHAPTER THIRTEEN

# An Interview with John Carpenter

Conducted by Ronald V. Borst
Compiled by Ian Conrich and David Woods

*Formative Years*

Ronald V. Borst: *Your father taught music at Western Kentucky University. He also gave you an 8mm camera, when you were aged eight. To what extent has your father been an influence on your career?*
John Carpenter: Well, huge. I mean, my Dad and my Mom have both given me great gifts – genetic creativity. My Dad gave me music, and my Mom was also musical. My father was an intellectual. He gave me the 8mm camera at the beginning and told me, 'go create something. Don't sit around here with your thumb up your ass, go out and do something.' So like every other kid I get practising; I write a horror magazine and produce a horror science fiction movie. I started learning about editing from working with the assumption that you didn't have to do it in the camera, but later on you could edit the material and so on. My Dad was an *extremely* important figure in my life – he gave me the gift of music, my Mom gave me the gift of sanity. You can't ask for more than that.
*Your father was a session player for artists such as Roy Orbison, Brenda Lee and Johnny Cash. Do you have memories of meeting these people?*
I would go down with my father to Nashville where he would record and met Brenda Lee and Roy Orbison. I didn't get to meet Elvis; he was one guy I wanted to

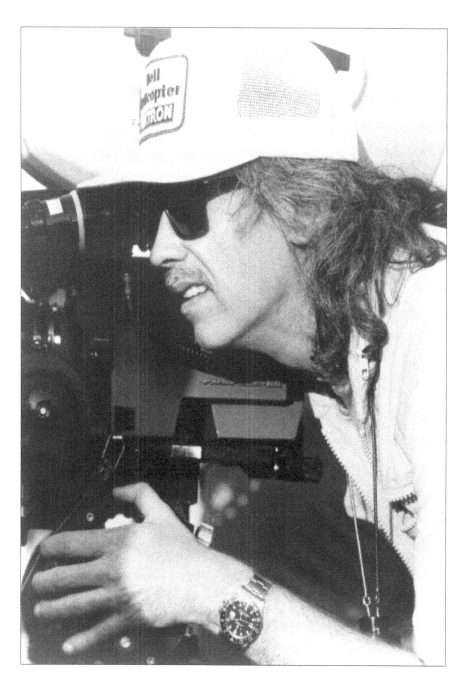

meet. I didn't get to meet Frank Sinatra, either. My Dad was one of the founding members of the Nashville Strings. They were a group of musicians from the Nashville symphony orchestra, and other places, who were hired to come in and play on sessions. They arranged the oboes and the violins and they arranged a whole lot of songs with this kind of sweet background – country music, rock 'n' roll, all sorts of things, I was a part of all that, watching that happen. But the most impressive guy I met was Roy Orbison, because he wore sunglasses all the way through when he used to play a session, and he had a guy who would sing harmony with him who also wore sunglasses. They would just go on up to the mike, these two guys with sunglasses, and then hit it. So instead of double-tracking, in other words, laying his voice over twice, he'd only do it once. My Dad would work five-hour sessions. That was good, that was the length of time they would do. They would rehearse twice, then cut the record, bring a back-up singer in, whoever was there – it was amazing.

*Apparently, you originally considered a career in music but then changed to film-making. Why?*

Well, my first love was always movies. I'd always wanted to be a director since I was a little kid, since I figured out that last credit, 'directed by'. I was watching films that had something in common about them, and I couldn't figure out what it was, except for the director. It was all that guy. He had something to do with the way it was being done; I very primitively began to figure out that that's the guy who makes the movie. So in '68 I was two years into university in Western Kentucky and I had to decide. I was in a rock 'n' roll band, making some good money, meeting good girls, having fun; do I stay here, or do I give it a shot? So I came out to Los Angeles and gave it a shot.

*What films were an initial influence? Horror and fantasy seem to have dominated your creative interests from an early age. You produced several fanzines and also 8mm shorts. Why have you been drawn to this genre?*

Because of a movie called *It Came From Outer Space*. I saw it in 3D when it first came out in 1953. I was five years old, and I was wearing those glasses when that first meteor exploded, and I didn't know it was 3D – I didn't know anything, I was just an innocent little kid – and it was overwhelming. It was quite terrify-ing but exciting; you thought, 'what an experience!' The first story I ever saw was Humphrey Bogart and Katherine Hepburn in *The African Queen*, with the leeches on his back; the most vivid memory for a little kid. I was going, 'What is *that*? Holy Toledo!' But then as time went on I think I began to appreciate there was a great kind of renaissance in horror and science fiction. Mostly science fiction. I really got into that because they seemed so subversive for the time. Unlike other staid kind of Hollywood productions, they seemed to have a little bit of something outlaw about them. I really dug that, and I think *Forbidden Planet* also had a big influence on me. It was the first movie I'd seen where it was in widescreen and colour and it took place on another world, and it was a lot of fun. But frankly, I got into the movie business to make westerns, that was my first love. I remember *Rio Bravo, Red River* – Hawks's films, mainly – but I saw Ford, I saw everybody, all the westerns, and that's what I wanted to make. But it didn't work out that way.

*In an interview you said of Bowling Green that 'everything that I know about evil I learnt in that little town'.[1] Could you elaborate?*

You have to understand, and as my Dad was telling me recently, jobs were hard to come by in the 50s. It wasn't a time of great plenty, and it was especially hard for someone with a PhD in music to find a position at a university. He had some offers, but the one that he liked the best was at a small college in Bowling Green, Kentucky. So we moved from Carthage, New York down to Kentucky. You've got to understand that my ancestors are all Yankees. My great great great uncle invented the elevator – Otis. James Otis, an even greater greater greater greater uncle ancestor was a patriot in the American Revolution. He was a firebrand who stood up and said, 'fuck the British, get rid of these taxes, get this tea out of here'. The problem came as he was sitting in a tavern one night and a tax collector came in with a club and beat him over the head so much that he lost it. He ended up in an asylum. So the patriot was silenced. My grandmother's family came from the Daughters of the American Revolution [DAR] believe it or not, and the DAR is a very strange organisation, but that's where I came from. Now you transplant these Yankees in Kentucky, in the middle of the Bible Belt. My Dad was kind of an intellectual, and here we are in Yahoo land with these country boys, and I was completely out of place. Completely. It's culture shock. I grew up in a little log cabin which my Dad rented behind the Kentucky Museum, so I grew up in a very strange environment, in this town that I didn't relate to at all. My family didn't relate to anybody there, so I was the outsider, and being interested in music and playing the violin, I wasn't the country boy from the farm. So I encountered a lot of looking at this culture from the outside. But then I went into high school … this was the Jim Crow South, and I saw some things that I will never, ever forget, things that human beings were doing to one another. It was astonishing stuff. So all the clichés about the South are true, and more. That's who they are. I had never encountered that kind of evil before, I just hadn't. I'd heard about Nazis, I'd heard about the war between the states, I'd heard about what was going on with Russia and the United States and the atomic bomb and all that stuff, but that was very abstract. But here it was right in the street, but here it was with my classmates, some pretty terrible things. I learned about it all.

*You attended the University of Southern California [USC] and studied filmmaking. What were your experiences of learning a film craft and what has been its effect on your subsequent creative output?*

Everything I really know about movie making I learned there; they taught us all the plumbing. We had to learn everything. We had to learn the camera, lighting, photography, moving photography, editing, sound, directing, acting, writing. I had to project, I had to work in a film lab and process – which is the worst job of all, running that stuff through the chemicals. Animation, history and criticism was not quite so big, but on production I learned everything. I was hungry for it. I always wanted to see what is this, how does this work, how do movies work? How do you make a movie? What's the process? What does the production manager do, what does an editor do, or a cameraman – why is he taking so long, what's the problem here? I learned about it, so I had a very deep technical background. But beyond that I learned the aesthetics. I was there in great, great times. My guest lecturers included Orson Welles, Howard Hawks, John Ford, Alfred Hitchcock, Roman Polanski. Everybody came through and spoke to us, and they answered questions and showed their movies. We had a big western retrospective, all the westerns made in the United States from *Birth of a Nation* on. Wild Bill Wellman, Delmer Daves, it just goes on and on, the directors that I met with and talked to and heard their experiences. John Ford got up and told anecdotes. It was a fascinating time to be there because we were in contact with the old Hollywood classic directors and even some of the new ones. And you got a real sense of being trained to go into Hollywood, because that's what the focus of USC was at the time. It was mainly on American films, Hollywood films, so that's what I wanted to do. It's meant everything to me.

*Industry*

*You have said that you would have been happiest working within the studio system of the 1940s. Why?*

They were very passionate guys. They may have been tough guys, they may have been mean, but they loved movies. They loved the process; they got involved in the process, they got involved in who were the actors. And they also shot longer too. They shot and *shot* some of these things.

*How important is it for you to be independent in your filmmaking?*

How important is it that the sun rises every morning? The movie business in Hollywood has changed so very much since I got in, and it keeps changing over the years. Certainly there are some big changes going on right now, though there were in the 80s too. And being independent and having control of your movie as a director is the biggest issue there is; all other issues pale in comparison with that. The minute that you give up control to someone else then it's no longer your film – it's someone else's film, someone else's vision. And really they can't do too much to you until you get into post-production. Post-production is where they can fuck with you. So you have a couple of options as a director. One is you can shoot so little coverage they can't re-cut it, but that's kind of cheesy. So, depending on what your movie is and how it goes, the only other thing you can get is final cut, which no-one wants to give, ever. There's all sorts of compromises in between, and some of them are not too bad. I've shared final cuts. I shared it once with Sherry Lansing. That was the easiest thing in the world. She didn't mean to give any problems, she just said 'I think your movie's a little long'.

*Which film?*

*Escape From L.A.* But when you get into a committee, I mean get into these previews, audience research, marketing research, then you start getting into some real problems. I've had some problems with my films, not too bad but a little bit. But control is the issue, and every movie is different. I've had final cut, I've had no cut – I've had it all. And in the happiest world that I could live in I would have total control of the film. But that's a highly idealised world.

*A director such as John Sayles has worked within the studio system to gain the financial freedom to pursue his own projects. To what extent has your own career followed this pattern?*

I've made some of their pictures – I mean some of the Hollywood movies that they offer to me. Assignments – *Starman* was an assignment, *Christine* was an assignment, *Big Trouble in Little China* was an assignment, *Memoirs of an Invisible Man* was an assignment. Those are movies that I didn't originate myself. Which is fine; I have no problem with that, and it's good to do it sometimes. Sometimes it works, sometimes it doesn't. In the case of *Starman*, that was a big apology for *The Thing*, because everybody was blaming me for it. It was not well received at the time.

*It needed no apology.*

Well, I had to go down on my knees, and then the only way to do it was to make a little love story, a girl movie. So I did, and it was fun to make; I enjoyed it, and I have no regrets.

*What have you learnt about the way the studio system works? In particular Big Trouble in Little China was a difficult production.*

It was difficult because of the administration at Fox at that time. I have worked with Barry Diller who's a notorious fellow, a well-loved businessman. But one of the changes that came about – really I guess from the 80s on, maybe earlier than that, to an extent in the 70s though I wasn't as active – was a lot of the people who were in charge of the studios, production companies and so forth, didn't know anything about making movies at all and had no passion for it. They came from Wall Street, they came from business administration school, they had business degrees, they were lawyers. Movies became more and more about product, and so passion was kind of lacking in there. By that I don't mean that great movies weren't made or good movies weren't made, because they always have been and always will be. But I remember Barry Diller saying he doesn't care what my problems are as a director, he doesn't care what goes on on the set. He doesn't care; it doesn't mean anything to him. At the same time he'll try to dictate what you do on the set. It would be like if I was in a bomb squad, and I was defusing a bomb, and somebody said, 'well I don't care how you do it, but I want you to do it this way. Here, don't do that, now take this cover off.' All of a sudden you answer to these same old pressures of the economics every time. That's what you have to be aware of in Hollywood: it's all about money. They want to make money, that's all; they don't care if it's good or bad, they want to make money. So that's always tricky, but I've been extremely lucky. Even the films that have been tinkered with a little bit have actually turned out okay, so I've been pretty lucky.

*You have directed a number of films and programmes for television. How does this differ from making feature films, and are you happy working with this medium?*

TV is not a great love of mine. Visually it's constrained, it's a tiny box. I like Panavision – widescreen movies – but we have to realise the future is going to be in different places. There will always be movie theatres; people will always go out, have an evening out, take the family. There will always be that kind of stuff, but the technological revolution is happening now, with digital, the Internet and satellite television, and all this is having an impact. Look at the growth of laserdiscs, DVDs and old movies that come back. They show complete cuts and have a director or a star or someone talking through it. This is great stuff. This is the way to keep movies alive. It's even better in some ways; it's not like we have to scrounge around to see a revival showing of a film, now you can see it in your home again and again, and study it. But again you're dealing with a tiny little screen. Even a big screen TV is a tiny little screen. I would be happy to make movies directly for the Internet or for the home audience. I could do that. I'd love to by-pass Hollywood; that would be great fun. But the only problem, and I go back to it again, is that small screen, small vision.

*Politics and Ideology*

*Critics have found both left- and right-wing motifs in your films. Do you feel your films have a consistent political agenda?*

People see things in films that are very odd to me. I got a letter from a religious group out in Wyoming or something, and they're associated with the Nordic Viking gods such as Thor. They have a booklet and it's pretty spooky. They call themselves 'folk', but it's almost Germanic; it's white 'folk' I guess. They sent me a letter saying thank you for all your good work. The folk – the people – love you for it. And I thought, what the hell are they talking about? *Assault on Precinct 13* was a western, and it was definitely about defending a police station, but I want to point out that the hero of the film was a convicted murderer, so I don't know that it was a right-wing film. I don't know, maybe it was. *Escape From New York* certainly wasn't. The bad guys were the authority figures. *They Live* was a criticism of unrestrained free enterprise; a definite criticism of the Reagan era, which was horrible.

*Many have found your films frightening, but you claim that if you were able to work without constraints you could produce a film which would really scare its audience. You have said that one of the factors which has restricted what you have been able to portray is that 'we're too scared in our personal lives these days'.[2] Can you explain?*

Every culture, everybody is afraid of the same things: fear of our own death, disfigurement, loss of a loved one, loss of identity. I fear the same things you do, you fear the same things that the people reading this book fear. We're all afraid. So we have police forces and we have religion to explain things to us, to protect us. We're frightened of forces of chaos, forces of evil, or of things happening – anything can happen; a plane could land and kill us right now. It's that knowledge that really things are beyond our control. We're afraid of all that, and to really scare people would be to open that little door and say life is really about chaos and it's not being directed. It's aimless, it's by chance. People don't want to hear that *at all*; *no-one* wants to hear it. That's the exact opposite of what people want. People want re-assurance that love triumphs, the hero triumphs. We're just too insecure to be able to admit that. That's what I think.

*Craft*

*You have sometimes been associated with a 'cinema of unease'. You have said that this is a matter of employing certain cinematic techniques. Can you elaborate?*

The tricks? Okay, visually it has to do with the size of the lenses that you're shooting with, the composition of the shots and the length of time the shot runs. It has to do with whether it's silent or whether there's music; it has to do with rhythm and tempo. It has to do with everything that goes into movie making. But in my experimentation at USC I discovered some tricks that can make people real uneasy. Silence makes people uneasy. I remember a film where I wanted outer space to be completely silent and the mixers added in noise. They said audiences can't stand it. I remember in *Assault on Precinct 13* we were mixing the reels – they were just dialogue scenes between the characters talking on a sound stage. The mixers again added noise in the background. I said why? 'Because it sounds too dead, it's too quiet.' Audiences get real uncomfortable when it's quiet. So, you start using some of this. Some sounds really bother them too. And you hold the shot too long, and it goes beyond boredom and you get uneasy. So it's all this stuff combined.

*One technique for which you are noted is the use of the widescreen process to create suspense and claustrophobia. How have you adapted widescreen for these effects?*

Fear, claustrophobia and isolation is not a process or an effect, it's a subject matter. It's a part of the story, it's a part of the movie you're creating. I just love widescreen, I always have since I was a little kid, and it just seems to be very cinematic, this big rectangular band across the screen. So it's getting a feel for it; I feel at home with that particular aspect ratio as opposed to a square or the 1.85 which is the matted, sort of semi-widescreen. So, the subject matter is something different. Perhaps my own experiences when I was a kid led me to this isolation and claustrophobia and being trapped.

*At certain points the visual impact of your films has been dependent on prosthetic effects. The Thing and Vampires, in particular, foreground the spectacle of body horror, and it could be argued that this leaves little to the viewer's imagination. Do you think this approach can be as effective as the less explicit techniques you have employed elsewhere?*

There's a cliché in Hollywood, and I think that maybe it came from *The Bad and the Beautiful,* where Kirk Douglas is the head of the studio or something, and they look at the *Cat People* costumes, which are all ratty, and he says 'we'll do it like the old days, we'll put them in the shadows – the effective way'. But that's just a cliché. If you can convince me that this monster from outer space has just landed, and here he is in the middle of our house, right there, under the light, I'm going to start screaming and running around. That's when you hit a home run. You see, it's easier to put everything in the shadows. That's just a cliché; it makes you feel better. An actress, Valeria Golino, was lecturing me one day, and she said you never show the face of the devil, never. And I thought to myself, yeah, but if you could, you'd scare the shit out of people.

*Music*

*Is music necessary to your films? In what way does it function?*

It's a secondary narrative. The music that I make functions to support the scenes that aren't good, that need support. If they don't need support you can stick the music away. Narrative, music is narrative.

*Has your attitude to the use of music changed over the course of your career?*

Absolutely. I don't write music. All my music's improvised, so for the most part – I'd say 90 per cent of the time – I don't have a prewritten theme. Occasionally I do; for *Vampires* I had a little theme that I had written at home, and occasionally I do some sketches. But primarily it's coming in with the cut of the movie, and I just start improvising music to the scenes, and then I go back and layer on top of that with a synthesiser, and keep layering until I have a piece done. It's the sense of timing of what's going on on the screen. In other words, I've watched, I see the cut,

I see the scene going by and ask, what does it need here? So it's a feel process. It's like jazz; it's like a jazz musician comes in and you start doing a vibe, and all of a sudden you're playing and it's not written music; it's improvised. So in that sense it's not like Mickey Mouse. John Williams is the biggest current user of Mickey Mouse music. Max Steiner was one of the big users of '*bom, bom*' with somebody's footsteps. *King Kong* has a gigantic Mickey Mouse score which is telling you *everything* that is happening. It's wonderful stuff, it's wonderful grand old movie making. But it's right on the nose. It tells you what to feel. The music I do tells you what to feel but it's trying to be very unobtrusive, almost like a sound effect.

*As a director what are the advantages of being able to compose your own music?*

Well, it gives me another voice in the film, another creative voice. The disadvantage is that it takes six to ten weeks to do it, every day. It's exhausting. After you've directed the film and you've cut it, then you have to go through a whole new creative process again. Almost like you're putting on a new set of clothes and a new hat and saying, 'I don't care what you did as a director, now I care as a composer'. After I'm done with that, I'm washed up. I am dead. That's the problem; it's complete exhaustion.

*Do you have musical ideas prior to post-production? Is the way you choose to shoot a film affected by this? For instance, many of your films, which use music with tight rhythms and repetitions, are claustrophobic and are built around specific time frames.*

It has nothing to do with the music. It's all about subject matter, what the story's about. Music enhances what the story is. I don't think about the music on the set. I don't think about the music until my editor puts on temp music. I don't even want to know where it's from. He gives it a try; he'll put on the Beach Boys or Stravinsky in the city, and sometimes that really is influential. I'll think 'wow, that Beach Boys song right there really sounds good', so that the tone of that song is something I like. So I'll go off with that in mind and maybe come up with something that doesn't have the same notes but feels the same. So that's often helpful, he gives me a little help with the temp scores.

*Under what circumstances have you played fuller or lesser roles in the composition and selection of music for your films? What are the disadvantages and advantages of collaborating on compositions?*

I've collaborated a couple of times. The advantage is that you have somebody to share the work with you, so that you can come in and listen to what they've done. The disadvantage is that it's like any other creative process. You can't tell a composer, 'I didn't like that, let's do something else'. What? What are you talking about? Different notes, different what? And it's hard, especially if I'm co-composing – I have to direct it a little bit. Any collaboration is hard when it's something specific like music.

*You have a distinctive style of composition. Which composers do you admire and also from where do you draw your musical influences? For instance, why did you use Debussy in Escape From New York? Have you been influenced by the music of Steve Reich or Philip Glass?*

No. I used Debussy because it was a good idea. My editor dropped it in and said how does this feel, and I thought 'Oh, that's great'. I've been influenced by three composers mainly: Bernard Herrmann, Bernard Herrmann and Bernard Herrmann. He got the most out of the least means. The simplest scores, the most beautiful. His scores are so evocative. I know the composers he rips off from the old days, like Stravinsky. He's borrowed a lot of techniques from classical music, but his music is astonishing. You can't think of some movies without him. What would *Vertigo* be without him? What would *The Seventh Voyage of Sinbad* be without Bernard Herrmann? It wouldn't be anything. What would *Psycho* be without him? It wouldn't be a scary movie. To me he is as much a part of Hitchcock's artistry as anything, with that score. So I've worshipped him. I also like Dimitri Tiomkin a great deal, he's an old-style composer in the same vein as Max Steiner, but some of his scores are just great.

*How did Ennio Morricone become involved with composing the music for The Thing? Could you describe the process of working with him and did you have a musical input? Initially, you were to be the composer.*

I didn't want to be composer on that movie, I wanted him. He was one of my favourite composers in movies. I loved his score for *Once Upon a Time in the West*. I think it's probably my favourite because it's just so astonishing. We couldn't speak the same language, but he saw a cut of the film and he got some ideas from that, and then I told him about keeping the score to a minimum in terms of the amount of notes and very few key changes. But then in certain cases I let him just go ahead and do something orchestral. This is an end-of-the-world movie, a movie almost without any hope as soon as this Thing, this disease starts spreading among the men. It's a disease. You can think of it as like a Quatermass Experiment that's been done, and pretty soon that thing is going to be spreading. And in a way I wanted to make a very tragic-feeling soundtrack; almost a hopelessness, a dread. That was communicated, and that's where a director and composer really should be talking – in those kind of terms. I wanted to have this feeling of doom. So once you give a composer that kind of a direction and an idea, that's what he's looking for; just like an actor, he's looking for the feel and emotion behind it, because music is emotion. But then he did that score himself; that was not me.

*Genre*

*In 1978, you said that cinema audiences 'are more sophisticated now and they've seen too many genre films'. You also said that Hollywood films 'are getting more and more pretentious' [Milne and Combs 1978: 95]. What is your view of the state of popular filmmaking in the USA today?*

Mainstream Hollywood movies have stolen all the genre dimensions from horror movies and incorporated them into their films. There are no real B-movies any more. Hollywood makes big-budget B-movies. Hollywood films have become less pretentious in many ways, and more stupid, more formulaic. It makes you long for the old days.

*You have often admitted an indebtedness to the horror, science fiction and western genres. In particular, Howard Hawks is an important influence – why, and does this affect the extent to which you see your films as your own?*

Howard Hawks to me personally was the greatest director because he made a great movie in every genre. He did musicals, he did gangster movies, he did westerns, he did comedies. He moved with ease through these different genres. But what he brings to it is his own personal vision of the world, his own personal concerns with people, with actors. He's a very deeply personal filmmaker who worked with genres. That's what inspires me about him.

*Writers have observed in the films of Hawks a motif of the contingent group under threat. Similarly, you appear interested in the relationships between individuals in extreme situations. What is it that fascinates you about how people behave and interrelate?*

It's endlessly fascinating. I mean, that's life. It's amazing to watch how people interact with each other under stress and in joy. So it's endlessly fascinating and endless in the number of stories, it seems to me, about people and how they respond to the environment they're in; whether they're in love or whether they're in hate, or whether they're in trouble, or whatever.

*There are certain genres within which you have never operated. Why is this? You once remarked that you would like to make a musical. Would you still like to do so?*

I'd love to. I have a great musical about a nuclear power plant accident. I really am dead serious. It came to me one day … there was a song back in the 40s and 50s which was trying to explain music – you pushed a little valve down and the music goes round and round and it comes out here. I thought you could do the same thing with a power plant explaining how it works. You put the core here, you put the rods in there. And you could have these guys dancing in those rat suits. Could be fun!

*You have directed several remakes of classic films – Village of the Damned and The Thing – yet you have only ever directed one sequel. Why?*

The only sequel I directed [*Escape From L.A.*] was because Kurt Russell begged me to do it. He wanted to do it, wanted to be involved creatively. He wanted to play the character [of Snake Plissken] again. It wasn't something that I had ever planned to do, but Kurt is my friend and he wants to do it – so okay, let's go do it. And it was fun. I got to work with Kurt as a writer. Kurt was a writer long ago, before *Elvis* and before *Escape From New York*, so he wrote some of the screenplay. Kurt's a real smart guy, he's a real movie guy. People underestimate Kurt; don't ever underestimate him. So he came up with a lot of that movie, a lot of that movie was his.

*Collaboration and Creativity*

*You have collaborated with various people – Larry Franco and Tommy Wallace. How have these collaborations contributed to your creative vision?*

I've been really lucky to have a lot of talented collaborators. The directors of photography and production designers that I've worked with were really fine people, really talented. But you're all working from a central vision and they bring in their own feelings about it. That's what you're looking for in a collaborative situation. They've saved my ass.

*Why have you worked with a relatively consistent group of actors, such as Charles Cyphers and Nancy Loomis?*

Why not? They're friends; they give me the performance I want. I've worked with Kurt Russell probably more than anybody else, and he's a friend, but he's also a really talented actor and I don't have to spend time with him and nurse him through a part. He doesn't need fathering. You see, most actors need a daddy, and depending on their background they need a good daddy or they need a bad daddy. They have issues in their lives they haven't resolved or they're going to try to resolve them with me, and I'm there to make them do their best; somehow give them what they need to do their best. If I have to be tougher on them, or have to be gentle or seductive, or whatever the father's role is, that's my role. So I look for people who do a job that makes it easy on them, because there's a lot of physical and emotional stress in directing. It's not the easiest job in the world to do, and over the years it gets harder and harder every time to start a new film. So I'll try to make things as easy as possible; that's really the answer.

*What level of control operates in your directing of actors? For instance, it has been said that Snake Plissken is a creation of both you and Russell.*

Oh, absolutely. There's no doubt that every performance that you see is mostly created by the actor. A director can tell an actor a million things and it doesn't matter. They're the ones that have to get up and do it. Insecure directors give line readings, green directors get up and say 'okay, say it like this'. Well, that's bullshit. You just help them get there when they get lost. But Kurt's a great example. Kurt and I are as different politically as you can possibly be. He's further to the right than Genghis Khan! I mean he's way out there; you've got to realise how different we both are. But we see the same things in Snake Plissken, and in other characters – and movies. We have an agreement on the direction we want to go in. So I think that's the biggest thing: that you have the same goal. James Woods said to me, 'I'll play all your lines, I just want to do it my way. It's got to be me doing it, I can't be anybody else.' Well, of course not, of course not. In the end it's the actor's performance, and I'm guiding, I'm helping.

*Are you concerned about how your work is perceived? You have been quoted as saying, 'In France, I'm an auteur. In Germany, I'm a filmmaker. In the UK, I'm a horror director. In the US, I'm a bum' [Jones 1999: 27].*

Concerned? Well, there's nothing I can do about it! Guys get typecast as horror directors – and I'm one of them. Like I said, I got in the business to make westerns but it didn't work out that way; I got typecast as a horror director after *Halloween*. Well, that's fine, I have no problem, it's been a great fun career and a great life, but what goes along with it is you get typecast, and horror directors are just a little bit more respectable than pornographers. Just a little bit! I've never really had much respectability as a director, certainly not like some of my peers. I've had my share of accolades and I've had my share of good reviews. But I can't control it, there's nothing I can do. I suppose I could change my style of directing but I can't really do that, so why worry about it?

The interview took place on 26 January 2000 in John Carpenter's office. The questions put by Ronald V. Borst were devised by Ian Conrich and David Woods in consultation with the contributors to this collection.

*Notes*

1  *The Night He Came Home: John Carpenter's Halloween,* BBC2, tx 30 October 1999.
2  *The Directors: John Carpenter* (Media Entertainment in association with the American Film Institute, 1997).

*References*

Jones, K. (1999) 'John Carpenter: american movie classic', *Film Comment,* 35, 1, 26–31.
Milne, T. and R. Combs (1978) 'The Man in the Cryogenic Freezer', *Sight and Sound,* 47, 2, 94–8.

# FILMOGRAPHY

(Early 8mm shorts directed, all pre-1969)
*Revenge of the Colossal Beasts*
*Terror from Space*
*Gorgon, the Space Monster*
*Gorgo Versus Godzilla*
*Sorceror from Outer Space*
*Warrior and the Demon*

*The Resurrection of Bronco Billy*, 1970
(short film)
Director: James R. Rokos
Screenplay: John Carpenter, Nick Castle, Trace Johnston, John Longenecker, James R. Rokos
Editor: John Carpenter
Music: John Carpenter

*Dark Star*, 1974
Director: John Carpenter
Producer: John Carpenter
Executive Producer: Jack H. Harris
Associate Producer: J. Stein Kaplan
Screenplay: John Carpenter, Dan O'Bannon

Director of Photography: Douglas Knapp
Editor: Dan O'Bannon
Special Effects: Dan O'Bannon
Spaceship Design: Ron Cobb
Music: John Carpenter
Production Company: Jack H. Harris Enterprises
Length: 83 minutes
Cast: Brian Narelle (Doolittle), Dre Pahich (Talby), Cal Kuniholm (Boiler), Dan O'Bannon (Pinback), Joe Saunders (Commander Powell), Miles Watkins (Mission Control), Cookie Knapp (Computer)

*Assault on Precinct 13*, 1976
Director: John Carpenter
Producer: J. S. Kaplan
Executive Producer: Joseph Kaufman
Screenplay: John Carpenter
Director of Photography: Douglas Knapp
Editor: John T. Chance [John Carpenter]
Makeup: Don Bledsoe
Special Effects: Richard Albain Jr
Music: John Carpenter
Production Company: CKK Production
Length: 91 minutes
Cast: Austin Stoker (Bishop), Darwin Joston (Wilson), Laurie Zimmer (Leigh), Martin West (Lawson), Tony Burton (Wells), Charles Cyphers (Starker), Nancy Loomis (Julie), Peter Bruni (Ice Cream Man), John J. Fox (Warden), Marc Ross (Patrolman Tramer), Alan Koss (Patrolman Baxter), Henry Brandon (Chaney), Kim Richards (Kathy), Frank Doubleday (White Warlord)

*Eyes of Laura Mars*, 1978
Director: Irvin Kershner
Screenplay: John Carpenter, David Zelag Goodman (Story by John Carpenter)

*Zuma Beach*, 1978
(TV movie)
Director: Lee H. Katzin
Teleplay: John Carpenter, John H. Sherman

*Someone's Watching Me! (High Rise)*, 1978
(TV movie)
Director: John Carpenter
Executive Producer: Richard Kobritz
Associate Producer: Anna Cottle
Teleplay: John Carpenter
Director of Photography: Robert Hauser

Editor: Jerry Taylor
Makeup: Karl Sillvera
Music: Harry Sukman
Production Company: Warner Bros. Television for NBC Television
Length: 98 minutes
Cast: Lauren Hutton (Leigh Michaels), David Birney (Paul Winkless), Adrienne Barbeau (Sophie), Charles Cyphers (Gary Hunt), Grainger Hines (Steve), Len Lesser (Burly Man), John Mahon (Frimsin), James Murtaugh (Leone), J. Jay Saunders (Police Inspector), Michael Laurence (TV Announcer), George Skaff (Herbert Stiles), Robert Phalen (Wayne)

*Halloween*, 1978
Director: John Carpenter
Producer: Debra Hill
Executive Producer: Irwin Yablans
Associate Producer: Kool Lusby
Screenplay: John Carpenter, Debra Hill
Director of Photography: Dean Cundey
Editor: Tommy Wallace, Charles Bornstein
Makeup: Erica Ulland
Music: John Carpenter
Production Company: Falcon International Productions
Length: 91 minutes
Cast: Donald Pleasence (Loomis), Jamie Lee Curtis (Laurie), Nancy Loomis (Annie), P. J. Soles (Lynda), Charles Cyphers (Brackett), Kyle Richards (Lindsey), Brian Andrews (Tommy), John Michael Graham (Bob), Nancy Stephens (Marion), Arthur Malet (Graveyard Keeper), Mickey Yablans (Richie), Brent Le Page (Lonnie), Adam Hollander (Keith), Nick Castle (The Shape)

*Better Late than Never*, 1979
(TV movie)
Director: Richard Crenna
Teleplay: John Carpenter

*Elvis (Elvis: The Movie)*, 1979
(TV movie; overseas theatrical release)
Director: John Carpenter
Producer: Anthony Lawrence
Executive Producer: Dick Clark
Associate Producer: James Ritz
Supervising Producer: Toni Bishop
Screenplay: Anthony Lawrence
Director of Photography: Donald M. Morgan
Editor: Ron Moler
Makeup: Marvin Westmore
Music: Joe Renzetti

Production Company: Dick Clark Motion Pictures
Length: 119 minutes
Cast: Kurt Russell (Elvis Presley), Shelley Winters (Gladys Presley), Bing Russell (Vernon Presley), Robert Gray (Red West), Season Hubley (Priscilla Presley), Pat Hingle (Colonel Tom Parker), Abi Young (Natalie Wood), Charlie Hodge (Himself), Randy Gray (Elvis, as a boy), Meg Wyllie (Grandma), Nora Boland (Teacher), Felicia Fenske (Lisa Marie), Larry Geller (Himself), Joe Mantegna, Melody Anderson, Ed Begley Jr, Charles Cyphers

*The Fog*, 1979
Director: John Carpenter
Producer: Debra Hill
Executive Producer: Charles B. Bloch
Associate Producer: Barry Bernardi, Pegi Brotman
Screenplay: John Carpenter, Debra Hill
Director of Photography: Dean Cundey
Editor: Tommy Lee Wallace, Charles Bornstein
Special Makeup Effects: Rob Bottin
Special Effects: Richard Albain Jr
Blake Effects: Rob Bottin, Dean Cundey
Music: John Carpenter; Electronic Realisation: Dan Wyman
Production Company: Debra Hill Productions. For Avco Embassy
Length: 89 minutes
Cast: Adrienne Barbeau (Stevie Wayne), Jamie Lee Curtis (Elizabeth Solley), Janet Leigh (Kathy Williams), John Houseman (Mr Machen), Tom Atkins (Nick Castle), Charles Cyphers (Dan O'Bannon), Nancy Loomis (Sandy Fadel), Ty Mitchell (Andy), Hal Holbrook (Father Malone), John Goff (Al Williams), George 'Buck' Flower (Tommy Wallace), Jay Jacobs (Mayor), Ric Moreno, Lee Sacks, Tommy Wallace (Ghosts), John Carpenter (Bennett; uncredited)

*Escape From New York*, 1981
Director: John Carpenter
Producer: Larry Franco, Debra Hill
Associate Producer: Barry Bernardi, Aaron Lipstadt
Screenplay: John Carpenter, Nick Castle
Director of Photography: Dean Cundey
Editor: Todd Ramsay
Makeup Supervisor: Ken Chase
Special Effects Supervisor: Roy Arbogast,
Music: John Carpenter in association with Alan Howarth
Production Company: Avco Embassy/ International Film Investors/ Goldcrest Films International
Length: 99 minutes
Cast: Kurt Russell (Snake Plissken), Lee Van Cleef (Hauk), Ernest Borgnine (Cabbie), Donald Pleasence (President), Isaac Hayes (The Duke), Season Hubley (Girl in Chock Full O'Nuts), Harry Dean Stanton (Brain), Adrienne Barbeau (Maggie), Tom Atkins (Rehme),

Charles Cyphers (Secretary of State), Joe Unger (Taylor), Frank Doubleday (Romero); John Strobel (Cronenberg), Ox Baker (Slag)

*Halloween II*, 1981
Director: Rick Rosenthal
Producer: Debra Hill, John Carpenter
Screenplay: John Carpenter, Debra Hill
Music: John Carpenter in association with Alan Howarth

*The Thing*, 1982
Director: John Carpenter
Producer: David Foster, Lawrence Turman
Executive Producer: Wilbur Stark
Associate Producer: Larry Franco
Co-Producer: Stuart Cohen
Screenplay: Bill Lancaster (Based on the story 'Who Goes There?', by John W. Campbell Jr)
Director of Photography: Dean Cundey
Editor: Todd Ramsay
Special Makeup Effects: Rob Bottin
Special Effects: Roy Arbogast, Leroy Routley, Michael A. Clifford
Music: Ennio Morricone
Production Company: Universal. A Turman-Foster Company
Length: 109 minutes
Cast: Kurt Russell (MacReady), A. Wilford Brimley (Blair), T. K. Carter (Nauls), David Clennon (Palmer), Keith David (Childs), Richard Dysart (Dr Copper), Charles Hallahan (Norris), Peter Maloney (Bennings), Richard Masur (Clark), Donald Moffat (Garry), Joel Polis (Fuchs), Thomas Waites (Windows), Norbert Weisser (Norwegian), Larry Franco (Norwegian Passenger with Rifle), Nate Irwin (Helicopter Pilot), John Carpenter (Norwegian in Video Footage; uncredited)

*Halloween III: Season of the Witch*, 1982
Director: Tommy Lee Wallace
Producer: John Carpenter, Debra Hill
Music: John Carpenter, Alan Howarth

*Christine*, 1983
Director: John Carpenter
Producer: Richard Kobritz
Executive Producer: Kirby McCauley, Mark Tarlov
Co-Producer: Larry Franco
Associate Producer: Barry Bernardi
Screenplay: Bill Phillips (Based on the novel by Stephen King)
Director of Photography: Donald M. Morgan
Editor: Marion Rothman
Makeup: Bob Dawn

Special Effects Supervisor: Roy Arbogast
Music: John Carpenter in association with Alan Howarth
Production Company: Columbia-Delphi Productions. A Polar film
Length: 110 minutes
Cast: Keith Gordon (Arnie), John Stockwell (Dennis), Alexandra Paul (Leigh), Robert Prosky (Darnell), Harry Dean Stanton (Junkins), Christine Belford (Regina Cunningham), Roberts Blossom (LeBay), William Ostrander (Buddy), David Spielberg (Mr Casey), Malcolm Danare (Moochie), Steven Tash (Rich), Stuart Charno (Vandenberg), Kelly Preston (Roseanne)

*The Philadelphia Experiment*, 1984
Director: Stewart Raffill
Executive Producer: John Carpenter

*Starman*, 1984
Director: John Carpenter
Producer: Larry J. Franco
Executive Producer: Michael Douglas
Co-Producer: Barry Bernardi
Associate Producer: Bruce A. Evans
Screenplay: Bruce A. Evans, Raynold Gideon
Director of Photography: Donald M. Morgan
Editor: Marion Rothman
Makeup: Peter Altobelli
Special Effects Coordinator: Roy Arbogast
Special Effects Supervisor: Bruce Nicholson
Starman Transformation: Dick Smith, Stan Winston, Rick Baker
Music: Jack Nitzsche
Production Company: Columbia-Delphi Productions II
Length: 115 minutes
Cast: Jeff Bridges (Starman), Karen Allen (Jenny Hayden), Charles Martin Smith (Mark Shermin), Richard Jaeckel (George Fox), Robert Phalen (Major Bell), Tony Edwards (Sergeant Lemon), John Walter Davis (Brad Heinmuller), Ted White (Deer Hunter), Dirk Blocker (Cop #1), M. C. Gainey (Cop #2), Sean Faro (Hot Rodder), Buck Flower (Cook), Russ Benning (Scientist), John Carpenter (Man in Helicopter; uncredited)

*Big Trouble in Little China*, 1986
Director: John Carpenter
Producer: Larry J. Franco
Executive Producer: Paul Monash, Keith Barish
Associate Producer: Jim Lau, James Lew
Screenplay: Gary Goldman, David Z. Weinstein
Adaptation: W. D. Richter
Director of Photography: Dean Cundey
Editor: Mark Warner, Steve Mirkovich, Edward A. Warschilka

Makeup: Ken Chase
Special Effects Coordinator: Joseph Unsinn
Creatures: Steve Johnson, Dave Kelsey, Screaming Mad George, Eric Fiedler
Martial Arts Choreography: James Lew, Jim Lau
Music: John Carpenter in association with Alan Howarth
Production Company: Twentieth Century Fox. A Taft-Barish-Monash production
Length: 100 minutes
Cast: Kurt Russell (Jack Burton), Kim Cattrall (Gracie Law), Dennis Dun (Wang Chi), James Hong (Lo Pan), Victor Wong (Egg Shen); Kate Burton (Margo), Donald Li (Eddie Lee), Carter Wong (Thunder), Peter Kwong (Rain), James Pax (Lightning), Suzee Pai (Miao Yin), Chao Li Chi (Uncle Chu), Jeff Imada (Needles), Rummel Mor (Joe Lucky), Craig Ng (One Ear), John Carpenter (Worker in Chinatown; uncredited)

*Black Moon Rising*, 1986
Director: Harley Cokliss
Executive Producer: John Carpenter
Screenplay: John Carpenter, Desmond Nakano, William Gray
Story: John Carpenter

*The Boy Who Could Fly*, 1986
Director: Nick Castle
Actor: John Carpenter (The Coupe de Villes band member)

*Prince of Darkness*, 1987
Director: John Carpenter
Producer: Larry Franco
Executive Producer: Shep Gordon, André Blay
Screenplay: Martin Quatermass [John Carpenter]
Director of Photography: Gary B. Kibbe
Editor: Steve Mirkovich
Makeup: Frank Carrisosa
Special Effects Coordinator: Kevin Quibell
Music: John Carpenter in association with Alan Howarth
Production Company: Alive Films
Length: 101 minutes
Cast: Donald Pleasence (Priest), Jameson Parker (Brian), Victor Wong (Birack), Lisa Blount (Catherine), Dennis Dun (Walter), Susan Blanchard (Kelly), Anne Howard (Susan), Ann Yen (Lisa), Ken Wright (Lomax), Dirk Blocker (Mullins), Jesse Lawrence Ferguson (Calder), Peter Jason (Dr Leahy), Robert Grasmere (Wyndham), Thom Bray (Etchinson), Joanna Merlin (Bag Lady), Alice Cooper (Street Schizo), Betty Ramey (Nun), Jessie Ferguson (Dark Figure)

*They Live*, 1988
Director: John Carpenter
Producer: Larry Franco

Executive Producer: Shep Gordon, André Blay
Associate Producer: Sandy King
Screenplay: Frank Armitage [John Carpenter] (Based on the short story 'Eight O'Clock in the Morning' by Ray Nelson)
Director of Photography: Gary B. Kibbe
Editor: Gib Jaffe, Frank E. Jimenez
Makeup: Frank Carrisosa
Special Effects: Roy Arbogast
Music: John Carpenter, Alan Howarth
Production Company: Alive Films
Length: 94 minutes
Cast: Roddy Piper (Nada), Keith David (Frank), Meg Foster (Holly), George 'Buck' Flower (Drifter), Peter Jason (Gilbert), Raymond St Jacques (Street Preacher), Jason Robards III (Family Man), John Lawrence (Bearded Man), Susan Barnes (Brown-haired Woman), Sy Richardson (Black Revolutionary), Wendy Brainard (Family Man's Daughter), Lucille Meredith (Female Interviewer), Larry Franco (Neighbour)

*Halloween 4: The Return of Michael Myers*, 1988
Director: Dwight H. Little
Music: Alan Howarth. *Halloween* theme by John Carpenter

*Halloween 5: The Revenge of Michael Myers*, 1989
Director: Dominique Othenin-Girard
Music: Alan Howarth. *Halloween* theme by John Carpenter

*El Diablo*, 1990
(TV movie)
Director: Peter Markle
Teleplay: Tommy Lee Wallace, John Carpenter, Bill Phillips

*Blood River*, 1991
(TV movie)
Director: Mel Damski
Teleplay: John Carpenter

*Memoirs of an Invisible Man*, 1992
Director: John Carpenter
Producer: Bruce Bodner, Dan Kolsrud
Executive Producer: Arnon Milchan
Screenplay: Robert Collector, Dana Olsen, William Goldman (Based on the book by H. F. Saint)
Director of Photography: William A. Fraker
Editor: Marion Rothman
Makeup: Rick Sharp, Lee Harmon
Special Effects Coordinator: Ken Pepiot

Music: Shirley Walker
Production Company: Warner Bros. A Cornelius production
Length: 99 minutes
Cast: Chevy Chase (Nick Halloway), Darryl Hannah (Alice Monroe), Sam Neill (David Jenkins), Michael McKean (George Talbot), Stephen Tobolowsky (Warren Singleton), Jim Norton (Dr Bernard Wachs), Pat Skipper (Morrissey), Paul Perri (Gomez), Richard Epcar (Tyler), Steven Bar (Clellan), Gregory Paul Martin (Richard), Patricia Heaton (Ellen), Rip Haight [John Carpenter] (Helicopter Pilot)

*Body Bags (John Carpenter Presents 'Mind Games')*, 1993
(TV movie)
Director: John Carpenter (segments 'The Morgue', 'The Gas Station', 'Hair'), Tobe Hooper (segment 'Eye')
Executive Producer: Sandy King, John Carpenter, Dan Angel
Producer: Sandy King
Co-Producer: Dan Angel
Screenplay: Bill Brown, Dan Angel
Director of Photography: Gary Kibbe
Editor: Edward A. Warschilka
Special Makeup Effects: Rick Baker, Howard Berger, Robert Kurtzman, Greg Nicotero
Special Effects: Howard Jensen
Music: John Carpenter, Jim Lang
Production Company: 187 Corp., Showtime Network
Length: 91 minutes
Cast: John Carpenter (Coroner), Tom Arnold (Man #1), Tobe Hooper (Man #2); 'The Gas Station', Robert Carradine (Bill), Alex Datcher (Anne), Peter Jason (Gent), Molly Cheek (Divorcee), Wes Craven (Pasty Faced Man), Sam Raimi (Bill – Dead Attendant), David Naughton (Pete), Buck Flower (Stranger); 'Hair', Stacy Keach (Richard), David Warner (Dr Lock), Sheena Easton (Megan), Dan Blom (Dennis), Greg Nicotero (Man with Dog), Deborah Harry (The Nurse); 'Eye', Mark Hamill (Brent), Twiggy (Cathy), John Agar (Dr Lang), Roger Corman (Dr Bregman), Charles Napier (Manager)

*Il Silenzio dei Prosciutti (Silence of the Hams)*, 1993
Director: Ezio Greggio
Actor: John Carpenter (Trench Coat Man)

*In the Mouth of Madness*, 1995
Director: John Carpenter
Producer: Sandy King
Executive Producer: Michael De Luca
Associate Producer: Artist Robinson
Screenplay: Michael De Luca
Director of Photography: Gary B. Kibbe
Editor: Edward A. Warschilka
Special Makeup Effects: Robert Kurtzman, Gregory Nicotero, Howard Berger

Special Effects: Martin Malivoire Pictures, Ted Ross
Music: John Carpenter, Jim Lang
Production Company: New Line Cinema
Length: 95 minutes
Cast: Sam Neill (John Trent), Julie Carmen (Linda Styles), Jürgen Prochnow (Sutter Cane), David Warner (Dr Renn), John Glover (Dr Sapirstein), Bernie Casey (Robbie), Peter Jason (Insurance Fraud Perpetrator), Charlton Heston (Jackson Harglow), Frances Bay (Mrs Pickman), Wilhelm von Homburg (Simon), Kevin Rushton (Guard no. 1), Gene Mack (Guard no. 2), Conrad Bergschneider (Axe Maniac), Hayden Christensen (Paper Boy)

*Village of the Damned*, 1995
Director: John Carpenter
Producers: Michael Preger, Sandy King
Co-Producer: David Chackler
Executive Producers: Ted Vernon, Shep Gordon, André Blay
Co-Executive Producers: James Jacks, Sean Daniel
Screenplay: David Himmelstein (Based on the book *The Midwich Cuckoos*, by John Wyndham, and the 1960 screenplay by Sterling Silliphant, Wolf Rilla, George Barclay)
Director of Photography: Gary B. Kibbe
Editor: Edward A. Warschilka
Special Makeup Effects: Robert Kurtzman, Gregory Nicotero, Howard Berger
Special Effects: Roy Arbogast
Music: John Carpenter, Dave Davies
Production Company: Universal. An Alphaville production
Length: 99 minutes
Cast: Christopher Reeve (Alan Chaffee), Kirstie Alley (Dr Susan Verner), Linda Koslowski (Jill McGowan), Michael Paré (Frank McGowan), Meredith Salenger (Melanie Roberts), Mark Hamill (Reverend George), Pippa Pearthree (Sarah), Peter Jason (Ben Blum), Constance Forslund (Cally Blum), Karen Kahn (Barbara Chaffee), Thomas Dekker (David), Lindsey Haun (Mara), Rip Haight [John Carpenter] (Man at Gas Station Phone)

*Halloween: The Curse of Michael Myers (Halloween 666: Curse of Michael Myers; Hall6ween)*, 1995
Director: Joe Chappelle
Music: Alan Haworth. *Halloween* theme by John Carpenter

*Escape From L.A.*, 1996
Director: John Carpenter
Producer: Debra Hill, Kurt Russell
Screenplay: John Carpenter, Debra Hill, Kurt Russell (Based on characters created by John Carpenter, Nick Castle)
Director of Photography: Gary B. Kibbe
Editor: Edward A. Warschilka
Special Makeup Effects: Rick Baker
Special Effects Coordinator: Marty Bresin

Special Effects Supervisor: Dale Ettema
Music: Shirley Walker, John Carpenter
Production Company: Paramount. In association with Rysher Entertainment
Length: 102 minutes
Cast: Kurt Russell (Snake Plissken), A. J. Langer (Utopia), Steve Buscemi (Map to the Stars Eddie), George Corraface (Cuervo Jones), Stacy Keach (Malloy), Michelle Forbes (Brazen), Pam Grier (Hershe), Jeff Imada (Saigon Shadow), Cliff Robertson (President), Valeria Golino (Taslima), Peter Fonda (Pipeline), Ina Romeo (Blonde Hooker), Peter Jason (Duty Sergeant), Bruce Campbell (Surgeon General of Beverly Hills), Paul Bartel (Congressman), Tom McNulty (Com Officer), Robert Carradine (Skinhead)

*Vampires*, 1998
Director: John Carpenter
Producer: Sandy King
Executive Producer: Barr Potter
Co-Producer: Don Jakoby
Screenplay: Don Jakoby (Based on the novel 'Vampire$' by John Steakley)
Director of Photography: Gary B. Kibbe
Editor: Edward A. Warschilka
Special Makeup Effects: Robert Kurtzman, Gregory Nicotero, Howard Berger
Special Effects Coordinator: Darrell D. Pritchett
Music: John Carpenter
Production Company: Columbia and Largo Entertainment. A Storm King production
Length: 108 minutes
Cast: James Woods (Jack Crow), Daniel Baldwin (Montoya), Sheryl Lee (Katrina), Thomas Ian Griffith (Valek), Maximilian Schell (Cardinal Alba), Tim Guinee (Father Adam Guiteau), Gregory Sierra (Father Giovanni), Mark Boone Junior (Catlin), Cary-Hiroyuki Tagawa (David Deyo), Tommy Rosales (Ortega), Henry Kingi (Anthony), Frank Darabont (Man with Buick)

*Halloween H20: 20 Years Later*, 1998
Director: Steve Miner
Music: John Ottman. *Halloween* theme by John Carpenter

*Silent Predators*, 1999
(TV movie)
Director: Noel Nosseck
Teleplay: John Carpenter, William Gilmore, Matt Dorff

*Ghosts of Mars*, 2001
Director: John Carpenter
Producer: Sandy King
Screenplay: Larry Sulkis, John Carpenter
Director of Photography: Gary B. Kibbe
Editor: Paul C. Warschilka

Special Makeup Effects: Robert Kurtzman, Greg Nicotero, Howard Berger
Special Effects Coordinator: Darrell Pritchett
Music: John Carpenter
Production Company: Screen Gems. A Storm King production
Length: 98 minutes
Cast: Ice Cube (James 'Desolation' Williams), Natasha Henstridge (Melanie Ballard), Jason Statham (Jericho Butler), Pam Grier (Helena Braddock), Clea Duvall (Bashira Kincaid), Joanna Cassidy (Whitlock), Liam Waite (Michael Descanso), Wanda DeJesus (Akooshay), Duane Davis (Uno), Rodney A. Grant (Tres), Lobo Sebastian (Dos), Robert Carradine (Rodale), Peter Jason (McSimms)

*Vampires: Los Muertos*, 2001
Director: Tommy Lee Wallace
Executive Producer: John Carpenter, Sandy King

*Halloween: Resurrection*, 2002
Director: Rick Rosenthal
Music: Danny Lux. *Halloween* theme by John Carpenter

Carpenter as interviewee or discussant in programmes and documentaries – a selection:
*Fear on Film: Inside 'The Fog'* (1980, Steven A. Wacker)
*Horror Café* (1990, Janet Fraser Crook)
*Fear in the Dark* (1991, Dominic Murphy)
*Moving Pictures* (feature on CinemaScope) (1993, Louis Heaton)
*Masters of Illusion: The Wizards of Special Effects* (1994, Gary R. Benz)
*After the Sunset: The Life and Times of the Drive-in Theatre* (1995, Jon Bokenkamp)
*Clive Barker's A-Z of Horror* (1997, Ursula Macfarlane)
*The Reality Trip* (1997, Louis Heaton)
*The Directors: John Carpenter* (1997, Robert J. Emery)
*The Night He Came Home: John Carpenter's Halloween* (1999, Andrew Abbott)
*Faces of Evil* (2000, Phil Tuckett)
*The American Nightmare* (2000, Adam Simon)
*Guns for Hire: The Making of 'The Magnificent Seven'* (2000, Louis Heaton)
*Dario Argento: An Eye for Horror* (2000, Leon Ferguson)
*Mario Bava: Maestro of the Macabre* (2000, Garry S. Grant)
*AFI's 100 Years, 100 Thrills: America's Most Heart-Pounding Movies* (2001, Gary Smith)
*Hidden Values: The Movies of the Fifties* (2001)
*Music Behind the Scenes: Suspense* (2001, Howard Hill)
*Masters of Horror* (2002, Mike Mendez, Dave Parker)
*Halloween: A Cut above the Rest* (2003)
*Super Secret Movie Rules: Slashers* (2004)

# BIBLIOGRAPHY

Compiled by Ian Conrich and David Woods; information on movie tie-in paperbacks supplemented by Ronald V. Borst.

[R] = film review

*Books on Carpenter*

Boulenger, G. (2003) *John Carpenter: The Prince of Darkness.* Los Angeles: Silman-James Press.

Cumbow, R. C. (1990) *Order in the Universe: The Films of John Carpenter.* Metuchen, NJ: Scarecrow Press [2nd edn, 2000].

D'Agnolo Vallan, G. and R. Turigliatto (1999) *John Carpenter.* Turin: Lindau [in Italian].

Lagier, L. and J.-B. Thoret (1998) *Mythes et Masques: Les Fantômes de John Carpenter.* Paris: Dreamland éditeur [in French].

Loderhose, W. (1990) *John Carpenter: Das Grosse Filmbuch.* Hamburg: Bastei Lubbe [in German].

Muir, J. K. (2000) *The Films of John Carpenter.* Jefferson, NC and London: McFarland.

Odell, C. and M. Le Blanc (2001) *The Pocket Essential John Carpenter.* Harpenden: Pocket Essentials.

*Movie tie-in paperback novels*

Etchinson, D. (1980) *The Fog.* New York: Bantam/London: Corgi.

Foster, A. D. (1974/9) *Dark Star.* New York: Ballantine/London: Futura.

_____ (1982) *The Thing.* New York: Bantam/London: Corgi.

_____ (1984/5) *Starman.* New York: Warner Books/London: Corgi.

King, S. (1983/4) *Christine.* New York: Signet/London: NEL.

McQuay, M. (1981) *Escape From New York.* New York: Bantam/London: Corgi.

Richards, C. (1979/80) *Halloween.* New York: Bantam/London: Corgi.

Saint, H. F. (1992) *Memoirs of an Invisible Man.* Harmondsworth: Penguin.

Steakley, J. (1998/9) *Vampires.* New York: Roc Books/Harmondsworth: Penguin.


*General*

Bankston, D. (2003) 'Wrap Shot', *American Cinematographer,* 84, 4, 144.

Bernstein, J. (1996) *Guardian: The Guide,* 13 April, 97.

Caetano, A. I. (1995) 'El cine de los pobres', *Amante Cinema,* 45, 36 [in Spanish].

Carpenter, J. (1975) 'The Gods Hate Hollywood', *Photon,* 26, 6.

_____ (1983) 'On Composing for *Halloween*', *Fangoria,* 30, 38–9.

_____ (1996) 'John Carpenter's Guilty Pleasures', *Film Comment,* 32, 5, 50–3.

_____ (2001) 'Facing the Evils', *Fangoria,* 200, 6.

Clarke, F. S. (1980) 'Roots of Imagination', *Cinefantastique,* 10, 1, 11.

Crawley, T. (1981) 'John Carpenter: The Dark Star Behind The Fog', *Films Illustrated,* 112, 132–7.

Dempsey, P. (1995) 'Cinema of Ideas', *Screen International,* 995, 31.

Fischer, D. (1991) *Horror Film Directors 1931–1990.* Jefferson, NC: McFarland,117–43.

Gans, C. (1980) 'Au-dela des brumes de l'Angoisse', *Écran Fantastique,* 13, 26–34, 38–40 [in French].

Garsault, A. (1995) 'John Carpenter un fantastiqueur classique et moderne', *Positif,* 409, 8–9 [in French].

Gilbey, R. (1994) 'Budget brat-packer', *Independent* London Supplement, 5 July, 8.

Hasted, N. (1996) 'Why he never sold his soul', *Independent* Section 2, 19 September, 8.

Hoffmann, C. (1984) 'Die Welt des John Carpenter', *Retro,* 25, 11–12 [in German].

Holms, P. (2003) *Music From the Movies,* 38, 56.

Jones, K. (1999) 'John Carpenter: american movie classic', *Film Comment,* 35, 1, 26–31.

Keyser, G. (1999) 'Genremeester voor lege zalen', *Skrien,* 231, 18–21 [in Dutch].

Klewer, D. (1981) 'Der Howard Hawks Der Moderne: Die Horror Trips Des John Carpenter', *Vampir,* 23, 5–16 [in German].

Lagier, L. (2001) 'John Carpenter et les effets spéciaux (Portrait du cinéaste en artiste inaisissable)', *Cinémaction,* 102, 139–45 [in French].

Lucas, T. (1995) 'The Panavision World of John Carpenter', *Video Watchdog,* 27, 49–55.

Martin, B. (1980) 'John Carpenter', *Fangoria,* 8, 22–6.

McCarty, J. (1995) 'John Carpenter', in J. McCarty (ed.) *The Fearmakers: The Screen's Directorial Masters of Suspense and Terror.* London: Virgin, 166–75.

Moules, P. (1979) 'Carpenter's Craft', *Film Making,* 17, 2, 77.

Nichols, D. B. and B. Martin (1981) 'An Anatomy of Terror', *Fangoria,* 10, 19–22, 48–9.

Noriega, G. (1995) 'Dossier Carpenter. El reino de los noventa minutos', *Amante Cinema,*

45, 32–5 [in Spanish].

Rayns, T. and S. Meek (1978) '…And An Ascendant Star', *Time Out*, 414, 14–15.

Ross, R. (1984) 'Les rythmes de l'Angoisse', *La Revue du Cinema*, 391, 39–43 [in French].

Rouyer, P. (1995) 'L'Antre de la folie retour a Hobb's End', *Positif*, 409, 6–7 [in French].

Strick, P. (1984a) '*Christine* and *The Dead Zone*', *Sight and Sound*, 53, 2, 150.

Sullivan, D. (1995) 'Carpenter Meets the Wolf Man', *Fangoria*, 143, 45.

Swires, S. (1988) 'The Curse of "Halloween"', *Fangoria*, 78, 24.

Thonen, J. (1998a) 'Vampires. Carpenter's Web', *Cinefantastique*, 30, 7/8, 60.

____ (1998b) 'John Carpenter: Cinema of Isolation', *Cinefantastique*, 30, 7/8, 64–73.

Wesley, M. (1987) 'The Films of John Carpenter', *Samhain*, 2, 6–9.

Wiater, S. (1992) *Dark Visions*. New York: Avon, 19–29.

Zapiola, G. (1982) 'Para devaluar a John Carpenter', *Cinemateca Revista*, 35, 18–20 [in Spanish].

Ziegler, R. E. (1983) 'Killing Space: The Dialectic in John Carpenter's Films', *Georgia Review*, 37, 4, 770–86.

*Interviews*

Appelbaum, R. (1979a) 'From Cult Homage To Creative Control', *Films and Filming*, 25, 9, 10–16.

____ (1979b), 'Working with numbers', *Films and Filming*, 25, 12, 20–4.

Assayas, O., S. le Péron and S. Toubiana (1982) 'Entretien Avec John Carpenter', *Cahiers du Cinema*, 339, 15–23 [in French].

Auty, C. (1980) 'B-Souper', *Time Out*, 551, 14–15.

Bauer, E. (1999) 'Things That Go Bump in the Night', *Creative Screenwriting*, 6, 1, 62–5, 76.

Calcutt, I. (1994) 'A Method in Madness', *Samhain*, 47, 22–6.

Chase, C. (1982) *New York Times*, 26 June.

Crawley, T. (1981) 'A Starburst Interview with John Carpenter', *Starburst*, 36, 32–7; 37, 46–50.

Delorme, G. and A. Brillant (1998) 'Entretien Avec Un Faiseur De Vampires', *Premiere*, 254, 110–11 [in French].

Egan, A. and K. Higgins (2000) 'John Carpenter. An Interview', *Focus*, 20, 23–8.

Elmer, D. (1996) 'Boom Towns', *Time Out*, 11–18 September, 28.

*Empire* (2004) 'Public Access', 176, 60–1.

Ferrante, A. C. (2001) 'Carpenter's Tools', *Cinescape*, 54, 20–1.

Fox, J. R. (1980) 'Riding High On Horror', *Cinefantastique*, 10, 1, 5–10, 40, 42–4.

Fox, J. R., J.-M. Lofficier and R. Lofficier (1982c) 'Entretien avec John Carpenter', *Écran Fantastique*, 28, 49–57 [in French].

Frappat, H. and O. Joyard (2001) 'John Carpenter: La peur voyage', *Cahiers du Cinema*, 562, 54–61 [in French].

Garris, M. (1982a) 'Landis, Cronenberg, Carpenter', *Fangoria*, 19, 30–3 [part 1].

____ (1982b) 'Landis, Cronenberg, Carpenter', *Fangoria*, 20, 26–9 [part 2].

____ (1982c) 'Landis, Cronenberg, Carpenter', *Fangoria*, 21, 26–9 [part 3].

Goodman, J. (1989) 'The sharp shooter', *Guardian*, 22 June, 21.

Henry, M. (1995) 'Entretien avec John Carpenter. "Nous sommes tous des démons"', *Positif*, 409, 10–18 [in French].

Hope, A. (1978) 'John's low cost star vehicle', *Screen International*, 122, 10–11.

Jaehne, K. (1985) 'The Man Behind Starman', *Films*, 5, 5, 10–11.

Johnston, S. (1989) 'Cheap thrills and dark glasses', *Independent*, 22 June, 16.

Jones, A. (1994) 'Novel Horror', *Shivers*, 12, 24–6.

Julius, M. (1995) 'The Carpenter's Tale', *Shivers*, 15, 38–41.

Lofficier, J.-M. (1980) 'Entretien avec John Carpenter', *Écran Fantastique*, 13, 35–7 [in French].

Mauceri, J. (2001) 'Life on Mars?', *Shivers*, 92, 34–7.

McCarthy, T. (1980) 'Trick and Treat', *Film Comment*, 16, 1, 17–24.

Migliore, A. and J. Strysik (2000) *The Lurker in the Lobby: A Guide to the Cinema of H. P. Lovecraft*. Seattle: Armitage House, 36–43.

Milne, T. and R. Combs (1978) 'The Man in the Cryogenic Freezer', *Sight and Sound*, 47, 2, 94–8.

Newman, K. (1988a) 'Prints of Darkness', *City Limits*, 344, 16–17.

____ (1988b) 'They Live!', *Fear*, 1, 12–15.

Nilsson, T. and S. Biodrowski (1991) 'The Return of John Carpenter', *Cinefantastique*, 22, 3, 4–6.

Oddie, A. (1980) 'An Interview with Director John Carpenter. *The Fog*', *Filmmakers Monthly*, 13, 5, 16–21.

Pirie, D. (1982) 'Low Budget Highs', *Time Out*, 628, 25.

Pulleine, T. (1978) 'Fire in the streets', *Guardian*, 8 March.

Rosenthal, D. (1980) 'Rated H For Horrors', *New York*, 18 February, 50, 52, 54.

Saada, N. (2000) 'Unis par la peur – Dario Argento rencontre John Carpenter', *Cahiers du cinéma*, 542, 4–5 [in French].

Salisbury, M. (1992a) 'John Carpenter', *Starburst Yearbook*, 17–21.

____ (1992b) 'Thrilled Beyond Belief', *What's On in London*, 20 May, 10–11.

*Screen International* (1979) 'A man who knows where he's going', 182, 6.

Slot, O. (1994) 'It didn't turn me into one', *Independent*, 14 April, 32.

Smith, A. (1996) 'Carpenter's Log', *Empire*, 89, 94–6.

Spelling, I. (2000) 'John Carpenter Goes to Mars', *Fangoria*, 193, 16–17.

Stevenson, J. (1980) 'Profiles: People Start Running', *New Yorker*, 28 January, 41–8, 50, 55–8.

Swires, S. (1985) '*Starman*: Entretien Avec John Carpenter', *Écran Fantastique*, 56, 54–8 [in French].

Tinkerbelle (1980) 'suspense builder. John Carpenter', *Interview*, 10, 5, 30–2.

Turan, K. (1980) 'Carpenter: A Fringe Hollywood Hero', *Now*, 24 October.

Wansell, G. (1982) 'Interview: John Carpenter. The monstrous conception', *Times*, 25 August, 7.

Wells, J. (1980) 'New Fright Master John Carpenter', *Films in Review*, 31, 4, 218–24.


*Dark Star* (1974)

Anderson, C. W. (1985) *Science Fiction Films of the Seventies*. Jefferson, NC: McFarland, 84–9.

Andrews, N. (1978) *Financial Times*, 24 February [R].

Beau (1974) *Variety*, 1 May, 18 [R].

Bernades, H. (1995) *Amante Cinema*, 45, 37 [R, in Spanish].

Bilbow, M. (1978) *Screen International*, 122, 18 [R].

Brien, A. (1978) *Sunday Times*, 5 February [R].

Castell, D. (1978) *Films Illustrated*, 78, 206 [R].

*Cinefantastique* 2, 3, 4–7 [interview with Dan O'Bannon].

Coleman, J. (1978) *New Statesman*, 3 March [R].

Combs, R. (1978) *Monthly Film Bulletin*, 529, 22–3 [R].

Cruce, B. (1994) *Perfect Vision*, 6, 23, 130–1 [R].

Fuller, N. (1974) *Scotsman*, 30 August [R].

Gibbs, P. (1978) *Daily Telegraph*, 24 February [R].

Gow, G. (1978) *Films and Filming*, 24, 8, 35–6 [R].

Howard, A. (1974) *Hollywood Reporter*, 29 March, 3 [R].

Hutchinson, T. (1978) *Sunday Telegraph*, 26 February [R].

Jarecki, N. (2002) *Breaking In: How 20 Film Directors Got Their Start*. New York: Broadway, 90–6.

Malcolm, D. (1977) *Guardian*, 22 December [R].

____ (1978) *Guardian*, 23 February [R].

Maslin, J. (1979) *New York Times*, 3 February [R].

*Monthly Film Bulletin*, 529 (1978) 'The Genesis of *Dark Star*', 35.

O'Bannon, D. (1984) 'The Remaking of *Dark Star*', in D. Peary (ed.) *Omni's Screen Flights/ Screen Fantasies: The Future According to Science Fiction Cinema*. New York: Columbus, 147–51.

Peary, D. (1984) *Cult Movies 2*. Vermilion: London, 53–5.

Plowright, M. (1978) *Glasgow Herald*, 14 August [R].

Robinson, D. (1978a) *Times*, 3 February [R].

____ (1978b) 'The slow evolution of *Dark Star*', *Times*, 8 March.

Sigal, C. (1978) *Spectator*, 4 March [R].

Stanbrook, A. (1999) 'Epic story of war and friendship in Cambodia', *Daily Telegraph*, 3 July [R].

*Times Magazine* (1994) 22 January [R].

*Video Watchdog* (1992) 12, 50–51 [R].

Walker, A. (1978) *Evening Standard*, 23 February [R].

Wilson, C. (1979) *Daily Mail*, 24 February [R].

Winogura, D. (1974) '*Dark Star*', *Cinefantastique* 3, 4, 40–2.


*Assault on Precinct 13* (1976)

Andrews, N. (1978) *Financial Times*, 10 March [R].

Baily, K. (1978) *Sunday People*, 12 March [R].

Barker, F. (1978) *The Evening News*, 9 March [R].

Barkley, R. (1978) *Sunday Express*, 12 March [R].

Bernades, H. (1995) *Amante Cinema*, 45, 37 [R, in Spanish].

Bilbow, M. (1978) *Screen International*, 129, 30 [R].

Brien, A. (1978) *Sunday Times*, 12 March [R].

Canby, V. (1979) *New York Times*, 17 February [R].

Christie, I. (1978) *Daily Express*, 11 March [R].

Combs, R. (1977/8) *Sight and Sound*, 47, 1, 58–9 [R].

Coleman, J. (1978) *New Statesman*, 10 March [R].

Davies, R. (1978) *Observer*, 12 March [R].

Dignam, V. (1978) *Morning Star*, 10 March [R].

Divine, C. (2000) 'Noir Romantics: The Urban Poetry of *Assault on Precinct 13*', *Creative Screenwriting*, 7, 5, 20–2.

Gibbs, P. (1978) *Daily Telegraph*, 10 March [R].

Gow, G. (1978) *Films and Filming*, 24, 5, 45 [R].

Harmsworth, M. (1978) 'Cracker in the ghetto', *Sunday Mirror*, 12 March [R].

Hinxman, M. (1978) *Daily Mail*, 10 March [R].

Hutchinson, T. (1978) *Daily Telegraph*, 12 March [R].

Malcolm, D. (1978) *Guardian*, 9 March [R].

Milne, T. (1978) *Monthly Film Bulletin*, 529, 19–20 [R].

Plowright, M. (1978) 'A hoodlum siege that could happen', *Glasgow Herald*, 25 September [R].

Sigal, C. (1978) *Spectator*, 18 March [R].

S. M. (1978) *Films Illustrated*, 80, 289 [R].

Thirkell, A. (1978) 'Guts in the ghetto', *Daily Mirror*, 10 March [R].

Walker, A. (1978) *Evening Standard*, 9 March [R].

Whit. (1976) *Variety*, 17 November, 19 [R].

Williams, T. (1979) '*Assault on Precinct 13*: The Mechanics of Repression', in R. Wood and R. Lippe (eds) *The American Nightmare: Essays on the Horror Film*. Toronto: Festival of Festivals, 67–73.


*Someone's Watching Me!* (1978)

Davis, E. (1978) *Hollywood Reporter*, 30 November, 8 [R].

García, J. (1995) *Amante Cinema*, 45, 38 [R, in Spanish].

McCarty, J. (1986) *Psychos: Eighty Years of Mad Movies, Maniacs, and Murderous Deeds*. New York: St Martin's Press, 165–6.

Wolcott, J. (1978) 'Welcome to L.A. Revisited', *Voice*, 29 November [R].


*Halloween* (1978)

Andrews, N. (1979) *Financial Times*, 26 January [R].

Barron, F. (1978) '"Halloween" seen as perennial holiday fare by Irwin Yablans', *Hollywood Reporter*, 10 November, 19.

Calcutt, I. (1989) 'Death Has Come to Your Little Town', *Samhain*, 17, 22–5.

Canby, V. (1979) 'Chilling Truths About Scaring', *New York Times*, 21 January [R].

Carpenter, J. (1983) 'On Composing for Halloween', *Fangoria*, 30, 38–9.

Clover, C. J. (1992) *Men, Women, and Chain Saws*. London: British Film Institute.

Combs, R. (1979) *Monthly Film Bulletin*, 541, 27 [R].

Dika, V. (1990) *Games of Terror: Halloween, Friday the 13th, and the Films of the Stalker Cycle*. London and Toronto: Associated University Presses, 30–52.

Donga, R. (1999) *Music From the Movies*, 22, 19].

Fox, J. (1979) *Films and Filming*, 25, 6, 32–3 [R].

French, P. (1979) *Observer*, 28 January [R].

Garsault, A. (1989) 'Fantastique. Michael, Jason, Freddy ou le trio infernal', *Positif*, 343, 50–3 [in French].

Gibbs, P. (1979) *Daily Telegraph*, 9 February [R].

Hege. (1978) *Variety*, 25 October, 20 [R].

Henfield, M. (1990) 'Horror film "took over the mind of a killer"', *Daily Mail*, 1 May, 4.

Hinxman, M. (1979) *Daily Mail*, 2 February [R].

Humphries, R. (2002) *The American Horror Film: An Introduction*. Edinburgh: Edinburgh University Press, 139–50.

Hutchinson, T. (1979) 'Evil times', *Sunday Telegraph*, 28 January [R].

Iaccino, J. F. (1994) *Psychological Reflections on Cinematic Terror: Jungian Archetypes in Horror Films*. Westport, CT and London: Praeger, 129–36.

Jameson, R. T. (1979) *Movietone News*, February, 40–1.

Kael, P. (1979) *New Yorker*, 19 February [R].

Kapsis, R. E. (1982), 'Dressed to Kill', *American Film*, 7, 5, 53–6.

Malcolm, D. (1979) *Guardian*, 25 January [R].

McCarty, J. (1986) *Psychos: Eighty Years of Mad Movies, Maniacs, and Murderous Deeds*. New York: St Martin's Press, 162–7.

Meek, S. (1979) 'Ring Of Fear', *Time Out*, 458, 13 [R].

Mercer, S. (1979) 'John Carpenter's *Halloween*', *Cinemonkey*, 17, 5–7.

Milne, T. (1979) *Sight and Sound*, 48, 2, 128 [R].

Neale, S. (1981) '*Halloween*: Suspense, Aggression and the Look', *Framework*, 14, 25–9. [Reprinted in B. K. Grant (ed.) (1984) *Planks of Reason: Essays on the Horror Film*. Metuchen, NJ and London: Scarecrow Press, 331–45.]

Paul, W. (1994) *Laughing Screaming: Modern Hollywood Horror and Comedy*. New York: Columbia University Press, 319–24.

Peary, D. (1981) *Cult Movies*. New York: Delacorte Press, 123–7.

Pennington, R. (1978) *Hollywood Reporter*, 27 October, 3 [R].

Pinedo, I. C. (1997) *Recreational Terror: Women and the Pleasures of Horror Film Viewing*. New York: State University of New York Press, 69–81.

Plowright, M. (1979) *Glasgow Herald*, 14 May [R].

Quintín (1995) *Amante Cinema*, 45, 37–8 [R, in Spanish].

Rathgeb, D. L. (1991) 'Bogeyman from the Id: Nightmare and Reality in *Halloween* and *A Nightmare on Elm Street*', *Journal of Popular Film and Television*, 19, 1, 36–43.

Rockoff, A. (2002) *Going to Pieces: The Rise and Fall of the Slasher Film, 1978–1986*. Jefferson, NC: McFarland, 50–61.

Rosenbaum, J. (1980) '*Halloween*', *Take One*, 7, 2, 8–9.

Smith, A. (1997) 'Q & A', *Empire*, 97, 50.

Telotte, J. P. (1982) 'Through a Pumpkin's Eye: The Reflexive Nature of Horror', *Literature/ Film Quarterly*, 10, 139–49. [Reprinted in G. A. Waller (ed.) (1987) *American Horrors: Essays on the Modern American Horror Film*. Urbana and Chicago: University of Illinois Press, 114–28.]

Thomson, D. (1981) *Overexposures: The Crisis in American Filmmaking*. New York: William Morrow, 173–87.

Wapshott, N. (1979) *Scotsman*, 10 February [R].

*Western Mail* (1979) 'The night Elaine watched as a killer stalked…', 18 May.

*Elvis* (1979)

Bilbow, M. (1979) *Screen International*, 203, 19 [R].

Collis, J. (1979) 'Crying For The King', *Time Out*, 487, 21 [R].

Combs, R. (1979) *Monthly Film Bulletin*, 547, 170–1 [R].

Davis, E. (1979) *Hollywood Reporter*, 9 February, 19 [R].

de la Fuente, F. (1995) *Amante Cinema*, 45, 38 [R, in Spanish].

Marill, A. H. (1979) 'The Television Scene', *Films in Review*, 30, 6, 362, 366 [R].


*The Fog* (1979)

Allen, T. (1980) 'The Carpenter Touch', *Voice*, 25 February [R].

Andrews, N. (1980) *Financial Times*, 7 November [R].

Angell, R. (1980) *New Yorker*, 25 February [R].

Assayas, O. (1980) *Cahiers du Cinema*, 310, 43–5 [R, in French].

Bartholomew, D. (1980) *Cinefantastique*, 10, 1, 15 [R].

Bernades, H. (1995) *Amante Cinema*, 45, 38 [R, in Spanish].

Bilbow, M. (1980) *Screen International*, 266, 17 [R].

*Blitz* (1980) November, 10.

Brien, A. (1980) *Sunday Times*, 9 November [R].

Brosnan, J. (1980) 'John Carpenter's *The Fog*', *Starburst*, 29, 24–7.

Canby, V. (1980) 'Revenge From the Past', *New York Times*, 29 February [R].

Castell, D. (1980) *Sunday Telegraph*, 9 November [R].

Christie, I. (1980) *Daily Express*, 8 November [R].

Coleman, J. (1980) *New Statesman*, 7 November [R].

Crawley, T. (1980a) 'Keeping *The Fog* in the family', *Films Illustrated*, 109, 198.

_____ (1980b) 'Will John Carpenter Inherit Hitchcock's Crown?', *Photoplay*, 31, 11, 36–7, 39.

Denby, D. (1980) 'Foul is Fair', *New York*, 18 February, 78 [R].

du Pre, J. (1980) 'All Blood and Gore!', *Sunday People*, 9 November [R].

Fox, J. R. (1979) *Cinefantastique*, 9, 2, 39.

Frank, A. (1980) 'Shiver Me Timbers', *Daily Star*, 8 November [R].

Gibbs, P. (1980) *Daily Telegraph*, 7 November [R].

Harmsworth, M. (1980) *Sunday People*, 9 November [R].

Hinxman, M. (1980) 'A handful of horrors', *Daily Mail*, 7 November [R].

Hirschhorn, C. (1980) *Sunday Express*, 9 November [R].

Holm, P. (2001) *Music From the Movies*, 30, 48.

Hutchinson, T. (1980) *Now*, 7 November [R].

Knight, A. (1980) *Hollywood Reporter*, 15 January, 3 [R].

Lockhart, F. B. (1980) 'Autumn wave of ghosts, ghouls and poltergeists', *Catholic Herald*, 14 November [R].

Malcolm, D. (1980) *Guardian*, 6 November [R].

Martin, B. (1980) 'John Carpenter's *The Fog*', *Fangoria*, 5, 10–12, 37.

Migliore, A. and J. Strysik (2000) *The Lurker in the Lobby: A Guide to the Cinema of H. P. Lovecraft*. Seattle: Armitage House, 33–5.

Milne, T. (1980) *Monthly Film Bulletin*, 562, 214 [R].

O'Brien, T. (1980) *Leveller*, 14 November [R].

Plowright, M. (1980) *Glasgow Herald*, 15 December [R].

Poll (1980) *Variety*, 16 January, 31 [R].

Robinson, D. (1980) *Times*, 7 November [R].

Scanlon, P. (1979) 'The Fog: A Spook Ride on Film', *Rolling Stone*, 28 June.

*Screen International* (1979) 'Thriller that's become a family affair', 191, 6.

Spencer, C. (1980) 'All fright on the night', *New Standard*, 14 November [R].

Stannage, L. (1981) *Film Directions*, 4, 15, 31 [R].

Stavrakis, C. (2000) *Film Score Monthly*, 5, 8, 42–3.

Thirkell, A. (1981) 'Foggy phantoms of the deep', *Daily Mirror*, 7 November [R].

Tudor, A. (1980) 'Beware of the bogey man', *New Society*, 20 December [R].

Vassie, G. (2001) *Legend*, 35, 8–11.


*Escape From New York* (1981)

Aitken, M. (1981) *Daily Mail*, 25 September [R].

Barkley, R. (1981) *Sunday Express*, 4 October [R].

Beeler, M. (1996g) 'Escape From N. Y.: Filming the Original', *Cinefantastique*, 28, 2, 24–5.

Braun, E. (1981) *Films*, 1, 10, 32 [R].

Brown, G. (1981) *Financial Times*, 25 September [R].

Canby, V. (1981a) 'A Very Tall Tale', *New York Times*, 10 July [R].

\_\_\_\_ (1981b) 'They Make Movies Look Good', *New York Times*, 2 August.

Cart. (1981) *Variety*, 17 June, 14 [R].

Chase, D. (1981) 'Panater Lenses and Computerised Fire Effects in *Escape From New York*', *Filmmakers Monthly*, 14, 11, 27–30.

Castell, D. (1981) *Sunday Telegraph*, 4 October [R].

Christie, I. (1981) *Daily Express*, 26 September [R].

Coleman, J. (1981) *New Statesman*, 2 October [R].

Combs, R. (1981) *Monthly Film Bulletin*, 572, 174–5 [R].

Dhont F. and J. M. Trevor (1981) '*Escape From New York*', *Ciné-Revue*, 61, 25, 18–21 [in French].

Dupre, J. (1981) *Sunday People*, 27 September [R].

Edwards, P. (1981) *Starburst*, 38, 16–9.

Frank, A. (1981) 'The great escape – U. S. style!', *Daily Star*, 26 September [R].

French, P. (1981) *Observer*, 27 September [R].

Harmsworth, M. (1981) *Sunday Mirror*, 27 September [R].

Holms, P. (2000a) *Music From the Movies*, 28, 60–1.

\_\_\_\_ (2000b) *Music From the Movies*, 29, 60.

Hughes, D. (1981) *Sunday Times*, 23 August [R].

Kaye, S. (1995) '*Escape From New York*: Mythic Structure', *Creative Screenwriting*, 2, 4, 69–75.

Lévy, F. A. (1981) *Écran Fantastique*, 20, 75 [R, in French].

Lofficier, J.–M. (1981) 'Sur le tournage de *Escape From New York*', *Écran Fantastique*, 17, 58 [in French].

Lofficier, J.–M. and R. Lofficier (1981) 'John Carpenter's *Escape From New York*', *Écran Fantastique*, 17, 16–25 [in French].

Malcolm, D. (1981) *Guardian*, 20 August [R].

____ (1981) *Guardian*, 24 September [R].

Nurse, K. (1981) 'Snake in the criminal jungle', *Daily Telegraph*, 21 August [R].

Rebello, S. (1981) *Cinefantastique*, 11, 3, 47 [R].

Robinson, D. (1981) *Times*, 25 September [R].

Russo, E. A. (1995) *Amante Cinema*, 45, 38–9 [R, in Spanish].

Sarris, A. (1981) *Voice*, 8 August [R].

Sineux, M. (1981) *Positif*, 246, 56–7 [R, in French].

Sragow, M. (1981) 'John Carpenter's escape to nowhere', *Rolling Stone*, 20 August [R].

Stavrakis, C. (2000) *Film Score Monthly*, 5, 6, 47–8.

Strick, P. (1981) *Films and Filming*, 325, 37–8 [R].

*Sunday Times Magazine* (1981) 'B (for bleak) movies', 20 August [R].

Thirkell, A. (1981) *Daily Mirror*, 25 September [R].

*Times Magazine* (1995) 29 July [R].

Turner, G. (1981) *Cinefantastique*, 10, 4, 12.

Walker, A. (1981) *Evening Standard*, 24 September [R].

Waterman, I. (1981) *News of the World*, 27 September [R].


*The Thing* (1982)

Andrews, N. (1982) *Financial Times*, 27 August, 4 [R].

Bernades, H. (1995) *Amante Cinema*, 45, 39 [R, in Spanish].

Billson, A. (1997) *The Thing*. London: British Film Institute.

Boon, K. A. (1999) 'In Defense of John Carpenter's *The Thing*', *Creative Screenwriting*, 6, 1, 44, 66–73.

Brown, G. (1982) 'Return of *The Thing* that stalked the thirties', *Times Preview*, 20 August [R].

Bruzenak, K. (1982) 'Thing: A Classic Tale of Terror by John Carpenter', *Prevue*, 48, 58–61.

Canby, V. (1982) 'Bloody Protoplasm', *New York Times*, 25 June [R].

Carlomagno, E. (1982) 'Rob Bottin and *The Thing*', *Fangoria*, 21, 13–16, 63.

Cart. (1982) *Variety*, 23 June, 26 [R].

Castell, D. (1982) 'One damned Thing after another', *Sunday Telegraph*, 29 August [R].

Chase, C. (1982) *New York Times*, 25 June.

Christie, I. (1982) 'A thing that goes slurp in the night', *Daily Express*, 27 August [R].

Cook, R. (1982) 'Quite Some Thing', *New Musical Express*, 4 September [R].

Dignam, V. (1982) *Morning Star*, 30 August, 4 [R].

Edwards, P. (1982) *Starburst*, 50, 22–3.

Ferguson, F. (1982) *City Limits* 47, 4 [R].

*Film Review* special 25 (1998) 'The Science Fiction Hall of Fame: *The Thing*', 62–3.

Fischer, D. and R. Strauss (1991) 'Makeup Miracle Maker II', *Samhain*, 25, 26–7.

Fox, J. R. (1982) '*The Thing*', *Cinefantastique*, 12, 4, 52–3.

Fox, J. R., J.-M. Lofficier and R. Lofficier (1982a) '*The Thing*: Premiere Partie', *Écran Fantastique*, 28, 40–4 [in French].

____ (1982b) 'Entretien avec David Foster, producteur', *Écran Fantastique*, 28, 45–8 [in French].

____ (1982d) 'Entretien Avec Stuart Cohen, Co–Producteur', *Écran Fantastique*, 29, 33–4 [in French].

_____ (1982e) 'Entretien avec Bill Lancaster, scénariste', *Écran Fantastique*, 29, 35–6 [in French].

_____ (1982f) 'Entretien avec Roy Arbogast, responsible des effects spéciaux', *Écran Fantastique*, 29, 36–8 [in French].

_____ (1982g) 'Entretien avec Kurt Russell', *Écran Fantastique*, 29, 38–40 [in French].

Frank, A. (1982) *Daily Star*, 26 August, 8 [R].

French, P. (1982) *Observer*, 29 August, 28 [R].

Guerrero, E. (1990) 'AIDS as Monster in Science Fiction and Horror Cinema', *Journal of Popular Film and Television*, 18, 3, 86–93.

Harmsworth, M. (1982) *Sunday Mirror*, 29 August, 25 [R].

Hinxman, M. (1982) *Daily Mail*, 27 August, 20 [R].

Hirschhorn, C. (1982) '*The Thing* that brings terror from outer space', *Sunday Express*, 29 August, 18 [R].

Hogan, D. J. (1982) 'The Making of *The Thing*', *Cinefantastique*, 13, 2–3, 49–58, 63–75.

Hughes, D. (1982) *The Sunday Times*, 29 August [R].

Hutchinson, T. (1982) 'The latest Thing from outer space', *Mail on Sunday*, 29 August, 25 [R].

Jackson, P. (1982) 'A Splendid and slithery thing', *Western Mail*, 7 October, 7 [R].

Jenkins, S. (1982) *Monthly Film Bulletin*, 583, 158–160 [R].

Landon, B. (1992) *The Aesthetics of Ambivalence: Rethinking Science Fiction Film in the Age of Electronic (Re)production*. Westport, CT and London: Greenwood Press, 27–44.

Lockhart, F. B. (1982) *Catholic Herald*, 10 September [R].

Lucas, T. (1982) *Cinefantastique*, 13, 1, 49 [R].

Mackie, L. (1982) *Glasgow Herald*, 28 August, 9.

Malcolm, D. (1982) *Guardian*, 26 August, 9 [R].

Marsh, J. (1982) 'Things That Go Bump! In The Night (or Recipe for Disaster)', *Stills*, 1, 5, 30–3.

Martin, B. (1982a) 'On Location With The Thing', *Fangoria*, 18, 48–51.

_____ (1982b) 'On Location With The Thing', *Fangoria*, 19, 17–20.

_____ (1982c) 'Carpenter, The Thing, & Other Things', *Fangoria*, 20, 9–12.

Maxford, H. (2001) 'Things Ain't What They Used To Be', *Starburst*, 277, 76–81.

McCarthy, T. (1981) 'What Hawks Discarded (1951) Back in Carpenter "Thing" Re–Do', *Variety*, 27 July.

Migliore, A. and J. Strysik (2000) *The Lurker in the Lobby: A Guide to the Cinema of H. P. Lovecraft*. Seattle: Armitage House, 51–2.

*Motion Picture Product Digest* (1982) 10, 3, 10 [R].

Neale, S. (1990) '"You've Got To Be Fucking Kidding!": Knowledge, Belief and Judgement in Science Fiction', in A. Kuhn (ed.) *Alien Zone: Cultural Theory and Contemporary Science Fiction Cinema*. London and New York: Verso, 160–8. [Reprinted in Sean Redmond (ed.) (2004) *Liquid Metal: The Science Fiction Film Reader*. London: Wallflower Press, 11–16.]

Nurse, K. (1982) *Daily Telegraph*, 3 September, 9.

Osborne, R. (1982) *Hollywood Reporter*, 21 June, 4 [R].

Peary, D. (1988) *Cult Movies 3*. New York: Fireside, Simon and Schuster, 250–4.

Parente, W. (1982) 'Dedicated follower of fashion', *Scotsman*, 28 August, 3 [R].

Pennacini, C. (1985) 'Inquietudine cronometrica', *Cinema e Cinema*, 44, 69–75 [in Italian].

Pinedo, I. C. (1997) *Recreational Terror: Women and the Pleasures of Horror Film Viewing*. New York: State University of New York Press, 34–8.

Plowright, M. (1982) *Glasgow Herald*, 30 August, 8 [R].

Preston, J. (1982) *New Statesman*, 27 August, 27 [R].

Prince, S. (1988) 'Dread, Taboo and *The Thing*: Toward a Social Theory of the Horror Film', *Wide Angle*, 10, 3, 19–29. [Reprinted in S. Prince (ed.) (2004) *The Horror Film*. New Brunswick, NJ and London: Rutgers University Press, 118–30.]

Pulleine, T. (1982) *Films and Filming*, 336, 36–7 [R].

Robinson, D. O. (1982) *Times*, 27 August, 7 [R].

*Rolling Stone* (1982) 5 August, 33 [R].

Rosenbaum, J. (1982) 'Mefiez–Vous Des Imitations', *Cahiers du Cinema*, 339, 24–6 [in French].

Thirkell, A. (1982) 'Shivers on ice', *Daily Mirror*, 27 August, 27 [R].

Walker, A. (1982) *Evening Standard*, 26 August, 18 [R].

Warren, B. (1982) 'John Carpenter's *The Thing*', *Starburst*, 42, 40–1.

Wigan, M. (1982) *Scotsman*, 26 August, 4.


*Christine* (1983)

Andrews, N. (1984) *Financial Times*, 2 March, 25 [R].

Bergson, P. (1984) 'Pole position', *What's On*, 1 March [R].

Byrge, D. (1983) *Hollywood Reporter*, 7 December, 3, 6 [R].

Cart. (1983) *Variety*, 7 December, 14 [R].

Castell, D. (1984) *Sunday Telegraph*, 4 March, 14 [R].

Collings, M. R. (1986) *The Films of Stephen King*. Mercer Island: Starmont House, 101–12.

Corliss, R. (1984) 'Season's Bleedings in Tinseltown', *Time*, 19 March, 56 [R].

Dignam, V. (1984) *Morning Star*, 6 March, 2 [R].

Ferguson, F. (1984) *City Limits*, 126, 28 [R].

Ferguson, K. (1984) 'John Carpenter's Christine: A Four–Wheeled Wicked Lady!', *Photoplay*, 35, 4, 40–1.

Gibbs, P. (1984) *Daily Telegraph*, 2 March, 17 [R].

Gill, A. (1984) 'Car Wars!', *New Musical Express*, 3 March, 21 [R].

Guerif, F. (1984) '*Christine*: de Stephen King à John Carpenter', *Écran Fantastique*, 42, 8–9 [in French].

Harron, M. (1984) *New Statesman*, 2 March, 30–1 [R].

Hogan, D. J. (1984) *Cinefantastique*, 14, 3, 56 [R].

Hutchinson, T. (1984) *Mail on Sunday*, 4 March, 38 [R].

Jackson, P. (1984) *Western Mail*, 10 March, 8 [R].

Jankiewicz, P. (1995) 'Roy Arbogast: Maker of Monsters', *Shivers*, 15, 42–4.

Johnson, K. (1984) *Prevue*, 54, 24–7 [R].

Johnston, S. (1984) *Monthly Film Bulletin*, 602, 77–8 [R].

Johnstone, I. (1984) *Sunday Times*, 4 March, 55 [R].

Karani, C. (1984) *Écran Fantastique*, 42, 6–7 [R, in French].

Kelley, B, (1983) 'John Carpenter's *Christine*', *Cinefantastique*, 13, 6 and 14, 1, 8–9.

_____ (1984) *Cinefantastique*, 14, 3, 56–7.

Lewis, B. (1984) *Nine to Five*, 19 March, 10 [R].

Lloyd, A. (1984) *Films and Filming*, 355, 34–5 [R].

Lucas, T. (1996) *Video Watchdog*, 33, 56–7 [R].

Magistrale, T. (2003) *Hollywood's Stephen King*. New York: Palgrave Macmillan, 147–72.

Martin, R. H. (1983a) 'Richard Kobritz and *Christine*', *Fangoria*, 32, 14–18.

_____ (1983b) 'Keith Gordon and *Christine*', *Fangoria*, 32, 19–22.

_____ (1984) 'Car Trouble', *Fangoria*, 33, 40–3.

Maslin, J. (1983) 'Car Crazy', *New York Times*, 9 December [R].

*Motion Picture Product Digest* (1983) 11, 12, 46 [R].

Poulle, F. (1984) *Jeune Cinéma*, 158, 34–6 [R, in French].

Pulleine, T. (1984) *Guardian*, 1 March, 11 [R].

*Retro* (1984) 23, 15 [R, in German].

Robinson, D. (1984) *Times*, 2 March, 14 [R].

Russell, W. (1983) *Glasgow Herald*, 31 December, 8.

_____ (1984) *Glasgow Herald*, 10 March, 8 [R].

Strick, P. (1984b) 'Uneasy lies the head', *Sight and Sound*, 53, 2, 150 [R].

Thirkell, A. (1984) 'Polished Killer', *Daily Mirror*, 2 March, 21 [R].

Underwood, T., C. Miller and J. Conner (1987) *Stephen King Goes to Hollywood*. New York: New American Library, 69–78.


*Starman* (1984)

Bergson, P. (1985) 'Shining', *What's On*, 9 May, 45 [R].

Brosnan, J. (1985) 'It's Only A Movie', *Starburst*, 41 [R].

Brown, G. (1985) *Times*, 10 May, 8 [R].

Byrge, D. (1984) '"Starman" b.o. potential shining', *Hollywood Reporter*, 3 December, 3, 6.

Canby, V. (1984) 'Seen in 1984, the Future Looks Bleak', *New York Times*, 21 December.

Case, B. (1985) *Stills*, 19, 75–6 [R].

Castell, D. (1985) *Sunday Telegraph*, 12 May, 18 [R].

Christie, I. (1985) 'Star turn from Jeff', *Daily Express*, 10 May, 30 [R].

Clinch, M. (1985) *MS London*, 13 May, 27 [R].

Coleman, J. (1985) *New Statesman*, 10 May, 29 [R].

Combs, R. (1985) *Monthly Film Bulletin* 616, 163–4 [R].

Corliss, R. (1984) 'The Lover from Another Planet', *Time*, 24 December, 37 [R].

Counts, K. (1985a) *Cinefantastique*, 15, 5, 47, 49, 56 [R].

_____ (1985b) 'Who really wrote *Starman* and why it looks like *Wavelength*', *Cinefantastique*, 15, 5, 47.

D. C. (1985) *Photoplay*, 36, 6, 27 [R].

Dewson, L. (1985) 'Jeff Bridges – A Starman At Last?', *Photoplay*, 36, 6, 40–3.

Dignam, V. (1985) *Morning Star*, 10 May, 2 [R].

Eisen, S. (1995) *Amante Cinema*, 45, 39–40 [R, in Spanish].

Eller, C. (1985) '*Starman*', *On Location*, 8, 7, 66–70, 178–79.

Enker, D. (1985) 'Alienation', *Cinema Papers*, 52, 66–7 [R].

Farmer, D. (1984) '*Starman*: Sur le tournage du nouveau Carpenter', *Écran Fantastique*, 46, 28–9 [in French].

_____ (1985) 'Starman: Une romance de science–fiction signée John Carpenter', *Écran Fantastique*, 52, 13–5 [in French].

Frank, A. (1985) *Daily Star*, 11 May, 18 [R].

French, P. (1985) *Observer*, 12 May, 19 [R].

Garsault, A. (1985) 'Beautés et dangers de la convention', *Positif*, 295, 59–60 [R, in French].

Harmsworth, M. (1985) 'Karen is Star Struck', *Sunday Mirror*, 12 May [R].

Harris, J. P. (1985) 'Makeup expert Dick Smith on the transformation effects of *Starman*', *Cinefantastique*, 15, 5, 48.

Hoberman, J. (1984) *Voice*, 25 December, 67–8 [R].

Jagr., (1984) *Variety*, 5 December, 17 [R].

Johnstone, I. (1985) *Sunday Times*, 12 May, 38 [R].

Jones, A. (1985) *Starburst*, 81, 16 [R].

Kael, P. (1985) *New Yorker*, 28 January, 88–9 [R].

Karani, C. (1985) *Écran Fantastique*, 58, 6 [R, in French].

King, A. S. (1984) 'On the set of "Starman"', *Starlog*, 89, December, 58–60, 66.

Malcolm, D. (1985) 'The lover from another planet', *Guardian*, 9 May, 13 [R].

Martin, G. (1985) 'Who Phoned E.T.?', *New Musical Express*, 11 May, 16 [R].

Maslin, J. (1984a) '"Starman" gets touch of Carpenter', *New York Times*, 20 July, C8.

_____ (1984b) 'Sci–Fi Love Story', *New York Times*, 14 December [R].

Newman, K. (1985) *City Limits*, 188, 21 [R].

Parente, W. (1985) 'Soft landing for Bridges', *Scotsman*, 11 May, 3 [R].

Pulleine, T. (1985) *Films and Filming*, 367, 41 [R].

Rabkin, W. (1985) '*Starman*: Bruce Nicholson et les magiciens de L' I. L. M.', *Écran Fantastique*, 58, 50–3 [in French].

Rayner, R. (1985) *Time Out*, 768, 53 [R].

Robertson, N. (1984) *New York Times*, 20 July, 66.

Shorter, E. (1985) *Daily Telegraph*, 10 May, 13 [R].

Steensland, M. (1985) '*Starman*', *Prevue*, 58, 30–3, 73.

Taylor, P. (1985) 'Another day, another alien', *Financial Times*, 16 May, 17 [R].

Thirkell, A. (1985) 'Baby Out Of The Blue', *Daily Mirror*, 10 May [R].

Usher, S. (1985) 'With a new look at our odd way of life', *Daily Mail*, 10 May, 26 [R].

van Poznak, E. (1985) *Girl About Town*, 13 May, 8 [R].

Walker, A. (1985) 'A husband in space', *Evening Standard*, 9 May, 22–3 [R].


*Big Trouble in Little China* (1986)

Andrews, N. (1986) *Financial Times*, 14 November, 21 [R].

Bartlett, J. (1986) *The Voice*, 22 November, 33 [R].

Bergson, P. (1986) 'Mixed noodles', *What's On*, 20 November, 87 [R].

Brit. (1986) *Variety*, 2 July, 13–4 [R].

Combs, R. (1986) *Monthly Film Bulletin*, 635, 364–6 [R].

Corliss, R (1986) *Time*, 14 July, 36 [R].

Dignam, V. (1986) *Morning Star*, 21 November, 8 [R].

Fischer, D. (1986) *Hollywood Reporter*, 30 June, 4, 12 [R].

Floyd, F. (1986) *New Musical Express*, 15 November, 22 [R].

García, S. (1995) *Amante Cinema*, 45, 40 [R, in Spanish].

Goldberg, L. (1986a) '*Big Trouble in Little China*', *Écran Fantastique*, 69, 18–21 [in French].

_____ (1986b) 'Entretien avec Kurt Russell', *Écran Fantastique*, 72, 26–7 [in French].

____ (1986c) 'Entretien avec Kim Cattrall', *Écran Fantastique*, 72, 28–9 [in French].

Goldberg L., J.-M. Lofficier and R. Lofficier R. (1995) *The Dreamweavers: Interviews with Fantasy Filmmakers of the 1980s*. Jefferson, NC and London: McFarland, 40–6.

Goodman, W. (1985) 'Mad Mélange', *New York Times*, 2 July, 29 [R].

Harmetz, A. (1985) 'A ghostly film that's no "kiddie movie"', *New York Times*, 9 August, C10.

Hoberman, J. (1986) *Village Voice*, 8 July, 66 [R].

Holms, P. (2000) *Music From the Movies*, 27, 45.

Horvilleur, G. (1986) *Cinématographe*, 123, 61 [R, in French].

Hutchinson, T. (1986) *Hampstead and Highgate Express*, 21 November, 103 [R].

*Independent* (1986) 14 November, 22 [R].

Jackson, P. (1987) 'Cowboy Kung-fu in Chinatown', *Western Mail*, 10 January, 12 [R].

Jones, A. (1986) *Starburst*, 99, 23 [R].

Lloyd, A. (1986) *Films and Filming*, 385, 35–6 [R].

Lucas, T. (1993) *Video Watchdog*, 20, 63–5 [R].

Malcolm, D. (1986) *Guardian*, 13 November, 15 [R].

Mars-Jones, A. (1986) 'A Chinese goulash', *Independent*, 12 November, 15 [R].

Mather, V. (1986) *Daily Telegraph*, 8 September, 8 [R].

Newman, K. (1986) *City Limits*, 267, 25 [R].

Norman, N. (1986) *The Face*, October, 124 [R].

Parente, W. (1986) 'Bamboozled in Chinatown', *Scotsman Weekend*, 22 November, 7 [R].

Peachment, C. (1986) *Time Out*, 847, 25 [R].

Pourroy, J. (1986) 'Putting Big Trouble Into Little China', *Cinefex*, 28, 30–49.

Robinson, D. (1986) *Times*, 14 November, 15 [R].

Robley, L. P. (1986a) 'Big Effects for *Big Trouble*', *American Cinematographer*, 67, 6, 60–71.

____ (1986b) 'Production Design for *Big Trouble*', *American Cinematographer*, 67, 6, 72–4.

____ (1986c) 'John Lloyd et la direction artistique de *Les Aventures de Jack Burton*', *Écran Fantastique*, 72, 30–2 [in French].

Russell, W. (1986) 'Enjoyable wok on the wild side', *Glasgow Herald*, 22 November, 8 [R].

Scotto, D. (1986) *Écran Fantastique*, 72, 6 [R, in French].

Steensland, M. (1986) 'Stirring Up *Big Trouble in Little China*', *American Cinematographer*, 67, 6, 52–8.

Usher, S. (1986) 'Macho magical mystery tour', *Daily Mail*, 14 November, 29 [R].

van Gelder, L. (1986) 'John Carpenter After "Big Trouble"', *New York Times*, 27 July, 110 [R].

Walker, A. (1986) 'Kurt's perpetual motion picture', *Evening Standard*, 13 November, 27 [R].


*Prince of Darkness* (1987)

Andrews, N. (1988) *Financial Times*, 13 May, 21 [R].

Camb. (1987) *Variety*, 28 October, 14, 16 [R].

Canby, V. (1987) *New York Times*, 23 October, 26 [R].

Castagno, G. J. (1995) *Amante Cinema*, 45, 40 [R, in Spanish].

Clarke, J. (1988) *Samhain*, 8, 30 [R].

Counts, K. (1987) *Hollywood Reporter*, 22 October, 3, 8 [R].

Dietrich, B. (1991) '*Prince of Darkness*, Prince of Light: From Faust to Physicist', *Journal of Popular Film and Television*, 19, 2, 91–6.

Edelstein, D. (1987) *Village Voice*, 3 November, 76, 80 [R].

Floyd, N. (1988) *Time Out*, 925, 37 [R].

French, P. (1988) *Observer*, 15 May, 39 [R].

Garsault, A. (1988) *Positif*, 329–330, 105–6 [R, in French].

Gilbert, J. (1988) *Fear*, 3, 38–9 [R].

Heal, S. (1988) *Today*, 13 May, 27 [R].

Hockley, M. (1988) *Samhain*, 8, 28.

Leayman, C. D. (1988) *Cinefantastique*, 18, 4, 46 [R].

Lucas, T. (1998) *Video Watchdog*, 46, 69–71 [R].

Malcolm, D. (1988) *Guardian*, 12 May, 27 [R].

Morley, S. (1988) *Mail on Sunday*, 22 May, 36 [R].

Murray, A. W. (1988) *Scotsman*, 20 June, 4 [R].

Newman, K. (1988c) *City Limits*, 345, 25 [R].

Parente, W. (1988) 'Schlocky horrors', *Scotsman*, 16 May, 9 [R].

Pulleine, T. (1988) *Films and Filming*, 404, 46 [R].

Robinson, D. (1988) *Times*, 12 May, 16 [R].

*Samhain* (1988) '*Prince of Darkness*: The Making of the Film', 8, 18–19.

Strick, P. (1988) *Monthly Film Bulletin*, 652, 147–8 [R].

Swires, S. (1987) 'John Carpenter's Prince of Darkness', *Fangoria*, 69, 28–31, 66.

Usher, S. (1988) *Daily Mail*, 13 May, 28 [R].

Walker, A. (1988) 'Messy deaths', *Evening Standard*, 12 May, 29 [R].

*What's On* (1988) 11 May, 67 [R].


*They Live* (1988)

Andrews, N. (1989) *Financial Times*, 22 June, 25 [R].

C. J. (1989) *The Voice*, 25 April, 36 [R].

Calcutt, I. (1989) 'They Came From Outer Space', *Samhain*, 15, 21–3 [R].

Cart. (1989) *Variety*, 9 November, 16 [R].

Castagna, G. J. (1995) *Amante Cinema*, 45, 40–1 [R, in Spanish].

Clarke, F. S. (1989) 'Stop–Motion and Matte Effects for *They Live*', *Cinefantastique*, 19, 4, 43.

Clarke, J. (1989) *Films and Filming*, 416, 44 [R].

Colette, M. (1989) *Time Out*, 983, 37 [R].

*Empire* (1989) 1, 88 [R].

Fischer, D. (1988) *Hollywood Reporter*, 4 November, 6, 41 [R].

_____ (1989) 'John Carpenter's *They Live*', *Cinefantastique*, 19, 1–2, 12–3, 124.

French, P. (1989) *Observer*, 25 June, 41 [R].

Garsault, A. (1989) 'Plaisirs de l'intelligence et du style', *Positif*, 340, 72–3 [R, in French].

Heal, S. (1989) *Today*, 23 June, 33 [R].

Heuring, D. (1989) 'From Outer Space, *They Live*', *American Cinematographer*, 69, 9, 64–70.

Hoberman, J. (1988) 'Morning After in America', *Village Voice*, 15 November, 61 [R].

Hutchinson, T. (1988) *Hampstead and Highgate Express*, 23 June, 105 [R].

Johnston, S. (1989) *Independent*, 22 June, 16 [R].

Johnstone, I. (1989) *The Sunday Times*, 25 June, C8 [R].

Jones, A. (1989) *Starburst*, 131, 21–2 [R].

Jones, S. (1989) *Shock Xpress*, 3, 1, 38.

Leayman, C. D. (1989) *Cinefantastique*, 19, 4, 42, 58 [R].

Lucas, T. (1998) *Video Watchdog*, 46, 69–71 [R].

Maslin, J. (1988) 'Subliminal Persuasion', *New York Times*, 4 November [R].

McCracken, H. (1989) *Cinefantastique*, 19, 3, 56 [R].

Milne, T. (1989) *Monthly Film Bulletin*, 665, 163–4 [R].

Pulleine, T. (1989) *Guardian*, 22 June, 16 [R].

Quantick, D. (1989) *New Musical Express*, 17 June, 27 [R].

Robinson, D. (1989) *Times*, 22 June, 18 [R].

Rodman, H. A. (1988) 'Trailers, Spots, 'n' Teasers', *Village Voice*, 1 November, 73–4.

Sawtell, J. (1989), 'Sci-fi parable of alienation', *Morning Star*, 23 June, 8 [R].

Sellers, R. (1989) *Melody Maker*, 1 July [R].

Shapiro, M. (1988) 'Run! Run! Run For Your Life!: They Live', *Fangoria*, 78, 20–4.

_____ (1989) *Fear*, 7, 21.

Sims, R. (1989) 'Unwelcome visitors', *What's On*, 21 June, 71 [R].

Tookey, C. (1989) *Sunday Telegraph*, 25 June, 41 [R].

Usher, S. (1989) *Daily Mail*, 23 June, 28 [R].

Wigan, M. (1989) 'Unlimited sedition', *Scotsman Weekend*, 24 June, 3 [R].

Wise, D. (1989) 'Live and let die', *Sounds*, 26 June [R].


*Memoirs of an Invisible Man* (1992)

Amdon, S. (1992) *Financial Times*, 14 May, 17 [R].

Biodrowski, S. (1991) '*Memoirs of an Invisible Man*', *Cinefantastique*, 22, 3, 7.

_____ (1992) '*Memoirs of an Invisible Man:* John Carpenter on Directing', *Cinefantastique*, 22, 4, 10–11.

Bradley, L. (1992) *Empire*, 36, 28 [R].

Brett, A. (1992) 'Funnier than his films?', *What's On*, 20 May, 11–12.

Brown, G. (1992a) *Times Life and Times*, 14 May, 3 [R].

_____ (1992b) *Sight and Sound*, 2, 2, 48 [R].

Cameron-Wilson, J. (1992) 'Call him inconspicuous', *What's On*, 13 May [R].

Chua, L. (1992) *Village Voice*, 10 March, 64 [R].

Collins, D. (1992) *Sun*, 15 May, 15 [R].

Floyd, N. (1992) *Time Out*, 13 May, 61 [R].

French, S. (1992) *Observer*, 17 May, 52 [R].

García, S. (1995) *Amante Cinema*, 45, 41 [R, in Spanish].

Gentry, R. (1991a) 'Fraker Records. *Memoirs of an Invisible Man*', *American Cinematographer*, 72, 12, 46–53.

_____ (1991b) 'Now You See Him, Now You Don't', *American Cinematographer*, 72, 12, 54–6, 58, 60–1.

Heal, S. (1992) *Today*, 15 May, 19, 22 [R].

Horowitz, J. (1992) 'Memoirs of a Ya–hi Ya–ho', *Premiere*, 5, 8, 49–54.

Hughes, D. (1992) 'Chevy gets in on the vanishing act', *Mail on Sunday*, 17 May, 38 [R].

Hutchinson, T. (1992) *Hampstead and Highgate Express*, 15 May, 87 [R].

Jackson, K. (1992) 'Transparent bid for stardom', *Independent*, 15 May, 16 [R].

Jones, A. (1992a) *Starburst*, 166, 29–30, 32 [R].

_____ (1992b) 'Chasing Chevy: Memoirs of an Invisible Comedian', *Starburst*, 167, 16–9.

Lane, A. (1992) *Independent on Sunday*, 17 May, 17 [R].

Lawson, N. (1992) 'An old–fashioned vanishing trick', *Daily Telegraph*, 14 May, 14.

Lowry, B. (1992) *Variety*, 2 March, 55 [R].

Lucas, T. (1992) *Video Watchdog*, 13, 12–13 [R].

Maslin, J. (1992) *New York Times*, 28 February [R].

Maxford, H. (1992) 'E's invisible! That's wot's the matter with 'im!', *What's On*, 13 May, 42–3.

McDowell, E. (1987) 'A First Novel's Windfall in Film and Club Rights', *New York Times*, 28 January, C19.

Morley, S. (1992) 'Seeing is not believing', *Sunday Express*, 17 May, 63 [R].

Norman, N. (1992) *Evening Standard*, 14 May, 39 [R].

Perry, G. (1992) *The Sunday Times* Section 7, 17 May, 4–5 [R].

Pounder, L. (1992) '*Memoirs of An Invisible Man*', *Starburst* special, 12, July, 41–5.

*Premiere*, (1992) 'The Eyes Have It', 5, 11, 19.

Pulleine, T. (1992) *Guardian*, 14 May, 28 [R].

Pulver, A. (1992) *City Limits*, 14 May, 25 [R].

Sawtell, J. (1992) *Morning Star*, 16 May, 7 [R].

Tookey, C. (1992) *Sunday Telegraph*, 17 May [R].

Usher, S. (1992) 'Not one to keep an eye out for', *Daily Mail*, 15 May, 30 [R].


*Body Bags* (1993)

Biodrowski S. (1993) 'Tales From the Morgue: *Body Bags*', *Cinefantastique*, 24, 3–4, 112–15.

Moore, A. (1993) 'Body Bags of Fear and Fun', *Fangoria*, 126, 44–9.

*Samhain* (1995) 50, 33 [R].

Scott,T. (1993) *Daily Variety*, 8 September [R].


*In the Mouth of Madness* (1995)

Billson, A. (1995) *Sunday Telegraph* Review, 18 June, 5 [R].

Brown, G. (1995a) *Village Voice*, 7 February, 51 [R].

____ (1995b) *Times*, 15 June, 33 [R].

Buxton, D. (1995) *Samhain*, 51, 31 [R].

Curtis, Q. (1995) *Independent on Sunday*, 18 June, 20 [R].

Davenport, H. (1995) *Daily Telegraph*, 16 June, 22 [R].

Floyd, N. (1995) *Time Out*, 14 June, 11 [R].

Francke, L. (1995) *Observer* Review, 18 June, 11 [R].

Hagerty, B. (1995) *Today*, 16 June [R].

Johnston, S. (1995) *Independent* Section 2, 15 June, 10 [R].

Jones, A. (1995a) 'John Carpenter. Directing *In the Mouth of Madness* a la H. P. Lovecraft', *Cinefantastique*, 26, 2, 44–5.

____ (1995b) *Starburst*, 200, 14 [R].

Julius, M. (1995) *What's On*, 14 June [R].

Kemp, P. (1995) *Sight and Sound*, 5, 8, 52–3 [R].

Klady, L. (1995) *Variety*, 6 February, 73, 76 [R].

Leith, W. (1995) *Mail on Sunday*, 18 June, 27 [R].

Lucas, T. (1995) *Video Watchdog*, 29, 58–60 [R].

Malcolm, D. (1995) *Guardian* Section 2, 15 June, 9 [R].

Maslin, J. (1995) *New York Times*, 3 February [R].

Mauceri, J. (1995) 'Absolute Madness', *Shivers*, 16, 28–30.

Mendik, X. (1999) '"I Think, Therefore You Are". Or How I Lost Myself In The Mouth of Madness', in A. Black (ed.) *Necronomicon Book Three*. Hereford: Noir Publishing, 172–86.

Newman, K. (1995) *Empire*, 73, 40 [R].

Rowe, M. (1995) 'Master of Madness', *Fangoria*, 140, 32–5.

Salisbury, M. (1995) *Fangoria*, 140, 36–7 [R].

Schwartberg, S. (1994) '*In the Mouth of Madness*', *Cinefantastique*, 25, 5, 8–11.

Seguin, D. (1993) '*In the Mouth of Madness*', *Screen International*, 936, 20.

_____ (1995) *Screen International* 995, 31 [R].

Shone, T. (1995) *Sunday Times* Section 10, 18 June, 7 [R].

Tookey, C. (1995) 'Booked on a trip to hell', *Daily Mail*, 16 June, 45 [R].


*Village of the Damned* (1995)

Gehr, R. (1995) *Village Voice*, 9 May, 76 [R].

Lucas, T. (1995) *Video Watchdog*, 30, 67–9 [R].

Maslin, J. (1995) *New York Times*, 26 April [R].

Mauceri, J. (1995) 'Never Work with Children or Aliens', *Shivers* 19, 32–4.

McCarthy, T. (1995) *Variety*, 1 May, 36–7 [R].

Sullivan, D. (1995) '*Village of the Damned*. The Eyes (Still) Have It', *Fangoria*, 143, 40–5, 82.

Williams, L. (1995) *Legend* 18, 32.


*Escape From L.A.* (1996)

Alison, C. (1996) 'A free man in Tinseltown', *Times*, 16 September, 18 [R].

Bacal. S. (1996) 'Postcards From LA', *Starburst* special, 30, 54–6.

Beeler, M. (1996a) '*Escape From L.A.*', *Cinefantastique*, 27, 11–12, 8–9.

_____ (1996b) '*Escape From L.A.*', *Cinefantastique*, 28, 1, 32–3.

_____ (1996c) '*Escape From L.A.*', *Cinefantastique*, 28, 2, 16–7, 19, 21–2, 25, 27.

_____ (1996d) '*Escape From L.A.: Director John Carpenter*', *Cinefantastique*, 28, 2, 18–9, 62.

_____ (1996e) '*Escape From L.A.: Costume Design*', *Cinefantastique*, 28, 2, 20–1.

_____ (1996f) '*Escape From L.A.: Production Design*', *Cinefantastique*, 28, 2, 23.

_____ (1996h) '*Escape From L.A.: Trashing Los Angeles*', *Cinefantastique*, 28, 2, 26–7.

Brown, G. (1996) *Times*, 19 September, 31 [R].

Collis, C. (1996) *Select*, 73, 131 [R].

Curtis, Q. (1996) *Daily Telegraph*, 20 September, 18 [R].

Elias, J. (1996) *Village Voice*, 13 September, 64 [R].

Ferrante, A. C. (1996a) '*Escape From L.A.*', *Fangoria*, 153, 9.

_____ (1996b) 'To Live And Die in *Escape From L.A.*', *Fangoria*, 155, 20–5, 68.

_____ (1996c) 'Coming Back To Escape', *Fangoria*, 156, 20–5.

_____ (1996d) 'Back In Snake's Skin', *Fangoria*, 157, 71–3, 82.

Ferraro, M. X. (1996) '*Escape* Artists', *American Cinematographer*, 77, 9, 76–80.

French, P. (1996) *Observer* Review, 22 September, 12.

Harris, S. (1996) *Legend*, 22, 30–1.

Holden, S. (1996) *New York Times*, 9 August [R].

Hoyle, M. (1996) *Financial Times*, 19 September, 27 [R].

*Independent* Section 2 (1996) 'Heart of darkness', 19 September, 10.

Hutchinson, T. (1996) *Film Guide*, 1, 8, 32 [R].

Jones, A. (1996a) 'From New York To L.A.', *Film Guide*, 1, 8, 10–12.

\_\_\_\_ (1996b) '*Escape From L.A.*', *Starburst*, 213, 4.

\_\_\_\_ (1996c) 'Escape Artists', *Starburst*, 217, 44–7.

\_\_\_\_ (1996d) *Starburst*, 218, 41 [R].

Magid, R. (1996) 'Effecting A New *Escape*', *American Cinematographer*, 77, 9, 81–6.

Malcolm, D. (1996) 'Not a patch on the original', *Guardian* Section 2, 20 September, 9 [R].

McCarthy, T. (1996) *Variety*, 12 August, 32 [R].

Nathan, I. (1996) 'Snake Charmer', *Empire*, 89, 90–6.

Newman, K. (1996) *Empire*, 88, 34 [R].

O'Connor, D. (1996) 'carpentry for beginners', *Film West*, 26, 48.

Peachment, C. (1996) *Sunday Telegraph Review*, 22 September, 8 [R].

Shone, T. (1996) 'No patch on the original', *Sunday Times*, 22 September, 10 [R].

Strick, P. (1996) *Sight and Sound*, 6, 10, 44–5 [R].

*Time Out*, (1996) 18 September, 72 [R].

Tonkin, B. (1996) *New Statesman*, 20 September, 43 [R].

Vaz, M. C. (1996) '*Escape From L.A.* Hasta La Buena Vista', *Cinefex*, 67, 23–4, 134.

Walker, A. (1996) *Evening Standard*, 19 September, 26–7 [R].

Wright, S. (1996) 'This Snake doesn't adder up to much', *Sun*, 20 September, 19 [R].


*Vampires* (1998)

Anthony, T. (1998) 'An odyssey with vampires', *Asian Age*, 3 November, 14 [R].

Billson, A. (1999) *Sunday Telegraph*, 31 October, 11 [R].

Bradshaw, P. (1999) *Guardian* G2, 29 October, 5 [R].

Braund, S. (1999) *Empire*, 126, 34 [R].

Chrissinger, C. W. (1998a) '"Vampires": Waging an unholy war', *Fangoria*, 171, 9.

\_\_\_\_ (1998b) 'Vatican vs. Vampires', *Fangoria*, 176, 26–31, 76.

\_\_\_\_ (1998c) 'Nailing Vampires', *Fangoria*, 177, 38–41, 82.

\_\_\_\_ (1998d) 'To Play and Slay', *Fangoria*, 178, 36–40.

Christopher, J. (1999) *Times*, 28 October, 46 [R].

Cruz, O. and R. Guins (2000) 'Asphalt Veins: On and Off the Road with the Vampire', in J. Sargeant and S. Watson (eds) *Lost Highways: An Illustrated History of Road Movies*. London: Creation, 130–46.

Dahan, Y. (1998) 'Vampires: Le Mal ecclesiastique contre la maladie du bien', *Positif*, 446, 40–1 [in French].

de Beus, I. (1998) *Creative Screenwriting*, 5, 6, 11 [R].

Fisher, N. (1999) 'Try these vampires for thighs', *Sun*, 30 October, 49 [R].

Floyd, N. (1999) *Time Out*, 27 October, 91 [R].

Fischer, D. (1998) 'John Carpenter's Vampires', *Cinefantastique*, 30, 9/10, 16–7.

French, P. (1999) *Observer*, 31 October, 9 [R].

Gandolfi, M. (1998) *Film Tutti I Film Della Stagione*, 36, 19–20 [R, in Italian].

Grantham, S. (1999) *Video Watchdog*, 51, 64–7 [R].

J. B. (1998) *Film Score Monthly*, 3, 10, 26.

Jones, A. (1999) *Film Review*, 587, 39 [R].

Korman, L. (1998) *Screen International*, 1156, 24 [R].

Monahan, M. (1999) *Daily Telegraph*, 29 October, 22 [R].

Newman, K. (1999) *Sight and Sound*, 9, 12, 60 [R].

Patterson, J. (1998) 'out there in production', *Neon*, 14, 18–9.

Quinn, A. (1999) *Independent*, 29 October, 11 [R].

\_\_\_\_ (1999) *Independent on Sunday*, 31 October, 3 [R].

Taubin, A. (1998) *Village Voice*, 3 November, 135 [R].

Thonen, J. (1998c) 'John Carpenter's Vampires', *Cinefantastique*, 30, 1, 7.

\_\_\_\_ (1998d) 'John Carpenter's Vampires', *Cinefantastique*, 30, 4, 8–9.

\_\_\_\_ (1998e) 'John Carpenter's Vampires', *Cinefantastique*, 30, 7/8, 54–6, 59, 60–3.

\_\_\_\_ (1998f) 'Vampires. Dressed to Kill', *Cinefantastique*, 30, 7/8, 57.

\_\_\_\_ (1998g) 'Vampires. Sandy King', *Cinefantastique*, 30, 7/8, 58–9.

\_\_\_\_ (1998h) 'Vampire Brides', *Cinefantastique*, 30, 9/10, 17.

Tookey, C. (1999) *Daily Mail*, 29 October, 53 [R].

Walker, A. (1999) *Evening Standard*, 28 October, 31 [R].

Walsh, S. (1998) *Film Ireland*, 73, 37 [R].


*Ghosts of Mars* (2001)

Atkinson, M. (2001) 'Villages of the Damned. Market Driven', *Village Voice*, 4 September, 115 [R].

Andrews, N. (2001) *Financial Times*, 29 November, 20 [R].

Chrissinger, C. W. (2001a) '*Ghosts of Mars* Rule Their Planet', *Fangoria*, 205, 16–20 [R].

\_\_\_\_ (2001b) 'Host of Mars', *Fangoria*, 206, 30–3, 80.

\_\_\_\_ (2001c) 'Ghosts Girl', *Fangoria*, 207, 60–2.

Christopher, J. (2001) *Times*, 29 November, 13 [R].

Collis, C. (2001) *Empire*, 150, 120 [R].

Divine, C. (2001) 'Ghosts of Mars Script Review', *Creative Screenwriting*, 8, 4, 32–4.

Dumars, D. (2001a) 'John Carpenter's *Ghosts of Mars*', *Cinefantastique*, 33, 4, 6–7.

\_\_\_\_ (2001b) 'John Carpenter's *Ghosts of Mars*', *Cinefantastique*, 33, 5, 40–2, 45, 48–9.

\_\_\_\_ (2001c) '*Ghosts of Mars*. John Carpenter', *Cinefantastique*, 33, 5, 43–4.

\_\_\_\_ (2001d) '*Ghosts of Mars*: KNB Effects', *Cinefantastique*, 33, 5, 46–7.

\_\_\_\_ (2001e) *Cinefantastique* 33, 5, 60 [R].

French, P. (2001) *Observer*, 2 December, 7 [R].

German, D. (2001) 'Mars Needs A Rest', *Asian Age*, 12 November, 17 [R].

Grayson, S. (2001) 'Interstellar Overdone', *Q*, 184, 171 [R].

Hazelton, J. (2001) *Screen International*, 1322, 31 August 2001, 27 [R].

Jones, A. (2001) *Starburst*, 280, 52 [R].

Kerr, P. (2001) 'Mars bores', *New Statesman*, 10 December, 44 [R].

Kleinman, D. (2001) 'The Battle of the B's', *Cinefantastique*, 33, 6, 62 [R].

Koehler, R. (2001) 'Carpenter Nails Down Retro, Active Planet', *Variety*, 27 August, 31, 34 [R].

Newman, K. (2001) *Sight and Sound*, 11, 12, 51–2 [R].

Patterson, J. (2001) *Guardian* G2, 28 August, 13.

Quinn, A. (2001) *Independent*, 30 November, 10 [R].

Robey, T. (2001) *Daily Telegraph*, 30 November, 25 [R].

Sibard, C. (2001) *Sunday Telegraph*, 2 December, 7 [R].

Sotinel, T. (2001) 'Les monstres de Carpentre n'ont pas sommeil', *Le Monde*, 21 November, 32 [R, in French].

Stavrakis, C. (2001) *Film Score Monthly*, 6, 9, 43.

*Starburst* special (2001) 'Mars Attracts!', 49, 54–8.

Thonen, J. (2001) '*Ghosts of Mars*: Carpenter's Westerns', *Cinefantastique*, 33, 5, 50–1.

Whalen, T. (2002) '"This is About One Thing – Dominion": John Carpenter's *Ghosts of Mars*', *Literature/Film Quarterly*, 30, 4, 304–7.

White, D. (2001) *Starburst*, 280, 73.

Young, N. (2001) *Time Out*, 28 November, 86.

# INDEX

www.ingramcontent.com/pod-product-compliance
Ingram Content Group UK Ltd.
Pitfield, Milton Keynes, MK11 3LW, UK
UKHW020654120225
455006UK00006B/71